The International Library of Sociology

PSYCHIATRIC SOCIAL WORK
IN GREAT BRITAIN
(1939 - 1962)

I0129342

Founded by KARL MANNHEIM

The International Library of Sociology

THE SOCIOLOGY OF MENTAL HEALTH

In 7 Volumes

PSYCHIATRIC SOCIAL WORK
IN GREAT BRITAIN
(1939 - 1962)

by

NOEL TIMMS

ROUTLEDGE

First published in 1964 by
Routledge and Kegan Paul Ltd

Reprinted in 1998 by
Routledge

2 Park Square, Milton Park, Abingdon, Oxfordshire OX14 4RN
711 Third Avenue, New York, NY 10017

First issued in paperback 2014
Routledge is an imprint of the Taylor and Francis Group, an informa business

© 1964 Noel Timms

All rights reserved. No part of this book may be reprinted or reproduced
or utilized in any form or by any electronic, mechanical, or other means,
now known or hereafter invented, including photocopying
and recording, or in any information storage or retrieval system, without
permission in writing from the publishers.

The publishers have made every effort to contact authors/copyright holders
of the works reprinted in *The International Library of Sociology*.
This has not been possible in every case, however, and we would
welcome correspondence from those individuals/companies
we have been unable to trace.

British Library Cataloguing in Publication Data
A CIP catalogue record for this book
is available from the British Library

Psychiatric Social Work in Great Britain (1939 - 1962)
ISBN 978-0-415-17806-8 (hbk)
ISBN 978-0-415-86871-6 (pbk)
The Sociology of Mental Health: 7 Volumes
ISBN 978-0-415-17835-8
The International Library of Sociology: 274 Volumes
ISBN 978-0-415-17838-9

CONTENTS

TABLES, FIGURES
AND MAPS

vii

ACKNOWLEDGEMENTS

I AM grateful to the following for their informed and helpful criticisms: Miss Megan Browne, (Lecturer in Psychiatric Social Work, Edinburgh University), Mrs. Elizabeth Irvine (Senior Tutor, Tavistock Clinic), Mrs. Kay McDougall (Senior Lecturer in Social Work Education, London School of Economics) and Professor David Donnison. In acknowledging the benefits of their considered judgments I would like to exonerate them from any identification with the opinions I have expressed.

The Association of Psychiatric Social Workers has generously allowed me access to their records for the purpose of this study and I would like also to record useful and pleasant conversations with the late Margaret Ashdown, Miss Elizabeth Howarth and Miss Noel Hunnybun. Many other psychiatric social workers have discussed their work in child guidance clinics, mental hospitals and community care with me and I am particularly grateful to the Director and staff of the clinic studied in Chapter Five. Finally, I would like to thank Mr. Edward James for his help with the statistical analysis of some of the material.

Chapter One

INTRODUCTION

'What happens when half-baked social workers half-trained in analytical techniques apply them indiscriminately in the delicate task of social guidance can best be left to the imagination.'[1]

THE object of this book is to study a particular group of social workers, those trained as psychiatric social workers. It was begun in the belief that their work should not be 'left to the imagination'[2] and that an accurate factual picture of their training, practice, professional activities, research and writing would inform and clarify. It has been designed to answer certain questions: who are psychiatric social workers? What do they do? Are they 'half-baked' or adequately trained? How has psychiatric social work been moulded? What attitudes do psychiatric social workers have towards other forms of social work and to what extent have these attitudes (conditioned by the setting of psychiatric social work) set the tone for social work in other settings for which they may or may not be appropriate?

Psychiatric social work, as we shall see later in this chapter, can be variously defined, but any of the possible interpretations of the term refer to a specialization within the wider field of social work. Its significance can perhaps be most easily appreciated against this general background. Attempts to define social work, however, have met with little success. This is so whatever the nature of the attempt; whether it has been to convey the essence of the activity or to denote what people who were called, or called themselves, social workers actually did; or even to decide to whom the title could properly be given. Social work has changed as society and our social knowledge have changed; it has been transformed because the social agencies from which it is practised (hospitals, local authorities, voluntary societies) have modified their original aims and conceptions. Some of the agencies have been unable to adapt to change and have ceased to exist; new agencies have been created to meet freshly appreciated needs, sometimes in novel ways. Thus, because social work is the product of many changing forces, a historical approach provides the most serviceable approach to understanding its operations. This has the additional advantage of enabling us to judge the impact of the new psychiatric specialization that first appeared in Britain around 1930.

Social work covers a wide range of activity which overlaps with ordinary neighbourliness at one end and psychotherapy at the other. Its origins as a separate and specialist series of activities can be found in the general changes brought about by the Industrial Revolution and, more particularly, in the response of certain philanthropists to conditions in the middle decades of the last century. Of special importance are the principles and procedures involved in the first forty years of the life of the Charity Organisation Society. It is these that most clearly show the gradual emergence of a new social role, that of the informed and professional friend, whose activity was different from that of the squire, clergyman or usual family friend. The aims of such agencies as the C.O.S. were often couched in terms of offering a helping relationship to assist the person or family in trouble in solving problems of everyday living (to find a job, a home etc.), but actual decisions more often than not revolved around granting or withholding material relief. For the majority of the destitute, however, recourse was usually to the statutory Poor Law Service. Until its abolition in 1948 this service was unaffected by the principles of social work as evolved by the voluntary bodies in the late nineteenth and early twentieth centuries. It is important to appreciate that theorizing about social work flourished initially under special circumstances. It developed in voluntary (i.e. non-statutory) bodies, such as Settlements and Charitable agencies, who had no responsibility for ensuring a uniform and general service. These agencies were often small and their primary discipline and purpose was that of social work. Not all voluntary agencies, however, were influenced by the main stream of social work. Probation officers who were in the first two or three decades of this century drawn predominantly from religious and social organizations, preferred to define themselves as court missionaries or court officers rather than social workers.

Introduction

The first extension of social work occurred in the medical field when in 1895 the first almoner was appointed. This established a social worker in a large, though still voluntary institution, in which medicine was clearly the first discipline and healing the main purpose. At this early stage—and indeed at intervals throughout the history of almoning—the function of the almoner could be more accurately described as a subsidiary rather than an auxiliary to medicine, since she was concerned largely with questions of payment and the abuse of free services. However, the almoners' connections with social work were firmly maintained throughout the present century. Their specialist training, for example, up to the Second World War was partly a university social science course (such training courses for general social work at a diploma level were established at several provincial universities from 1904 onwards) and partly an extended apprenticeship under the direction of an almoner at a hospital training centre.

Around 1930 when psychiatric social work was beginning in this country the general field of social work showed a number of significant features. Training for social work by means of the two year diploma course, combining theoretical study with practical work, was an established part of the curriculum of several universities, but its full professional character was never firmly recognized either inside or outside the universities. There were some branches of what would today be called social work that had a specialized training (e.g. moral welfare and almoning) and probation was to participate, to an extent, in university training in the near future. The actual field of social work consisted partly of such specialized workers and partly of a heterogeneous collection of workers in local education authorities, child welfare visitors, property managers and workers in voluntary societies, such as Settlements, Mental Welfare Associations and so on. Finally, there was little or no governmental interest in training for social work and little pressure from any quarter to staff the social services with trained personnel. The large statutory services of today did not exist.

It was into this world of welfare that psychiatric social work was introduced. The details of its introduction will be considered in Chapter Two, but a reference to the main implications of the new specialization is appropriate at this stage. Training for psychiatric social work consisted of a year's professional course at a university

3

given normally to those who had experience of social work and also a university qualification in social science. It was thus a post-graduate training for relatively experienced social workers. This represented a development of very great importance in social work training. Students were trained in two settings, the mental hospital and the child guidance clinic, and many of them worked in one or both of these fields. Work in a mental hospital had some similarities with that of the almoner, though from the beginning the psychiatric social worker was more clearly involved as an auxiliary, assisting the psychiatrist in diagnosis through her social history of the patient and his family, and gradually taking some part in treatment. The child guidance clinic was a more obviously new setting, aiming to help the family rather than the individual, without statutory obligations and relieved of decisions about material relief. In many ways these were the conditions for a new beginning in social work. The voluntary agency in the nineteenth century had claimed to help the family as a whole, but lack of psychological knowledge made this a largely empty claim. With the establishment of the child guidance clinic realization of the aim at least became possible. In both mental hospital and child guidance clinic social workers were implicitly or explicitly concerned for the first time with human behaviour and relationships as their primary function. In both settings they encountered and began to explore a crucial problem in welfare, the relationship between social worker and doctor.

An investigation of psychiatric social work assumes considerable importance at the present time for two main reasons. In the first place, social work itself has recently become a subject of general interest. What began in the second half of the nineteenth century as a marginal activity, the concern of a small group of philanthropists and a small collection of recipients, has become by the second half of the present century the subject of a well-known series of Government Reports[3] and the object of spirited attack by distinguished critics who assume it has developed to the point at which it constitutes a social danger.[4] Social work certainly touches an increasing proportion of the population through the increase in the number and complexity of the social services. Many social workers at the turn of the century were scornful of attempts to cure individual problems by the creation of general social services, but these services have grown and extended their range of opera-

4

tion and are now accepted as part of a way of living. Social workers carry important responsibilities in the work of these services which now employ a considerable number. What these workers do is, therefore, of growing interest to the general public. It can no longer be generally characterized as the voluntary activity of a small group of the well-to-do, but is the professional occupation of many drawn from a heterogeneous social group. The modern social workers' concern is not simply for sectional groups (for example, the poor, the 'deserving' etc.) but with the development of more comprehensive social services their work may impinge on any member of the community. Social work is gradually becoming recognized as one of the institutionalized means by which some of the unfavourable results of urbanization and industrialization are modified.

Such developments are obviously exerting an influence on social workers themselves. A succession of Government Committees has called for a great increase in the number of social workers and successive measures in the treatment of the offender, and of the mentally disordered, to name only two important groups, have placed considerable burdens of responsibility on the trained social worker. Social workers (and others) are asking if their training is adequate and appropriate, and if their methods of work can be improved. This questioning of training and methods of work is comparatively recent. Nineteenth century philanthropy had, of course, its thoughtful and critical social workers, women, for example, like Octavia Hill and Helen Bosanquet. The latter, in particular, expressed thoughtful concern in connection with training, the first objective of which she considered 'to make the student realize more fully and more definitely the issues involved in the work he is undertaking, to know more clearly what he wants, and to want higher things.'[5] But for the most part the philanthropists were confident in the sufficiency of their own beneficience and supremely untroubled by any uneasiness concerning the respective positions of donor and recipient. Their calm assurance is epitomized in the following advice to a friendly visitor at the turn of the century: 'A chat about your holiday in Scotland or Rome or Clacton-on-Sea, a description of the last play you saw, ball you went to, book you read, or even your brother's or uncle's latest fishing story, may carry you a great way into the affection of some tired housewife resting after Monday's washing.'[6]

Finally, social workers are seeking to become professional people. Most of the groups of specialist workers (e.g. child care officers, almoners etc.) have their own professional organizations which are attempting to create a professional image for their members, to exercise on governmental and other bodies a real influence, and to further the professional development of their members. To some critics this growth of professionalism is simply an absurd attempt at imitation, to others its significance is more sinister, whilst social workers themselves are hesitant and often timid in assuming professional status and working towards a united, single profession of social work.

These important developments in social work require a great deal of study. One approach would be to attempt the study of developments in all the separate fields, probation, child care etc. A more realistic approach would be to make a preliminary study of each field and it is within such an approach that the present work is orientated. The field of psychiatric social work provides an exceptionally strong vantage point from which social work developments as a whole can be surveyed. Psychiatric social work has behind it some years of tradition; training for such work has been well established in this country since the end of the Second World War. Psychiatric social workers have a considerable and justified reputation for their writings on social work and their professional association is perhaps the strongest, though by no means the largest, of the professional social work organizations. The study of psychiatric social work provides an opportunity of discovering some of the strengths and weakness of social work. Psychiatric social work can both be taken as a case example for the study of social work and also be seen as itself one of the most important developments in social work in this country. Without psychiatric social workers the history of social work in England from 1930 would lose a good deal of its significance.

A study of psychiatric social work has a special relevance at the present time in view of the increasing importance being given to our social policy in regard to the mentally ill. Psychiatric social workers were originally some of the storm troopers of the mental hygiene movement and their contribution to the mental health services has been significant.

In the treatment of the maladjusted child psychiatric social workers have played an essential part in the establishment and development of the child guidance service. It may well be that 'the child guidance movement is still little more than an act of faith',[7] but the service that does exist has influenced both its direct clientele and in profound, if untraced, ways the manner of child rearing in our society. In mental hospitals psychiatric social workers were not originally seen as part of the team, but they have played an important part in humanizing the institution and their work has developed in scope and complexity since the days when their primary function was seen as collecting data for psychiatrists. At the present when more patients are entering mental hospitals for the first time and when more are being re-admitted, the work of the only group of social workers so far trained to work in a psychiatric setting must be of importance. Such importance is increased when the new emphasis on care for the mentally disordered in the community is considered. If families and social workers of all kinds are to render the necessary support and help to the mentally disordered living in the community then they themselves must also be helped towards greater effectiveness. This is at least partly the work of the psychiatric social worker and it is necessary to ask if she is by training and temperament fitted to work outside the clinical setting of hospital or child guidance clinic. In view of the new policy for mental health are we training enough psychiatric social workers and are we training them well enough?

The contribution, actual and potential, of psychiatric social workers to the community, has become increasingly appreciated by the committees of enquiry concerned with different aspects of the field of social work. The Younghusband Report stated that 'We have no doubt that a great increase is urgently needed in the number of psychiatric social workers trained each year, so that they may meet a variety of demands . . .'[8] What is it that we are demanding more of? An historical investigation of psychiatric social work should shed important light on this question.

There has always been a considerable amount of public ignorance and misconception about psychiatric social workers, and, from time to time, an inadequate and misleading gloss on the profession has been given by commentators from psychiatry, public health, the universities, and from social work. A recent pilot survey into public knowledge of, and attitudes to, social work and the social services[9] showed that 75 per cent of the sample inter-

7

viewed had not heard of psychiatric social workers, while 80 per cent could not say what they did. Of the remainder most associated them with the actual treatment of mental patients. For example, the wife of a veterinary surgeon thought that they were 'people who treat the mentally ill—that is psychological experts'. The wife of a shop manager considered that 'they actually looked after people with some sort of phobia'. Others saw the psychiatric social worker doing the same sort of work as Health Visitors. It was just this kind of misunderstanding which earlier led the Association of Psychiatric Social Workers to consider a possible change in name. As Margaret Ashdown said at the General Meeting in January 1941: 'We must all have felt the burden of our name. It is certainly ponderous, perhaps a little pompous. The first element is still a mysterious word to many people and it is a teaser to spell . . .' However, with such suggested alternatives as 'social therapist', 'psychological' or 'psychiatric assistant' it is hardly surprising that after a lengthy discussion members concluded that the time was not opportune for change.

Misinterpretation and unrealistic criticism of psychiatric social work has been fairly constant in the development of the work and has derived from many sources. At times it seems that the psychiatric social worker was unacceptable to the 'ordinary' social worker because of her contamination with some of the undesirable side-effects of psychoanalytic thought. A writer in the Charity Organisation Review in 1931 commented that 'the psychiatric social worker, who has very likely been psychoanalysed herself, finds the psychopathic elements in a case of absorbing and dominating interest. But, we submit, she must not despise the worker who says: "I am not interested in psychopaths but in citizens" and I have a suspicion that some of the clients would be a good deal less psychopathic if the old fashioned civic ideal could be instilled into them a little more successfully.'[10] This is a particular form of the common criticism that psychiatric social workers are 'ivory tower' specialists, both speculative and ineffective. The history of psychiatric social work can show examples of this, but also examples (as in the establishment of the early hostels for maladjusted children) of work realistically geared to meeting previously unacknowledged need.

Social workers have not been alone in expressing criticism of their colleagues in psychiatric social work, but the main burden of their complaint has been that the psychiatric social worker is engulfed in purely psychoanalytic understanding and techniques. Psychoanalysts, on the other hand, are sometimes the critics, as the quotation at the head of this chapter shows, but their target is not the excess of analytic understanding that the psychiatric social worker brings to her work, but its insufficiency. Thus, the psychiatric social worker is rejected in both spheres, either because of superfluous knowledge or deleterious ignorance. In the more recent criticisms of social workers originating from Wootton's wholesale dismissal of much contemporary theorizing about social work the psychiatric social worker is next treated with some ambivalence. Some critics deplore the psychiatric influence on social work in general. McGregor, for instance, objects that such an influence 'has taught social workers to interpret many behavioural difficulties arising from nothing more complicated than shortage of money as problems of psychological maladjustment.'[11] Yet it remains obscure how far such critics would allow a place for specialized psychiatric social work. Others suggest that psychiatric social workers are one of the few social work groups to have attained something like professional organization and status and, it is implied, this is a notable and praiseworthy achievement. The following study will show, in part at least, the activities of psychiatric social workers and thus form a basis from which the truth of these criticisms can be assessed and their force understood.

It is usual to begin the study of any group by describing briefly or defining broadly the sort of group that is the object of interest.

On one level the definition of a psychiatric social worker is both easy and uninteresting. If we accept the recommendation of the Macintosh Committe (1951), endorsed recently in the Younghusband Report, (S.747), the term 'psychiatric social worker' should be restricted to persons holding a university qualification in mental health or psychiatric social work (or who are eligible for membership of the Association of Psychiatric Social Workers). The time and energy devoted by the Association to securing adequate protection of the title and the fact that the Younghusband Working Party felt it necessary to reiterate the recommendation of an earlier committee suggests that in practice people may use the title without the required qualification. However, even if the definition has a persuasive element, its use for most practical purposes is clear.

If we ask the related and necessary question, what is psychiatric social work, clarity gives way to interest. This is an apparently simple question, but in many ways the history of psychiatric social work can be seen as the continual attempt to answer it satisfactorily. This is true of psychiatric social work in the country of its origin, the United States, and in Great Britain. One of the main themes of the standard work on psychiatric social work in America[12] is the question, is psychiatric social work simply social work carried out in association with a psychiatrist or is it a special kind of social work that can be practised in any setting? The same kind of question is implicit in the discussions about psychiatric social work in England. In a paper in 1946, for example, the 'psychiatric' aspect of the work is seen at one point as simply skill in human relations and at another as a direct clinical function. It is suggested that material aid may be given 'psychiatrically, that is to say, at the right moment, within the framework of a treatment plan . . .' and that 'in clinic work the psychiatric social worker is usually concerned with the more psychiatric aspects of the patient or the family's problem, and problems of social and material care are entirely left to the appropriate agencies . . .'[13] Another writer stresses that 'we are *psychiatric* social workers: our casework . . . is based on the psychological understanding of . . . our own behaviour, our own reactions as well as those of our clients.'[14] There a psychiatric social worker is one who has psychological, or more properly, psychoanalytic understanding. Yet another writer discussing the two sides of the psychiatric social worker as a contributor to a medical diagnosis and as 'a social caseworker concentrating on making a usable relationship with her client who might be some other member of the patient's family . . .' gives the term a completely different emphasis. 'If she concentrates too much on her auxiliary functions she might just as well not have had a full social worker's training and if she gets too involved in her particular client's needs that she forgets that there is a patient and that she is employed by the hospital caring for him, then she might as well not be a *psychiatric* social worker.'[15] Here 'psychiatric' refers not to knowledge or understanding but to clinical setting.

One definition of psychiatric social work that is frequently

quoted is that offered by Noel Hunnybun, one of the first English
women to be trained as a psychiatric social worker. 'Psychiatric
social work' she writes 'is case-work based on the psychological
understanding of human behaviour, undertaken by social caseworkers who have received a special training to equip them for
work with children and adults suffering from mental illness or
problems of behaviour or personality. Whilst the training offered
was originally planned to provide workers in child-guidance
clinics and mental hospitals to work with psychiatrists and educational psychologists as members of a team, psychiatric social
workers are now employed . . . in many branches of social and
educational work.'[16] This is at least a comprehensive definition,
but its very virtue in this respect obscures the differences of view
on this topic that a history of psychiatric social work reveals.
American psychiatric social workers have perhaps appreciated
more clearly the possible definitions of their work, but the role of
the psychiatric social worker has been the subject of keen debate
amongst their British colleagues. In many ways to ask what is
psychiatric social work is to ask what is the history of that occupation.

The history of psychiatric social work which follows will consider firstly the origins and training of psychiatric social workers.
The training is of primary importance since it is only through such
training that social workers become psychiatric social workers and
become eligible for membership of the professional association.
An account is then given of those who have successfully completed
training for psychiatric social work. This is followed by a consideration of the careers of psychiatric social workers after training
and by an attempt to describe the work of psychiatric social
workers. The psychiatric social worker is then considered as a
research worker and writer. The concluding chapters are devoted
to the history of the Association of Psychiatric Social Workers,
with particular reference to training, influence on social policy, the
definition of psychiatric social work, and professional welfare.

NOTES

[1] Glover, E., *The Roots of Crime*, Imago, 1960, p. 67. He refers on the
previous page to the misguided enthusiasm of teachers of psychiatric social
work who encourage 'all sorts of interpretive techniques'.

Introduction

[2] Some aspects of psychiatric social work have, of course, been considered in Ashdown and Brown's book, *Social Service and Mental Health* (1953) and this work has been of considerable help in the preparation of the present book, even though, as will be clear from the text, I am not always in agreement with it.

[3] *Report of the Committee on Social Workers in the Mental Health Services,* Cmd. 8260. H.M.S.O. 1951.

Reports of the Committee on Medical Auxiliaries, Cmd. 8188, H.M.S.O. 1951.

Report of the Committee on Maladjusted Children.

Report of the Working Party on Social Workers in the Local Authority Health and Welfare Services. H.M.S.O. 1959.

Report of the Departmental Committee on the Probation Service, Cmnd. 1650, H.M.S.O. 1962.

[4] The most publicised criticisms are those made by Wootton: *Social Science and Social Pathology* (Chapter IX); 'Daddy Knows Best', *Twentieth Century,* October 1959; '*The Image of the Social Worker*', *British Journal of Sociology,* December 1960.

[5] Bosanquet, H., 'Methods of Training', *Charity Organisation Society Occasional Papers,* Third Series, No. 3.

[6] Shairp, L. V., *Hints for Visitors,* 1910, Introduction by C. S. Loch.

[7] Morris, J. N., Symposium on Operational Research in the National Health Service, *Proceedings of Royal Society of Medicine,* Vol. LI, 1958.

[8] *Report of the Working Party on Social Workers in the Local Authority Health and Welfare Services,* S.804.

[9] Timms, N., 'The Public and the Social Worker', *Social Work,* January 1962.

[10] Review of Robinson, V., *The Changing Psychology of Social Casework, Charity Organisation Review,* October 1931.

[11] McGregor, O. R., 'Social Facts and the Social Conscience', *Twentieth Century,* May 1960.

[12] French, L. M., *Psychiatric Social Work,* The Commonwealth Fund, 1940.

[13] Paper by E. M. Goldberg on 'Psychiatric Social Workers in the Community'.

[14] Myers, E., 'The Caseworker's Problems in Meeting the Inner and Outer Needs of Clients', *British Journal of Psychiatric Social Work,* No. 10, October 1954.

[15] McDougall, K., 'The Psychiatric Social Worker in the Mental Hospital', *Case Conference,* June 1958.

[16] Hunnybun, N., 'Psychiatric Social Work', in *Social Case-Work in Great Britain,* (ed.) Morris, C., p. 100.

Chapter Two

THE ORIGINS AND DEVELOPMENT
OF TRAINING FOR PSYCHIATRIC
SOCIAL WORK

'The very high value which is to-day placed by all on the work
done by the psychiatric social worker is in large part due to the
excellence of the type and of the training.'[1]
'If you want to train for social work find an A1 worker, work
under her, live on the spot, and read Balzac.'[2]

TRAINING in psychiatric social work is now an established
part of the education offered at several British universities; the
courses attract a large number of applicants and those who have
qualified are to be found in senior positions in the several fields of
social work, in social research and in teaching posts in universities
and other institutions of higher education. How did this training
begin and how has it developed? What have been the objectives of
training and how successfully have they been achieved? These are
among the questions that should be asked of the longest established
form of university training for professional social work in Great
Britain.

They are not questions of simply historical interest nor are they
of concern only to a limited group of professional workers. The
training and the objectives of social workers (be they psychiatric
social workers or not) cannot be exclusively described in technical
terms, since they are made up largely of the stuff of political and
moral judgment. It is one amongst many of the uncertainties for
which social workers must be prepared in and through training
that the 'layman' in discussing the objectives and methods of
social work is not intruding into a mystery, but exercising his
rights.

The Origins and Development of Training

Training in psychiatric social work in this country had unspectacular beginnings. The number of students was small[3] as was the membership of the group of early enthusiasts responsible for the first course of training in 1929. The Mental Health Course at the London School of Economics began as a small-scale operation supported as a cause by a few enthusiasts for mental hygiene and the story of its origins and early years may seem at times personal or even parochial. Yet it is on such a scale and in these terms that training and ideas about training developed. There was, however, forming a background to such changes, a developing tradition in the wider field of service for the mentally ill and subnormal which had its origins in the nineteenth century.

Social work on behalf of the mentally ill outside mental institutions began in the second half of the nineteenth century with the foundation in 1877 of 'The After-Care Association for the Female and Friendless Convalescent on leaving Asylums for the Insane' (to become in 1940, after various changes of title, The Mental After-Care Association). Care for mental defectives in the community did not begin to establish itself until the early twentieth century, when the Mental Deficiency Act of 1913 encouraged its development. In this year a number of voluntary associations were formed, of which the most important was the Central Association for the Care of Mental Defectives (to become in 1921, the Central Association for Mental Welfare). By the mid-twenties of the present century, then, there was a developing tradition of social work on behalf of the mentally ill and defective apart from service to such patients in institutions. There was, however, no recognized training for such work, and the importance of training was hardly appreciated. The Report of the Royal Commission on Lunacy and Mental Disorder in 1926, for example, recognized the importance of after-care, but made no mention of training. 'The transition from asylum life to the everyday world is a stage of peculiar difficulty for the recovered patient . . . There is here a great opening for philanthropic work and we heard, with admiration, of the public service rendered by the After-Care Association.'[4]

The impetus for training for social workers in the principles of mental hygiene came largely from those interested in children,

14

but developments in the mental hospital field enabled psychiatrists and administrators primarily concerned with the treatment of adults to co-operate in a common training for workers in both child guidance clinics and mental hospitals. The First World War had already directed some public interest towards psychology and the needs of those who were psychologically handicapped but not to the extent that they required mental hospital care. Gradually, after-care was being appreciated as a part of treatment and the social factors in both illness and recovery were receiving some attention.

The Mental Treatment Act of 1930 was an important landmark in the development of a mental health policy that was not exclusively preoccupied with legal restraint and definition and which recognized some at least of the social implications of mental illness. Under the Act public mental hospitals could receive voluntary and temporary patients without certification and could undertake out-patient and preventive work. Changes of attitude implicit in the Act only slowly became effective, but the beginnings of change were there to be fostered and encouraged.

However, the effective impetus for the development of mental health training came from those concerned with children, particularly the 'problem' delinquent child. Here again there was a tradition of concern arising from a nineteenth century background. By the end of the nineteenth century a number of factors were emphasizing the need for a social policy in regard to children. This was to be partly a policy for the poor and underprivileged and thus a continuation of the concern shown by such men as Kay Shuttleworth earlier in the century and partly a new policy beginning to focus on the school child as such. Among reasons for the implementation of such policies were the fears at the turn of the century for our national intellectual heritage and for the physical well-being of the population. There was also a growing interest in the application of scientific methods to the measurement of ability. Of importance in this development was the foundation in 1893 of the British Child Study Association. The main object of this society, founded at the suggestion of Galton by Sully, professor of mental philosophy at University College, London, was to encourage teachers to study the individual child and seek advice on their more difficult pupils. Advice could be obtained from certain of the school inspectors or from Sully himself. Burt has described this as 'the real origin of the child guidance movement,'[5] but there were in fact two strands in the development of this movement. The first, [historically, came from an emphasis on the study of the individual child and contained the origins of a school psychological service. The second strand developed from the idea of the team of psychiatrist, psychologist and social worker which found its first concrete expression in America. This second development did not influence British social work until the late 1920's.

Meanwhile, Kimmins, chief inspector of the London Schools, had been impressed by the possibilities of the British Child Study Association and began to press for the appointment of an educational psychologist to his inspectorate. In 1913 Cyril Burt was appointed 'to investigate cases of individual children who present problems of special difficulty and who might be referred for examination by teachers, school medical officers, or care committee workers, magistrates or parents, and to carry out, or make recommendations for, suitable treatment or training of such children.'[6] Towards the end of the war the appointment originally made 'for three years, but no more', was made permanent. The Underwood Report described this appointment as 'a landmark in the history of child guidance in this country.'[7]

The idea of the child guidance team (psychiatrist, psychologist and social worker) was being developed at this time in America, though the origins of psychiatric social work are to be found in the mental hospital field in that country. This specialization in social work arose from the interest in mental hospital after-care. The first after-care agent in America was appointed in 1906. Very soon after, the need for specialized training was recognized in a scheme of apprenticeship at the Boston Psychopathic Hospital under Mary Jarrett. It was at this hospital that the term psychiatric social worker was first used. In 1918 Smith College offered the first training in psychiatric social work. Of great importance in the spreading of psychiatric social work was the work of Healy in the Chicago Juvenile Psychopathic Institute (1909), which emphasized the team approach to the study and treatment of delinquency. In 1920 the Commonwealth Fund consulted the National Committee for Mental Hygiene in connection with the Fund's programme. At a Conference in Lakewood in 1921 the Fund agreed to finance a five-year plan for the prevention of juvenile delinquency; the main part of the programme was to consist in an extension of the type of work begun by Healy, who with Bronner, a psychologist, had in 1917 started the new Judge Baker Foundation at Boston. The first Commonwealth Fund Demonstration clinic was established in St. Louis. The Fund also gave financial support to the New York School of Social Work to establish a Bureau of Children's Guidance headed by Dr. B. Glueck and Dr. M. Kenworthy. It was to this School, as we shall see, that the first British social workers in the psychiatric field were sent to study.

In 1925 an English Magistrate Mrs. St. Loe Strachey was on a visit to America with her husband and saw something of the work of Child Guidance Clinics. She met representatives of the Commonwealth Fund and began preliminary negotiations with them with a view to establishing Child Guidance Clinics in England. It was agreed that she should call a meeting on her return of representatives of all the different kinds of social work in England which were primarily concerned with the prevention of delinquency. If this group requested help in establishing a demonstration clinic, the Directors of the Commonwealth Fund would put this before their Committee.

Mrs. Strachey on her return called together an informal group to discuss the subject. The organizations represented included the Central Association for Mental Welfare, the Howard League for Penal Reform, the Magistrate's Association and the National Council for Mental Hygiene. As a result of this preliminary conference the Executive Assistant of the Commonwealth Fund, Miss Scoville, was invited to visit England with a view to submitting a report to the Commonwealth Fund based on first-hand knowledge of the possibility of establishing Child Guidance.

Miss Scoville came to England in 1926. In the same year the Commonwealth Fund defined its policy. The Fund would not finance the proposed plan unless it had the interest and support of a widely representative group of leading members of the medical, educational and social services. It would not consider the establishment of a demonstration clinic unless it was used for training social workers and the desirability of affiliation to a University was stressed. This firm and clear indication of policy had the immediate effect of helping those concerned with British developments to focus their activities. In the long run the emphasis on training within an existing social science department of a university has had a considerable effect on the status and the development of training for psychiatric social work. When the Mental Health Course began at the London School of Economics in 1929 it was the first course within a British University which had the acknowledged aim of giving professional training in social work.

Evidence of the wide support required by the Commonwealth Fund was given in May 1927 in a letter signed by over 30 people, representing a wide field of interest including leading British psychologists, representatives of the London County Council, London University, the Central Association for Mental Welfare and of other bodies. The letter requested help in the establishment of a Child Guidance Clinic 'for training, service and research' and stressed the absence of 'the psychiatric viewpoint in social work'. This statement supports the view that behind the efforts of particular individuals, like Mrs. Strachey, there was a general and growing interest in psychology and the help it could give to social work. Part of this interest arose from the field of delinquency. Burt's study *The Young Delinquent* 1925 is of importance in this context. He mentions in fact in *An Autobiographical Sketch* that Mrs. Strachey came to talk about the possibility of enlisting the help of the Commonwealth Fund after she had read his study, which included a long memorandum on the need for more psychological centres or clinics. Social workers themselves were looking to psychology, as can be seen both from the action of probation officers in seeking individual consultation about their cases from psychiatrists in the 1920's and also from the invitation of Cyril Burt to give two lectures to the C.O.S. in 1917, because 'social workers are deeply anxious to know whether they can improve their efforts by a study of psychology in a technical and specific way'.[8] Burt's answer was encouraging:[9] 'The nature of the mental differences in different individuals, the frequency with which particular differences occur among certain classes, the signs by which they may be recognized, the causes which will produce or remove them—these problems one and all, may legitimately form the theme of scientific enquiry. To the social worker they are plainly of the greatest interest: indeed, it is very largely to the social worker that we must look for their solution.' Yet, at this very early stage there appeared also signs of the splitting between work with the environment and work with the personality that has been one of the greatest single hindrances to the development of social work—'With the circumstances of the case—income and liabilities, employment or causes of unemployment, available assistance from relatives, clubs, and so forth—with these psychology cannot directly be concerned. But where character or personality is in question, there psychology, were it in any way a complete or well-established discipline, should be the master science.' This, however, is to anticipate.

The letter referred to above was favourably received by the Commonwealth Fund and detailed proposals were worked out. Suggestions were made for general educational propaganda and for the loan of workers, once they had been trained in England, to Child Guidance Clinics and psychological departments of hospitals. The Commonwealth Fund invited a group of ten people, representing the different types of social work which the demonstration clinic would serve to visit the U.S.A. for a period of three months. An offer was also made to finance five social workers to undertake a year's training in America to prepare for work in the new clinic. In 1927 selection was made of those for Observation Visits and of social workers for a year's training. The group of social workers consisted of Kathleen Butler (Mrs. Wallace), an almoner, Catherine Craggs, working for the Central Association for Mental Welfare, Elizabeth Horder, a locum Probation Officer, Noel Hunnybun, assistant organizer in the School Care Committee of the London County Council, and Doris Robinson, a social worker at the Tavistock Clinic.

Some idea of the rather haphazard selection of these early days can be gained from the reminiscences of those selected. One of the 'psychiatric social workers' chosen has stated that one morning her superior asked her if she would like to go to America—'Something to do with children'. Another, who went to America later has described her selection interview in the following way. She was interviewed by a number of people. 'The first one asked her if she felt that going to America was likely to interfere with her religious or sex life. The second gave her the joyful news that £50 out of the grant must be spent on clothes, a fur coat which could be purchased for £12 being one of the items considered necessary. Attention at the same time was drawn to the fact that cotton stockings were unknown in America.'

The kind of training given to these English social workers, groups of whom went to America in 1927 and 1928, had as far as can be discovered three main features—the combination of theoretical and practical work, emphasis on social histories (at the Institute of Child Guidance it was important to obtain full information about relatives, if possible, to the third or fourth generation) and a particular form of case analysis, which emerged from the psychological teaching of Dr. Marion Kenworthy at New York, and was termed ego-libido analysis. Cases were minutely analysed using these two headings. This rather strange mechanical process emphasized, like most psychiatric teaching at that time, the classification of behaviour rather than the understanding of relationships, but it did lead students to a necessary and careful study of observations and statements in an interview. To this extent it represented a more hopeful basis for professional training than the views current at that time amongst leading social work teachers in Great Britain. Macadam, for example, some two years before, had expressed the view that case discussion 'may produce that mediocre uniformity and rigidity of outlook that is fatal in a social worker . . . The best type of "case worker" is endowed with inborn gifts, and will gain her experience in actual work, not in the class-room dissection of case papers.'[10] This was a typical view that expressed the anxiety of many British social workers that people might be mishandled as 'cases', and that students would become unsympathetic to the humanity of their clients if they learned about their *libido* in the detachment of the classroom. The concern to sustain a human contact with clients was, of course, sensitive and sensible, since little help can be given or accepted outside its context, but the anxiety was (and is still where present,) misplaced. It inhibited British social workers from any ordered analysis of problems connected with their clients lest they should be accused of introducing 'uniformity' or clinical dissection into what should be reverently regarded as a highly individual process. This view has its counterpart in literary criticism also—'we murder to dissect'; it indicates one of the main reasons why in the development of a new form of social work training it was necessary to learn from American experience. The condition of social work training in this country had appeared potentially strong at the turn of the century, but it failed to develop largely because of a split between the social 'reformers' who thought real social change could only take place through the expansion of the social services and social workers who looked to the development of potentialities within the personality of their clients through a personal relationship between client and helper.

DEVELOPMENTS IN TRAINING

The first course of training began in England at the London School of Economics in 1929. The Child Guidance Council, which was concerned in spite of its name with fostering developments in both the child guidance and mental hospital fields, awarded six scholarships and defrayed the whole cost of the course. It took, naturally, two or three years for firm outlines of the training to emerge. One of the early trained psychiatric social workers has described the situation as follows: 'Many of the tutors had only just come back from America. They had to try and fit the training into an English setting and it did not altogether fit. Furthermore, the outcome of the training was not known.' Two important principles were, however, established from the start. Firstly, there was an emphasis on a close interconnection of fieldwork and academic study on a concurrent basis, so that the week was divided into days spent in study at the School and in supervised work in mental hospitals and child guidance clinics. Secondly, the fieldwork was divided between these two fields and experience in each was considered essential. Insistence on experience in child guidance and the mental hospital was not at that time in accord with American practice which was based almost entirely on experience in the former type of agency. Why when so much was being learned from America, was this particular variation introduced? It seems to have been due partly to the strong interests of certain psychiatrists working in the mental hospital field (Dr. Mapother at the Maudsley was perhaps particularly influential) and partly to pressures within the group sponsoring the Course. Many in this group saw the two fields of work as completely different— hence neither could serve as a substitute for the other.

The Mental Health Course at the London School of Economics has changed its acknowledged aims over the years, but it has never been concerned solely with training psychiatric social workers as such. In 1929 its aims were stated as the preparation of 'men and women for social work in the field of mental health'.[11] Students were to be 'given practical experience of the social aspect of Mental Health Work . . .' and such experience was to be 'under skilled supervision' and to consist of 'visiting and observation of cases at Child Guidance and other clinics and hospitals as well as attendance at case discussions, conferences and demonstrations'. In 1930, it was stated in addition that 'Home visiting will form part of their training'. This was a reflection of the view common amongst observers outside social work that the distinguishing mark of the social caseworker was not so much what she did as where she did it.[12] The psychiatric social worker, however, very soon came to question this for a number of different reasons, partly because she had to distinguish herself from the 'general' social worker of the time and the disciplines from which she was learning (psychiatry but mainly psychoanalysis) relied on the office or clinic interview which had a higher status than the home visit. Moreover, if she was borrowing something from the technique of psychoanalysis this would encourage her to think of treatment conducted in an environment the physical features of which were controlled by the therapist.

The aims of the Course as stated in the printed syllabus were enlarged in 1933 and again in 1943. In 1933 the alternative was added 'or to widen the knowledge of those already engaged in social case work.' Finally, in 1943 it was stated that 'The course is designed for trained and experienced social workers, who wish to gain further understanding of the causes and treatment of personal difficulties and problems of behaviour in children and adults.' This aim is maintained to the present. In general it seems that the objective has widened from preparation for a particular field of work, described perhaps 'ideologically' as mental health, to furthering the understanding of problems of behaviour, described more generally. The constant focus of the course has been on providing a full year's training for social workers, in spite of attempts in the early years to shorten the course or to introduce students from other disciplines. In 1931, for example, a member of the Mental Health Consultative Committee drew attention to the large number of teachers who applied for the course. There was considerable discussion of this question, and it was finally agreed that the course should provide specialized training only to those already engaged in social work.

Statements of general objectives, however, do not tell us very much about developments in training and for a more detailed account we shall now have to consider changes in selection for training and in its actual content. Such changes can best be studied by focusing attention on one particular training course, the Mental Health Course at the London School of Economics. This was the first, and until 1944, the only course of training for psychiatric social work in Great Britain and it has trained not simply the majority of psychiatric social workers (73 per cent), but almost all those who hold specific appointments in research or fieldwork teaching and 70 per cent of those who have become teachers in institutions of higher education. Yet while attention will be concentrated on one particular course, it is important to realise that the spread of the training of psychiatric social workers to other universities constitutes a development of significance. There is a tendency in the Association of Psychiatric Social Workers (and outside) to equate training simply with the Mental Health Course and this has resulted in some failure to appreciate the problems and perhaps the special function of the courses outside London. A full consideration of these courses is not possible because of limitations of space, but some brief observations will be made in a later section of this chapter.

SELECTION

The task of selection is of considerable importance and its significance has always been stressed in the official views of the Association of Psychiatric Social Workers. It is worth considering for this reason and also because of the importance of selection in social work training generally. Selection procedures for the different branches of social work and for the different training courses show considerable variation and varying amounts of dissatisfaction have been expressed about each method. With such a high demand for trained social workers and the high costs of training it is obvious that much more attention should be given to selection.

Selection for the Mental Health Course in particular has always been subject to a fairly extensive mythology. It has been held, for example, that it is extremely difficult to get a place on the course. McDougall, in a study of applications in two consecutive years,[13] suggested that this idea of stringent selection served two purposes —it was a comfort to those who failed and it encouraged those selected to feel themselves an élite. She showed that about 50 per

23

cent of all applicants to the London School of Economics managed to train on one of the three courses existing at that time and that between 75 and 80 per cent of those who reached the selection committee either gained a place or were encouraged to apply again at a later date. She concluded that 'students with a social science certificate or degree and some social work experience stand a very good chance of getting a place in one of the present training courses.' The more recent figures concerning applications to the three courses at London, Manchester and Edinburgh suggest that this is still basically true. In Edinburgh, for example, in the five-year period 1955-59, almost all applicants were interviewed and usually about half of these were offered a place. For the session 1961-62, however, the relaxation for an experimental period of admission requirements produced for all courses a considerable increase in the number of applications. At London, for example, there was an increase of 47 per cent compared to the previous year, but an increase in those accepted of just under 20 per cent.

How has a selection been made from the number of people who apply each year for training?[14] Selection has always been made on information obtained from three main sources, references, personal statements from applicants and interviews. No use has been made of any kind of psychological tests, though in 1950 some experimental testing was carried out on students from the Course who volunteered. This was not taken very far beyond a beginning stage, partly because of what was considered to be the disturbing effect on the students.

The procedure for selection first became settled in 1932 and consisted of the following stages: Some applicants were seen for an initial discussion and of these some, of course, would be deterred from formal application. If the application was proceeded with, application forms were sent and references obtained; reports were received from Social Science Departments and Social Agencies; the student's essay (e.g. on Family Problems) was received and separate interviews arranged with each of three members of the selection committee, including one psychiatrist; scholars submitted medical certificates and foreign students who were not available for interview supplied a personal recommendation from a psychiatrist. This basic procedure was continued for some years and in 1937 an attempt at an assessment of its effectiveness was made. Since its inception it was found that there had been no rise in the proportion of students assessed 'A' but a fall in the proportion of 'C' students; students under 25 had a larger concentration of 'A' and 'C' than those over 25. Students holding a social science diploma only were more often successful in their examination than those with degrees only, but those with both had a lower proportion of failure. Those with nursing training had a lower proportion of success and with teaching *and* social work experience higher success. Students with no previous employment showed a considerable scatter. In 71 per cent of the cases initial and final assessment were the same. This study of selection procedure and the effect on outcome of training of different experience and qualification could well be repeated.

In January 1938 serious questions were raised concerning the psychiatric interview. One of the psychiatrists concerned voiced ethical doubts about this part of the procedure. In May the issues were discussed at length, and arguments propounded on both sides. Students after qualification would have to do work for which a psychiatrist was ultimately responsible and so it was reasonable for him to play some part in their selection. The interview itself was not based on the assumption that the applicant was a patient. Reports were understood by the applicants to be confidential to the selection committee and it was not contrary to medical etiquette to report to the selection committee on the health of a student if the purpose of the examination was understood by the student. Against these arguments doubts were expressed about the special expertise of a psychiatrist. Would he in an hour's interview be able to form a better judgment of a candidate than other experienced people? It was suggested that the very existence of the psychiatric interview helped to form a misleading impression that the Course was intended to alter personal attitudes and not give students the equipment for a profession. This was largely a false antithesis since certain personal attitudes are part of the professional equipment of the worker and they may require development and sometimes correction. The question of confidence, it was argued, did arise because on some occasions the doctor-patient relationship was established. Finally, the time consuming nature of the procedure was emphasized. A compromise, that psychiatric interviews should be requested only in certain instances, was rejected because of the consequent lack of standardization. The final decision was that such interviews were to continue for all students and that the psychiatrist should continue to be a member of the selection committee. In 1947, however, the psychiatric interview was discontinued as part of the routine procedure for every candidate, though psychiatrists remained on the selection committee. After this date each candidate was interviewed separately by a psychiatric social worker on the academic staff and by one of the fieldwork supervisors involved in the Course. The procedure has remained basically unchanged since then.

What can be said by way of appraising the methods of selection on the Mental Health Course which have also acted as a model or supporting precedent for courses of training for other kinds of social work? Appraisal is concerned, of course, with judging the degree of success in the attainment of objectives and the objectives in this case can be seen as short-term and ultimate. The short-term objective of the selection procedure can be described as the successful completion of the course itself. Selection, however, is not just for a course, but for successful membership of the profession and this objective can be considered as ultimate. Judging the procedure in the light of short-term objectives it would seem to have varying success. In the period 1945-49 between eight and 20 per cent of the students starting the Mental Health Course withdrew before completing the Course or failed in their examinations. In the period 1955-59, however, the proportion is very much lower, ranging from nil to seven per cent. No system can be expected to attain 100 per cent success over a period of time and it certainly seems that the short-term predictive value of the selection procedure has increased in recent years. It is, of course, impossible to say how far this is due to changes in the procedure, but the cessation of routine psychiatric interviews (largely because of the psychiatric time they consumed) has had no harmful effects on short-term objectives.

The selection interview fulfils a number of functions. It enables the candidate to meet and question those who may be teaching him in the near future and it enables the teacher to make a judgment on a number of issues. How does the candidate see himself now, as he was in the past and as he hopes to be in the future? In the light of this are his present goals reasonable and is he pursuing them in a reasonable way? How does the candidate speak of himself as a helping person? How does he respond to the opportunity to explore the way he relates to people or the implications of what he is saying? The interview as a selection tool has been heavily criticized,[15] but if we want considered judgments on questions like these just outlined, it is difficult to see what could replace it. What can be attempted, of course, is an improvement in the accuracy and sureness of these judgments. This can be achieved mainly through searching for clear answers to questions such as, what values should be expected from those interviewd in addition to 'reasonableness', what are the main objectives of the selection procedure and what additional methods might be used to serve as a check or complement to the individual interviewer?

It is certainly true that the selection interview gives the candidate an opportunity to display attitudes, but we are still uncertain of the attitudes required for minimum performance as a psychiatric social worker or for performance approaching the average. Lists of qualities have certainly been compiled in imagination and reality. The Training Sub-Committee of the Association of Psychiatric Social Workers in 1955, for example, saw the following personal qualities and capacities as a requisite for casework: a warm concern for people and a lively interest and curiosity; real tolerance of, and respect for, another's individuality and for their right to make their own decisions; intelligence, capacity for careful observation and objectivity; an adventurous attitude and a capacity to learn from mistakes; a capacity to face aggression in oneself and others, and, finally, personal integrity and the capacity to treat work as a vocation. These are admirable capacities and attitudes, but can their presence or absence be ascertained in the selection interview? It seems in fact likely that these attitudes are built up from one or two more basic personality sets and if this is the case some forms of psychological testing might well be considered. As this or any other list stands we do not know if all psychiatric social workers should possess all these capacities and attitudes or whether there is some order of priority. These questions are to some extent answerable by research[16] and the answers would be a considerable help in giving interviewers a more informed basis for their judgments.

The question concerning the main purpose of the selection interview, however, cannot be answered by research. This requires a decision, which is admittedly difficult. To consider the long-term objectives of selection, for example, that the person selected should make a sufficiently good use of the Course that he becomes a reasonably efficient member of his profession, is to consider the objectives of the whole Course, which will be discussed later. Yet there is evidence that psychiatric social workers have in the past made the decision even more difficult by attempting to give the situation of selection a therapeutic definition. This is clearly the case in Ashdown and Brown's treatment of selection. They saw the selection interview 'as a co-operative attempt to solve a vocational problem'.[17] This attempt to sweeten the reality of power and to hide from the full implications of judging people's suitability seems a reaction typical of the social worker placed in virtual command of scarce resources. The selection interview should certainly be conducted in the light of general social work values, but to treat the applicant as a person who has come for help with a vocational problem is to confuse possible side-effects with the main purpose of deciding whether the person is suitable for *this* Course and what use he is likely to make of it.

The decision to accept or reject a candidate is serious both for the candidate and in terms of the investment of time and money in the successful applicants. Are the two selection interviews a sufficient basis for the decision? It is frequently urged that by participating in an interview the candidate gives the selector the chance to observe and judge him in a situation which is the replica of that in which his future work will be carried out. There is some truth in this view (though we are not, of course, sure of the predictive value of the perceived attitudes, knowledge and skill) but it is possible that the interview of one person by another is a misleading paradigm case for social work. The emphasis on the 'one-to-one' relationship is clearly important, but social work in any setting is also a matter of relationships with groups whether clients, colleagues or other non-social work staff in an institutional setting composed of formal and informal groups. May not some of the apparent failure in long-term prediction be due to the fact that performance in these areas is not tested at selection?

CONTENT OF THE COURSE

Considerable emphasis has always been given on the Course to the fieldwork. This has taken the form of placing the students in selected mental hospitals and child guidance clinics where they are responsible for a small caseload carried under the supervision of fieldwork teachers usually called supervisors. The written reports of the students on the work carried out on their cases forms the basis of 'tutorial' or supervisory sessions which are regularly held by the supervisor. The satisfactory progress of the student in fieldwork has always been a necessary condition of his remaining on the Course and an evaluation of the fieldwork forms a part of the decision on whether to award the Diploma or not.

The arrangement of practical work has undergone three main changes after the experimentation of the first year or so when it was considered important to give the student experience of several different psychiatric agencies. Fieldwork was consolidated after this period into two main placements, one in child guidance and one in a mental hospital, with a small period assigned to work with mental defectives. The syllabus for 1932-33 stated that opportunities for specialization in Child Guidance, Adult Work or Mental Deficiency were given during the third term. In 1933 it is stated that 'a short period of training in mental deficiency work is arranged through the co-operation of the Central Association of Mental Welfare' and this remained a feature of the Course until 1940-41. The discontinuation of this kind of fieldwork is in fact one of the main changes in the arrangement of practical work even though the amount of time involved was very small, approximately one week. The second change was the increase in the number of fieldwork placements. For a long period the only placements used were the Maudsley Hospital and the London Child Guidance Clinic. In 1944 the Committee for Training Social Workers in Mental Health (established in 1940 when consideration was given to the future of the Course on the withdrawal of the Commonwealth Fund) considered the estimated number of psychiatric social workers that would be required. Their Practical Training Committee had previously considered three possible plans, (1) that the present training centres should offer their services to other clinics and hospitals, (2) that students should be scattered in ones and twos in as many hospitals and clinics as were required and should be assembled for special clinical teaching at the two present practical training centres, (3) that further training centres should be established for groups of not less than six students with specially provided supervision. The Practical Training Committee reported that they had decided in favour of (3) and, with the approval of the Director of the L.S.E. had opened negotiations with five clinics and hospitals. Towards the end of the War, for the first time since the beginning of the Course two hospitals other than the Maudsley were used for training, Warlingham Park and Guys, and the Tavistock Clinic was used for child guidance. Since then there have been several changes in hospitals and clinics used.

The third change concerned the extension of the Course by a period of two months fieldwork after the examinations in 1948. The Association of Psychiatric Social Workers had for some time been pressing for an extension of the Course and they expressed a hope that the two months addition of fieldwork would be used to give students experience of a provincial clinic or hospital. The additional placement was used in this way for some time, but for the last two years most students have continued in their second placements after the examinations. This has certainly increased the length of time in which they can carry cases 'in treatment', but students have also lost the opportunity of observing contrasts between the work and its setting in London and the provinces. This may have contributed to the reluctance of psychiatric social workers to spread more evenly over the British Isles. It certainly does not help the student who at the end of training applies for a provincial job where she has to meet and accept conditions of work which in terms of both psychiatric and social work resources may be very different from those in London.

Some idea of the changes in academic subjects taught can be obtained from a comparison of early and late syllabi. For these purposes the syllabus of the first two years proved atypical so that the year 1932-33 has been selected as representative of the earlier years of training.

1932-33	1959-60
General Psychology (10) Fildes	Psychiatry (12) plus 15 demonstrations Dr. K. Taylor
Administration of Acts (8)	
Individual Differences (10) Burt	The Mental Health Services (10) Mrs. McDougall
Mental Subnormality (10) Dr. Tredgold	
Psychiatric Social Case Work (15) Dr. Posthuma	The Study of Personality (10) Mr. Price Williams
Physical Causes (10) Dr. Posthuma	Mental Deficiency (3 plus 2 demonstrations) Dr. Thomas

The Origins and Development of Training

1932-33	1959-60
Applied Social Psychology (10) Clement Brown	A Sociological Approach to Social Problems (10) Mr. Wright
General Psychiatry (10) Dr. Moodie	Group Work in Psychiatric Settings (6)
Psychology of Childhood and Adolescence (10) Burt	Psychology of Family Relations (10) Mrs. Bannister
Mental Health in Early Childhood (10) Dr. Hadfield	Applied Physiology (6) Dr. Gibbons
Mental Disorder in Childhood (10) Dr. Moodie	Child Development (12) Miss Gardner
	Clinical Aspects of Child Development (14) Dr. Gillespie
	Social Casework Weekly class (29)
	Social Administration Weekly class (29):
	Children's Services (10)
	Delinquency Services (10)
	Mental Health (9)

This simple contrast shows both change and stability. One of the chief changes is the difference in time devoted to the study of mental deficiency. The subject is taught throughout the Course, but the time given varies from 17 lectures to the present arrangement of three lectures and two demonstrations. Much of the earlier teaching was, however, concerned with legislation. In other areas of learning there have been marked increases in time given and considerable differentiation in subject matter. The most noticeable increase has been in the time given to a consideration and identification of the methods to be used i.e. casework and group work. There has also been a considerable change in the content of casework teaching. This is not evident from the syllabi, but can be illustrated by a contrast between the examination questions asked on this subject in early and more recent years.

1932
(a) Assuming that 'bad companionship' is a frequent contributing factor in delinquency, what methods would you adopt towards discovery of its importance and towards adjustment in any particular case?
(b) A representative committee sets up a new Child Guidance Clinic in

a provincial city. Outline for the Social Worker some of her most important activities in the first few months.

(c) 'Only the individual himself can reveal the true meaning of his experiences. Therefore, the individual's own story is the first and most significant evidence in the history.' Discuss the implications of this statement for method in family casework.

(d) A child of 15 with co-operative parents of poor circumstances is attending a London Clinic on account of pathological stealing. Discuss the advantages and disadvantages of the alternatives open to you in arranging for the child to be placed away from home, including those with legal sanction for detention.

1960

(a) What do you understand by the term 'transference'? How is transference most likely to manifest itself in a casework situation?

(b) Discuss some of the main factors which you, as the psychiatric social worker, would consider in your first interview with the relative of a depressed patient newly admitted to hospital.

(c) What factors do you weigh up in deciding whether long term casework is the appropriate treatment in a particular case?

(d) 'The psychiatric social worker's task in child guidance is to concern herself with the problems and anxieties of the mother'. Discuss.

From the contrast between these two years a number of developments can be seen. The importance of psychoanalytic theory is clear from the first question in 1960 and questions about the difference between social casework and psychotherapy or, less understandably, psychiatry, began to appear in the examination papers after 1944. The 1932 questions seem to be more concerned than those of 1960 with the social history and in fact the term has not been used in examination papers since 1950. The early question concerning the pioneering of a child guidance clinic represents an issue which does not have as much importance for later years. There is in the later questions a greater differentiation in casework 'treatment' and a noticeable shift in its objectives. In the 1960 questions it is possible to see a differentiation between phases of casework (e.g. the *first* interview) and between treatments of varying duration (long term casework). It is also possible to see the objectives of casework as more clearly concerned with emotions (transference, the anxieties of the mother) than with the 'adjustment' and environmental manipulation of the earlier paper.

Although there are important differences between the content of the Course at its beginning and in 1960, it is important to remember also the basic continuities. From 1932 a core of subjects emerges which has a fairly continuous history. These subjects are: physiology, general psychology, general psychiatry, mental disorders in children, mental deficiency, the psychology of individual difference, and the psychology of childhood and adolescence. In addition attention is paid to the administration of particular acts. There are also case discussions and seminars on the wider aspects of mental health.

It would appear that psychology was given a greater emphasis in the earlier years of the Course. A series of lectures on general psychology ran from 1930 until 1941; and another on the psychology of individual differences from 1930 to 1941, with a break of one year. From 1943 to 1948 a course of lectures on 'Psychology and Mental Health' was given by Blackburn. The syllabus shows that this was concerned with 'Motivation and emotion. Reflexes and conditioned reflexes; the doctrine of instincts and its limitations . . . Mental mechanisms, the contribution of Freud and Adler . . . Perception . . . imagining . . . thinking . . . remembering . . . ability . . . Temperament and types. Vocational guidance and selection. Social conditions of work. Psychoneuroses of industry.' This represents a combination of general and social psychology, with some reference to the psychoanalysts. After 1948, however, the general psychology seems to be omitted and the areas of interest become personality (from 1953) and the psychology of family relations (from 1959). This last development forms part of a noticeable movement towards greater emphasis on the wider groupings of family and society. A course on social medicine ran from 1946 to 1951 and on sociological concepts from 1954 onwards. 'Greater emphasis' rather than a new emphasis because social work teaching seems for a great deal of the Course to have had the intention of linking social work to a social and ethical context. For example, a Course on 'Introduction to the Mental Health Course' aimed at an 'Historical introduction. Recent developments in (1) social attitude towards the study and treatment of the mentally unfit, (2) the study and treatment of delinquents and criminals, (3) objects and methods of social work. Implications of mental hygiene considered in terms of social institutions, public administration and social casework'. From 1943 to 1949 lectures were given on the Child Guidance Clinic as a social institution.

The other important change in regard to the teaching of psychology was the introduction in 1950 of the first course of systematic teaching in psychoanalysis with Dr. Gillespie's lectures on Clinical Aspects of Child Development. Students undoubtedly had contact with and were influenced by psychoanalysis before this, but the sources of their knowledge were incidental references in general psychology teaching and, of greater importance, the teaching provided in the fieldwork centres both in seminars held by psychiatrists and in individual supervisory sessions taken by psychiatric social workers.

OTHER TRAINING COURSES[18]

(1) Edinburgh
This course in Psychiatric Social Work was instituted by the Edinburgh Department of Social Studies, in 1944, in the face of considerable difficulties when, as the Association itself acknowledged, 'There were minimal facilities for giving Scottish students practical experience within reach of a teaching centre, and when the very novelty of the idea made the Association of Psychiatric Social Workers, the guardians of professional standards, cautionery rather than encouraging'.[19] Up to 1962 the Course trained 149 psychiatric social workers (23 men and 126 women). Perhaps the most important development on the Course in the last few years has been the extent to which students have come to take most of their lectures in common with students in medical social work and child care. This has produced something like a psychiatric social work stream in a more general Course of professional training for social work.

Students are selected after two interviews, one with one of the two psychiatric social work lecturers to the Course and the other with one of the fieldwork supervisors. As part of the selection procedure each candidate submits a statement (of not more than 500 words) on his or her reasons for wishing to take the training. Candidates should be over the age of 22 and should normally hold a social science qualification and it is explicitly assumed that this has involved attendance at 'a full university class in psychology'. The syllabus includes lectures and tutorials in: human growth and development; the field of work, including social administration; casework (with emphasis on the social aspects of mental disorders and mental deficiency; introduction to Medicine; psychological medicine, including child psychiatry and mental deficiency; psychology and social administration. Fieldwork is divided between a child psychiatric clinic and a mental hospital and during the summer vacation students gain full-time experience in psychiatric social work in centres outside Edinburgh.

(2) *Manchester*

The course began in 1946 in the Department of Psychology and was transferred in 1949 to the newly created Department of Psychiatry thus becoming the first and, so far, the only, course of training for psychiatric social work in a Faculty of Medicine. Up to 1962 the numbers of students averaged 9-10 because of the lack both of suitable accommodation and of approved fieldwork placements in the area. In 1962 the course was transferred to new premises and the number of students increased to 14 with an ultimate limit of 20, but it seems that the problem of fieldwork remains serious. The course has fed back into the region a fair proportion of its students, but these are spread over the large county of Lancashire and farther north and are not concentrated in Manchester itself.

The lecturer-in-charge of the Course has commented that the aim in the last few years has been increasingly to emphasize the purely psychiatric aspects of psychiatric social work. The Course hopes to give students a good grounding in their approach to psychiatric disorder and its treatment. The emphasis is on providing a reliable basis of medical understanding, with social work seen as auxiliary to the objectives of mental treatment. This represents to some extent an emphasis that differs from that of the Mental Health Course, and a definition of psychiatric social work that stresses its clinical function rather than 'psychodynamic' casework, though due attention is paid to the concepts of child guidance.

Since it began the Manchester Course has trained 144 psychiatric social workers (20 men and 124 women). Students are now accepted after interview with the University Selection Committee and only in exceptional circumstances are candidates under 23 years of age accepted for training. The theoretical content of the Course consists of lectures, tutorials and seminars in: psychiatry; including child psychiatry, psychopathology and physiology;

mental deficiency; psychology (including human development); principles and methods of psychiatric social work; historical, legal and social aspects of the mental health services; and social and psychological aspects of delinquency and crime. Fieldwork is divided into three periods over one calendar year. One of these is spent in the University Department of Psychiatry at the Manchester Royal Infirmary or other approved hospital; another at an approved child guidance clinic and the third in psychiatric units or local Health Authorities outside the Manchester area.

(3) *Liverpool*

A course of training for psychiatric social workers began in Liverpool in 1954 as a result of discussions between the University and the Regional Hospital Board on the serious shortage of trained psychiatric social workers on Merseyside. The course constitutes one of the specializations leading to the Diploma in Social Administration; the others are child care and, most recently, group and community work.

Much of the teaching is given in common to all the specialist groups, but each retains, to some extent, its own identity. The course has trained (1954-62, inclusive) 20 students, but just over half these have qualified in the last two years.

Students are selected from an average (since 1959) of about twenty applicants each year. Each candidate, provided the entrance requirements are met, is given four separate interviews. These interviews are taken singly by a psychiatrist, fieldwork supervisor, and two academic tutors. Decisions are reached on the basis of information supplied by the candidate, references and the interviews: candidates are not asked to submit any written statement concerning their personal motivation for social work. The subjects studied on the course include social psychiatry, the administration of the Mental Health services, Child health and development, deviations of personality and the theory and practice of psychiatric social work. Examinations are held covering these five subjects. Fieldwork consists of two days a week in a child psychiatric setting in the Autumn and Lent terms followed by a period of twelve weeks in the psychiatric social work department of a mental hospital.

The Origins and Development of Training

CRITICISMS OF TRAINING FOR PSYCHIATRIC SOCIAL WORK

There has been no sustained and detailed appraisal of training for Psychiatric Social Work. The Standing Advisory Committee on Training for Psychiatric Social Work, established in 1954 by the professional association, has the duty to 'review at regular intervals the adequacy of existing courses for granting qualifications in psychiatric social work', but its records are, of course, confidential and have not been made available for the present study. Certain criticisms have, however, been made of the training given to psychiatric social workers and others can be based on the content of the training described above. The training courses have, at different times, been seen as too specialized or insufficiently specialized, as too long or too short. What truth is there in such judgments?

The specialized nature of the training has, of course, been criticized in the light of the movement towards a common training for all branches of social casework. Younghusband, for example, has stated that 'The profound, though possibly inevitable, mistake that was made when this training was first instituted was that instead of making it a general course in social case work with the option of a psychiatric social work, medical social work or probation or family casework bias it was instituted as, and has remained, a specialized training in and for work with those who are seriously disturbed emotionally.'[20] Part of this criticism is, of course, based on wisdom after the event; one wonders exactly how mistaken *are* inevitable mistakes. No one would have recognized in 1930 or for many years after the extent to which training could be based on a common core of social casework knowledge which is 'generic' to all the specializations. In order for any 'break-through' in training to be made at all it was necessary to create a specialization so that effort and attention were made fruitful by emphasis on one aspect of social work. The criticism also fails to acknowledge the wider intentions of the training courses, even though it implicitly admits that the specialization was based on kind of client (i.e. the emotionally disturbed) rather than kind of setting (e.g. psychiatric). As we have seen the Course *intended* to prepare students to implement mental health principles in the wide field of social work and this intention was partly realized. Some critics even amongst psychiatric social workers were disappointed that the new workers

37

had not permeated general social work more deeply, but such criticism failed to appreciate both the unrealistic expectations other social workers held of psychiatric social work and also the extent to which from the beginning those trained on the Mental Health Course returned to, or entered, jobs outside the fields of psychiatric social work.

Younghusband fails to appreciate the extent to which psychiatric social work training might with justification be described itself as the first 'generic' training. The idea of 'generic' training is by no means clear, but essentially it seems concerned with imparting the knowledge and attitudes that are common to all branches of social work. This is accomplished by a considerable emphasis on the psychological and, to a lesser degree, the sociological influences on human behaviour and development and by an educational programme which combines fieldwork in two different social work agencies with concurrent academic work at the university. It appears that much of this description could apply to the Mental Health Course and other trainings in psychiatric social work. In particular, as we have seen, the principle of two fieldwork placements (child guidance and mental hospital) has been upheld from the beginning.

This principle is by no means self-evidently valid and it has been questioned from time to time. In 1933, for example, the Commonwealth Fund suggested that the Certificate might be endorsed 'Child Guidance Only' where students had not been placed in a mental hospital. However, the Mental Health Course Consultative Committee considered that this was undesirable since students should experience the whole range of problems in the psychiatric settings. Since then the principle of the two placements has been twice questioned. In 1951 Bowlby presented a memorandum to the Mental Health Course Committee on the inadequacy of the length of each separate placement. He considered that two short placements were inadequate if students were to carry cases long enough to develop their casework skill. The memorandum was considered, but no change was made in the Course and eventually Bowlby together with a leading psychiatric social worker, Noel Hunnybun established at the Tavistock Clinic an Advanced Casework Course based on a year's supervised fieldwork in a single institution. Finally, the Community Care Group of the Association of Psychiatric Social Workers suggested that there were now three fields of work rather than two, child guidance, the mental hospital and community care or work in the setting of the local health authority. The Training Sub-Committee of the Association considered the question in 1959 and was unanimously of the opinion that mental hospital experience was an essential preliminary to work in a community care service. It was considered that the newly qualified needed the support of a clinical setting before moving out to take responsibility on their own. The clinical setting, moreover, helped them to become immersed in the disciplines of diagnostic assessment and of working with people of different professional backgrounds. This could be said to represent a fairly general view amongst psychiatric social workers and certainly no major changes have been advocated along these lines by the tutors. Some changes, however, have occurred and in 1961 a number of students from the Mental Health Course spent one week each in a local authority where psychiatric social workers were employed 'in order to gain insight into the work in the local authority fields'.[21]

These are some of the questions that have been raised during the development of the Mental Health Course in connection with the policy of two separate placements. Important questions remain, however. How far are students expected to learn different things in each placement? There are certainly differences between social work in the child guidance clinic and mental hospital in terms of kinds of client, focus of work and responsibility taken by the psychiatric social worker. How far are these differences due to particular styles of work established as traditions in each setting and how far should students be encouraged to think of themselves as workers who can move easily between the settings, treating the differences as matters of relative unimportance? From the point of view of employment there seems to be considerable justification for the continuation of two kinds of placement, if what is learned in one cannot be learned in the other. It was estimated that before the War 16 per cent of psychiatric social workers had worked in both child guidance and mental hospital work and 25 per cent had worked at some time in clinics, catering for both children and adults.[22] Almost the same proportion of psychiatric social workers have followed this general pattern since the War, judging from the follow-up study of two groups of students (to be discussed fully in the following chapter). Of the students trained in 1947 and 1948

39

26 per cent had worked in both fields and 15 per cent in jobs that combined work with adults and children; of those trained in 1952 and 1953, the figures are 26 and 14 per cent respectively.

Yet, what of community care? How far can this be seen as a third field with parity with the two older fields? The answer to this question depends on what are thought to be the special features of this field, on what has to be learned for effective practice within it, and on what can be learned in this setting. All three considerations need to be assessed, though attention has hitherto been focused on only one element at a time. Perhaps most attention has been paid to the local authority setting of the work, but it is possible that the way this affects the work can be best appreciated at the stage of training through the general study of the psychology and sociology of institutions at work in our society. Such knowledge, or rather an approach to understanding such institutions through our knowledge of small groups and of large and small-scale institutions, could then be applied, adapted, and indeed augmented in whatever setting the social worker entered. One wonders why 'the local authority' setting has received so much emphasis that it has come to be regarded as a specialization in its own right? Again, this issue calls for empirical research, but it seems as if psychiatric social workers, judging by their employment records, regard this field as one to be entered after experience in child guidance or mental hospital. In the work study in the following chapter only about seven per cent of the students who qualified in the four years investigated went into community care as a first job. This proportion may increase, however, as community care develops. The Annual Report of the A.P.S.W. (1961) recorded that more newly qualified workers went into community care than into child guidance or into mental hospitals.

A more fundamental criticism of the training courses is raised implicitly by a psychiatric social worker concerned with the role of her colleagues in helping the mentally handicapped in the community. She suggested that: 'We might ask ourselves whether the techniques of intensive casework practised by Psychiatric Social Workers in Child Guidance Clinic, Psychiatric Out-Patient Departments, or even within Mental Hospitals are appropriate for dealing with stresses affecting all members of a family who have experienced breakdown in one of their number.'[23] This is really to ask how far the skills learned in training and consolidated in practice are transferable even within the field of mental health, let alone to other kinds of social work. The use of the term 'intensive' is, of course, misleading especially when applied to such a range of settings. It would appear, judging from the writings of psychiatric social workers and from informal discussions with them, that the most important results of a training in psychiatric social work are the increase in psychiatric knowledge and psychological understanding of oneself and others. This is certainly transferable to work in any setting. Its limitations are partly a reflection of the present state of knowledge and partly of imperfect adaptation to different settings. This faulty adaptation is in its turn partly the result of certain features of training. These will now be briefly considered.

In the Mental Health Course there has been a complete absence of teaching on research method or on the appreciation of the place of research in social work. A cultivated spirit of enquiry would have helped students to develop a keener sense of curiosity about the different settings in which they went to work. There has been a considerable emphasis throughout much of the Course on the child and on services on his behalf. Ashdown and Brown, for example, stated that 'In training . . . while the social history takes an important place and the need for a student to gain experience in interpreting her work to others is fully recognized, 'treatment', especially of the mother of a child patient at a child guidance clinic, is apt to be made the touchstone of the student's work.'[24] This emphasis has led to the over valuing of long-term work directed to the unfolding and working through of problems in parent-child relationships. It has also supported the tendency (which originated in psychoanalysis) to use, as one of the critical criteria for judging successful progress in casework, the extent to which the nature of childhood relationships are revealed in any particular case. I do not wish to deny the influence of the past on the present, but an overwhelming emphasis on childhood relationships has perhaps obscured for psychiatric social workers the significance of the changes that occur throughout life, the importance of 'Transformations of Identity'[25] not only in childhood and adolescence, but in marriage, work and retirement.

We have in this chapter considered changes in the Mental Health Course and some of the criticisms that have been made and could perhaps with more justice be made of the training involved. In considering these criticisms it is important to bear in mind that the teaching on such courses is determined to some extent by the content of the pre-professional courses. As this has changed so, for example, the Mental Health Course has been able to give less time to general psychology and more to the study of abnormal mental states. It is also important to remember that new developments in teaching are dependent on the recruitment of staff with the necessary knowledge and skill. For example, in 1962 no course is offering students teaching on groupwork, though this might be a significant part of their work in some agencies. This is mainly due to the shortage of teachers trained in groupwork methods. It should in theory be possible for existing staff to develop new subjects, but the length of the course and the time spent in interviewing candidates for selection etc. means that teachers on courses of training have much less time available than their colleagues in other university departments for such projects.

There have been two major opportunities in the last decade or so to review the training of psychiatric social workers. The Macintosh Report and the study by Ashdown and Brown. Both reported a general satisfaction amongst psychiatric social workers, but these are, of course, only one of the several groups who should be expected to judge these matters. The experience of taking the training has clearly a considerable influence on students, but that training must be judged also in relation to the fields of work for which students are prepared. Is there not at present, for example, some conflict between the objective of training a student so that she can learn to gain satisfaction from clinical practice, and pressure from many quarters, including the Macintosh and Younghusband Reports, that psychiatric social workers should also be prepared to offer an educational consultation to other social workers, as one of the main aspects of her job? She may be trained for long-term casework, but when she takes up her job find that she is expected to spend a considerable part of her time helping other social workers.

Future study of the training for psychiatric social work could profitably concentrate on two issues, what are the objectives of training and how is training related to the demands made on the student in learning and in her practice. The formulation of the objectives of training is peculiarly difficult for the training courses we have been considering. The main reason for this, of course, lies in the breadth of purpose entertained: the training is not simply for practise in psychiatric social work. This has encouraged (certainly until 1948) the formulation of aims so highly generalized that their meaning is not always clear. Thus, Ashdown and Brown stated that the goal of training is not the preparation of technicians, assuming that we know what a technician in human relations is. 'We think of it rather as the application within the field of mental hygiene of a certain way of seeing things—of seeing the individual and his environment (personal, social, cultural, material) always as one whole, of which the parts act upon and react to each other. Out of this way of seeing will arise appropriate ways of doing, according to the varied situations which arise.'[26] In such a panoramic and holistic context it is difficult to contemplate objectives of what might be termed the middle distance. Psychiatric social workers in general have found difficulty in formulating objectives which are, as it were, mid-way between such immediate aims as 'therapeutic listening' and the 'Great adventure of self-discovery.' It is doubtful whether an holistic point of view will of itself produce beneficial results. Indeed many philanthropists towards the end of the nineteenth century were so impressed with the interconnectedness of the social world that it became an object of contemplation rather than a field for action. It is significant that systematic appraisal of the adequacy of the mental health services developed slowly on the Mental Health Course and did not appear in the syllabus until 1947.

The objectives of training must be realistically conceived in ways which at least admit the possibility of some kind of test to ensure that they are being realized. Successful training should be judged largely by its effect on the work carried out after training. Training may not be concerned with passing on, in an intellectualized and condensed form, the detailed content of particular jobs, but we should expect to find meaningful connections between training and work. For the psychiatric social work courses such a demand represents a difficult challenge. Even from the early days of training successful students have gone into a wide variety of social work jobs. Even in psychiatric social work, workers have had to meet considerable difference in expectation both between different fields (e.g. child guidance and mental hospital) and in the same field. Psychiatric social workers in different fields and different areas (i.e. London as compared to the provinces) seem to have had differing expectations of themselves. Ashdown and Brown have commented on the increased uncertainty about role in the candidates of 1947 compared with those of ten years before, but if the distribution of posts in the early years is studied (see Chapter Four), it must be concluded that this is a change of emphasis only.

Yet, however diversified the jobs that successful students obtain, it is at present particularly important that some attempt be made to measure training against job. It is important for selection and for the continued high prestige of the profession. In the following chapters the greatly increased demand for psychiatric social workers is illustrated but this has only limited use in measuring the successful growth of the profession. How far does the demand represent an uncritical acceptance of what appears to be an essential part of fashionable policy and how far a response from people (psychiatrists, committees, etc.) who have experienced the work of psychiatric social workers and been satisfied?

An approach to the task of measuring training against job is to consider the role of the psychiatric social worker as student and as practitioner. This will highlight the kinds of uncertainty for which she should be prepared. Training for any kind of social work must always be, in varying degrees, a training for uncertainty. The identity of social work has to be created anew as society and our conceptions of society change and in each individual case the social worker is concerned with establishing her identity and creating a function specific to the case, albeit on a basis of a general identity and an established function. On the Mental Health Course, however, there have been and are still special factors that increase the uncertainty of role definition.

As a student the 'pyschiatric social worker' meets a number of strains in regard to her job. The need for the careful handling of clients is stressed and she is made aware of the great responsibilities involved in working with the emotionally disturbed, yet she knows she is comparatively inexperienced. She may be told to carry on as she did as a practising social worker, but she knows that she came on the course to improve her former practice. She is encouraged to show warmth to clients, to use her own feelings as a means of discovering the sort of person her client is and she is also warned about the damage 'unscrutinized' personal reactions can do. She usually enrolled for training because she had a

44

reasonably strong moral character, but moralizing is judged harmful, and the place of moral judgments in social work is obscure. She is encouraged to use psychoanalytic knowledge and at the same time she must not confuse her work with analysis. She gradually attempts to work out a professional identity as a psychiatric social worker, but here again uncertainty prevails.

The 'psychiatric social worker' is encouraged to make her diagnosis of a case as a social worker, but she is also a member of a team led by the doctor. She has to make her own role very often in child guidance clinics or in mental hospitals and she has to decide how far she sees herself as a therapist and how far, if necessary, others in the team can be led to accept her definition of her role. After training she tries to develop her professional skills and, for this reason, is attracted to centres where her colleagues are already established. Yet she knows that large areas of the country and whole groups of people are left without help. In her job she may try to develop her skill by 'intensive' work with a few cases and thus be in danger of failing to give sufficient attention or appropriate help to the remaining majority. In any case her work is punctuated by uncertainty. During training she absorbed varying amounts of psychoanalytic theory and has perhaps come to see that the problem which the client presents is not always the one with which he should be helped and that the 'sickest' member of the family is not always the one presented as client or patient. She has been taught to start where the client is and to proceed at the client's pace, but she has also appreciated the value of setting and achieving objectives in her work. She has perhaps read many references to social work knowledge yet she is aware how rudimentary and scattered this is. In spite of this she often has to act quickly and decisively.

These are some of the uncertainties for which the psychiatric social worker (and most other kinds of social worker) need to be trained. A detailed investigation of these role demands would be a fruitful way of beginning to measure training against performance. We should not, however, always have to rely on special research projects in order to appraise our training. Attention should be given to establishing or improving institutional ways of judging its results. Of special importance in this context is the existence of any machinery by which information about the effects of training is fed back to those responsible for the courses. There are several possible sources of such information, the employing bodies, psychiatric social workers in practice, their clients, and their colleagues. At present the only feedback mechanisms in existence are the formal appraisals of the Standing Advisory Committee and the informal reports on the training that individuals might make. If one examines the group of psychiatric social workers responsible for training it appears that very few are also in clinical practice themselves, the average time that has elapsed since their training is 15 years and it has been many years since many of them practised. The profession is thus deprived of a useful feedback mechanism that could exist in teachers themselves, though the close connection of some with the professional association and with research organizations does mean a continuing contact with development in the field.

NOTES

[1] Blacker, C. P., *Neurosis and the Mental Health Services*, 1946, p. 95.

[2] Anon. 'Eliminating the Subjective', *Charity Organisation Review*, June 1919.

[3] The average number of students qualifying in the first five years of the Mental Health Course at the London School of Economics was approximately 10 per year.

[4] *Report of the Royal Commission on Lunacy and Mental Disorder*, 1926, Cmd. 2700 S. 53.

[5] Burt, C., 'An Autobiographical Sketch', *Occupational Psychology*, Vol. XXIII, 1949.

[6] *Report of the Committee on Maladjusted Children* (Underwood) H.M.S.O. 1955, p. 8.

[7] *Ibid*, p. 8.

[8] Secretary of the C.O.S. quoted in Burt, C., 'Individual Psychology and Social Work', *Charity Organisation Review*, Vol. XLIII (New Series) January and February, 1918.

[9] The two following quotations are from the first article quoted above. My interpretation of Burt's answer is different from that recently given in Woodroofe, K., *From Charity to Social Work* (1962) p. 138. There his answer is described as 'decidedly ambiguous' and his attitude as 'lukewarm'. This view fails to mark his distinction between 'the abstract study of the mind in general' (which 'for the social worker . . . may indeed form an entertaining and even a suggestive hobby') and 'a newer psychology in the making', the psychology of individual differences. The study of the individual psychology of the applicant by the social worker is robustly advocated by Burt who looked for the day when psychological study would create 'social principles

(which) would no longer be mere rules of thumb. They would form like medicine, engineering, or industrial chemistry, an applied science, though one of a far higher order and a far nobler rank'.

[10] Macadam, E., *The Equipment of the Social Worker*, 1925 p. 189.

[11] Quotations in this and the following paragraph are taken from the Calendars of the London School of Economics.

[12] See, for example, the P.E.P. *Report on the British Social Services*, 1937, where it is stated that 'In view of the importance of *home contacts* in some of the constructive community services and of the *home visitation* in the administration of the social assistance services, there is plainly a real need for a comprehensive course of training in social case work . . .' p. 175 (italics not in original).

[13] McDougall, K., 'Chances of Selection for the Mental Health Course', *British Journal of Psychiatric Social Work*, No. 7, March 1953.

[14] Material on the development of the Mental Health Course has been obtained from Minutes of the Selection Committee, Minutes of the Mental Health Course Consultative Committee, Minutes of the Committee for Training Social Workers in Mental Health and Minutes of the Mental Health Course Committee.

[15] See, e.g. Eysenck, H. J., *Uses and Abuses of Psychology*, 1954. p. 129: . . .'no one who has examined the literature can have the slightest doubt that the interview as a clue to personality qualities is extremely unreliable and almost entirely lacking in validity'.

[16] It would, for example, be relatively simple and also instructive to discover professional opinion on the qualities of a good social worker. For an early attempt to investigate this question, in another profession, see Cattell, R. B., 'The Assessment of Teaching Ability—A Survey of Professional Opinion on the qualities of a good teacher'. *British Journal of Educational Psychology*, Vol. I, February 1931.

[17] Ashdown, M., and Brown, Clement, *op. cit.* p. 72.

[18] I am indebted for material on which these short accounts are based to the tutors of the training courses at Edinburgh (Miss Megan Browne), Manchester (Miss M. Hamilton) and Liverpool (Miss J. Simpson).

[19] *Report of the Association of Psychiatric Social Workers for the Years 1944-45-46.*

[20] Younghusband, E., 'Forward to 1903', *Social Work*, Vol. 10, No. 3, July 1953.

[21] *Annual Report of the Association of Psychiatric Social Workers*, 1961.

[22] Estimate given by Clement Brown at a general meeting of the A.P.S.W. July 1942.

[23] Castle, M., 'Mentally Handicapped People in the Community and the Role of the Psychiatric Social Worker', *Case Conference*, December 1955.

[24] *Op. cit.* p. 119.

[25] This is the title of a chapter by Strauss, A., (in Rose, A. (ed.), *Human Behaviour and Social Processes*, 1962), which attempts to demonstrate the importance of role changes in adult life.

[26] *Op. cit.*, p. 228.

Chapter Three

WHO ARE PSYCHIATRIC SOCIAL WORKERS?

THE question who are Psychiatric Social Workers, has up to the present received no firm empirical answer. This chapter presents certain basic information which has been collected on all students qualifying as psychiatric social workers up to 1962. This will enable us for the first time to discover the number who have trained, their ages, their academic qualifications, and their work experience before training. In order to obtain the necessary data information was collected from the training centres. These are the London School of Economics, and the Courses at Edinburgh established in 1945, Manchester, 1947, and Liverpool, 1954.[1]

Up to 1962 a total of 1202 people had qualified at these university centres as psychiatric social workers. Of these 136 were men.

The actual growth of psychiatric social work can be seen in a simple comparison of the numbers trained in the six quinquennial periods from 1930:

Table I: Numbers of Psychiatric Social Workers Trained
1930-1959 by Quinquennial Periods

Quinquennial Periods	Numbers Trained
1930–34	59
1935–39	106
1940–44	92
1945–49	224
1950–54	236
1955–59	224
(1960–62	161)

From these figures it is clear that we are now training just under

48

four times as many psychiatric social workers as we did in the first five years of training. Yet while the number trained 1935-39 was approximately double that trained in the previous period and this number was itself more than doubled in the period 1945-49, this figure was only very slightly increased 1950-54, and in the period 1955-59 we trained only as many psychiatric social workers as in the period 1945-49. More recent figures indicate, however, that the period 1960-64 will show an increase on the 1950-54 figures.

As a context for the preliminary interpretation of these figures it is helpful to compare them with recent figures for the recruitment of other social workers. In child care, for example, the number of officers increased between 1956 and 1960 from about 1,000 to almost 1,400; in probation between 1950 and 1961 the numbers of full-time officers increased from just over 1,000 to 1,749 (an increase of 74 per cent); between 1955 and 1959 twice as many almoners were trained as psychiatric social workers. Non-psychiatric social workers are maintaining or increasing their numbers, but a parallel increase cannot be expected in psychiatric social work because of the requirements for training. A significant proportion of child care officers (39 per cent in 1960) have no university qualification (either a social science diploma or a professional qualification in social work), while 45 per cent of the full-time probation officers appointed between 1958 and 1961 were direct entrants to the service without university qualification. For acceptance for training as psychiatric social workers students usually hold a social science degree or diploma or a non-social science degree followed by a social science diploma. Their training, like that of the Almoners, is in most cases, therefore, postgraduate, but psychiatric social work students, unlike Almoners, have usually had some experience in social work before starting their training. As a group psychiatric social work students are older and more experienced. A relaxation of admission requirements would undoubtedly increase the numbers of psychiatric social workers but this would affect the quality of training. This would be regrettable for psychiatric social work, and a generally retrograde step in view of the already uneven quality of social work as a whole.

An examination of the total of psychiatric social workers trained each year reveals interesting fluctuations within the quinquennial periods. The highest annual number of recruits was in 1947 (61), but the average recruitment between 1947 and 1959, the years after the Second World War is 46·6. The change in numbers since training began can be best illustrated by taking the average for two periods unaffected by the Second World War which initially reduced numbers and then produced the record figure just mentioned. Taking the ten year period 1930-39 the yearly average of recruits is 16·5 and for a similar period 1950-59 the average is 45. This increase is due to the beginning of training in other centres, and to the fact that the London School of Economics was admitting more students to the Mental Health Course. Yet the increase in numbers is not maintained in each year of training. Indeed the total of students trained on the four courses under consideration did not between 1956 and 1959 reach the 1955 total of 51. The L.S.E. Course shows a steady decline and so do the Manchester and Edinburgh Courses with the exception of 1957 for Edinburgh and 1958 for Manchester. It is not until 1961 that more than two students qualify on the Liverpool Course.

What are the possible reasons for such short-term and long-term fluctuations at a time when the prestige of psychiatric social work is high and when a succession of Government Committees has drawn attention to the importance of meeting the greatly increased demand for their services?

In the first place the increase in the period after the War is partly explained by exceptionally heavy recruitment in 1946. The London School of Economics, for example, admitted 54 students and 'for the first time good candidates had to be refused for lack of space.'[2] Secondly, the provincial training courses have succeeded in training only a small number of workers and even these small numbers have not always been sustained. Thus, in the quinquenneum 1955-59 Manchester trained 12 less workers than in the preceding period, and Edinburgh two less. Thirdly, there have been marked changes in the numbers applying for training and in those withdrawing before the Courses start. It is difficult to assess application figures, since the numbers recorded by the different Courses refer to applications rather than 'real' applicants. It is quite common practice for students to apply to more than one of the Courses. However, taking the London School of Economics, as an example, it seems clear that the period 1955-59 saw a significant decrease in the number of applicants, of interviews held to consider applications, and of students starting and finishing the Course compared with the period 1945-49. This seems due to a number of factors including a general uncertainty about the continued existence of psychiatric social work and training as such. The position has improved, however, as the training appears securely established and the experimental relaxation of entrance requirements has encouraged applications from a wider field. In 1961-62 there were 127 applications compared to an average of 78 in the previous seven years and 108 of these were considered compared to an average of 69 before. Yet whatever the number of candidates offered places there are always some who withdraw at such a late date that their places remain unfilled. In the session 1958-59, for example, 10 students withdrew before the Course started and there were insufficient suitable candidates to take their place. This is an unusually high figure, but the average seems around half this number. Reasons for withdrawal are various—personal (including marriage), failure in examinations, failure to obtain a grant. Yet whatever the reason withdrawal certainly presents a much more serious problem of loss at the present time than, for example, failure in the examinations.

A review of the numbers qualifying over the years does raise several significant questions. It seems that around 1945 we reached a kind of plateau in training for psychiatric social work and that any major extension of numbers since then has been extremely difficult. Does this mean that we can expect to train only a very limited number of psychiatric social workers and that we cannot expect to increase this number substantially even if we create new training courses in other universities? Judging from past experience this is true only to an extent. The Courses at Manchester and Edinburgh have trained respectively 144 and 149 students (up to 1962) and it is certain that places could not have been found for all of these students on the Mental Health Course at the London School of Economics, even though this Course has sometimes started without its full complement of students. The Course of training that began in the comparatively recent past (Liverpool) has produced a small number of psychiatric social workers, but it certainly seems that the creation of more new Courses for psychiatric social workers at this time will hardly do more than duplicate existing facilities at a high cost in money and manpower. There is, perhaps, a better case for attempting to ensure that existing

Courses take a larger number of students, but expansion is at present limited by the scarcity of fieldwork placements of sufficient quality and the need for a corresponding increase in the number and possibly the status of existing academic staff. Present government policy, of course, offers no hope of an expansion of this kind and financial support from the voluntary sector is at the moment focused on non-university training for social work.

If it appears likely that the number of students qualifying as psychiatric social workers will not be very greatly increased in the near future, a number of possible courses of action are open. We could accept the fact and try to use trained psychiatric social workers as economically and as strategically as possible. While accepting this fact we could remind ourselves that even if present figures indicate that in Great Britain there are approximately 20 psychiatric social workers for every million of the population, the number in Japan and Austria is between two and four, in Egypt and Pakistan between 0·1 and 0·9, in Canada, Finland and Switzerland, between five and nine. The British figure in fact as far as the available information goes is excelled only by Peru and the United States of America (20-39), and Israel (75)[3]. Alternatively, we could consider changes in the criteria by which psychiatric social workers are selected for training. Some changes in the requirements for admission are now in force for an experimental period of five years and these, in conjunction with the willingness of the Courses to take an additional number of students, may make a significant contribution to the problem of recruitment. The 'experiment' whereby students completing a 'generic' Course of social work training might become eligible for membership of the Association of Psychiatric Social Workers on completion of an additional fieldwork placement is to be reviewed in 1963, but very few students have qualified in this way up to 1961 (three at Newcastle and three at Southampton).

This, then, is one aspect of psychiatric social work training since 1930—a considerable increase in the number trained after the War and an increase in the number of training centres. At the same time the total numbers trained each year and over five-year periods show fluctuations which might well have implications for recruitment policies.

The other main feature is the increase in the number of men recruited to the profession since the war. The majority of psychiatric social workers are of course women; 1,066 of the total number trained. It was only in 1939 that a significant proportion of male psychiatric social workers qualified (about a quarter of the successful students). Between 1930 and 1939 11 men trained as psychiatric social workers, but between 1950 and 1959 the figure was 64 for all Courses. Put another way, in the period 1930-34 the proportion of male to female students successfully completing training was 1:28, while between 1955 and 1959 it was 1:6·5. With the exception of the War period the number and proportion of men qualifying as psychiatric social workers has increased in each quinquennial period. The relaxation of entrance qualifications has already led to an increase in the number of male students and 32 men trained in the years 1961 and 1962.

In the history of the professional Association, the influx of a larger group of men has had some effects in connection with salary questions and also with policies in regard to community care, the development of psychiatric social work in local health departments. Male psychiatric social workers have in fact an influence on the profession out of proportion to their numbers. For example, of those holding senior psychiatric social work posts over 30 per cent are men, though only 12 per cent of the profession are male. How do the male entrants to the profession compare with their female colleagues? Their age distribution follows the same broad trends, with the majority in the two groups 25-29 and 30-34. A higher proportion of the men had no university qualification (this is explained to some extent by the intake of an earlier period, 1935-39, and by very recent recruitment), about the same proportion held social science diplomas only, but a lower proportion held degrees or degrees with diplomas. The male entrant has a social work background less frequently than the female, and more often has clerical or industrial experience. However, when actual post on application is considered there seems to be little difference between the sexes.

Having established the number and sex distribution of the recruits to the profession trained in England, we shall next consider other features of this group—age, marital status, kinds and sources of university qualification before taking the Courses, kinds of previous experience and the posts actually held at the time of selection.

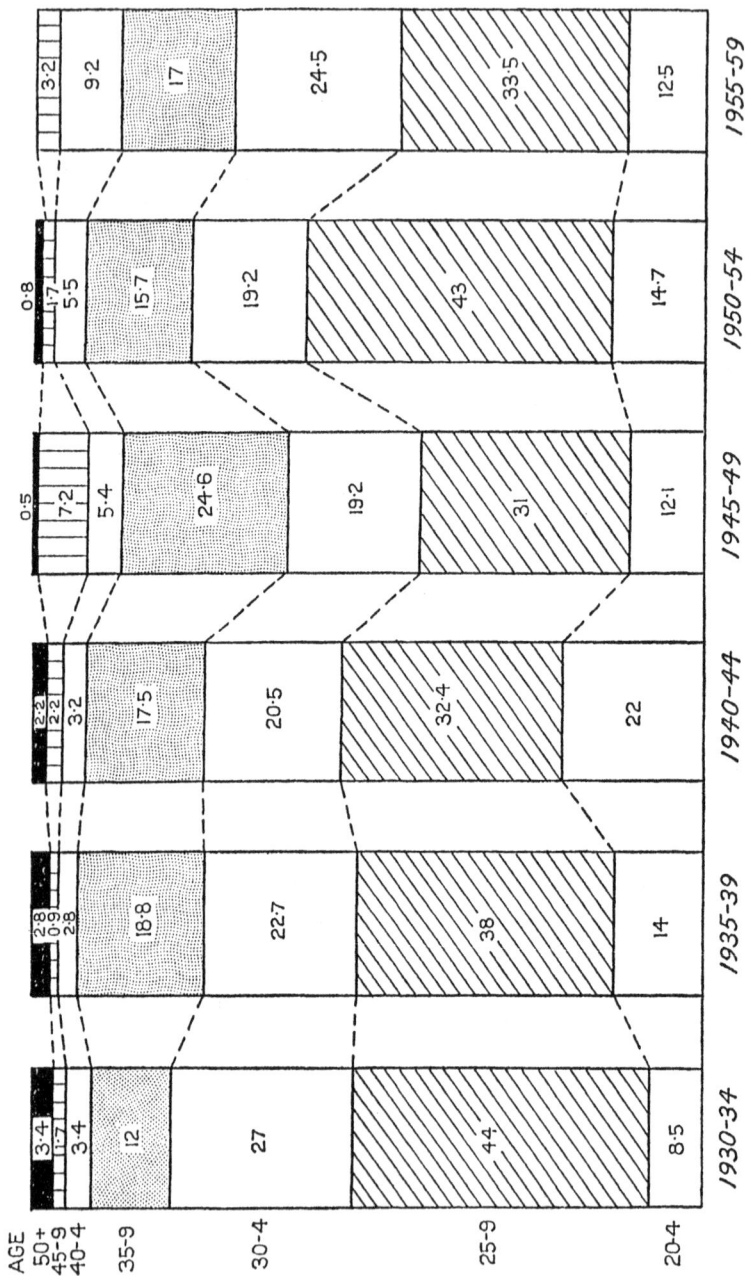

Figure I. Age Structure by Quinquennial Averages.

Who are Psychiatric Social Workers?

To ascertain the age structure of the new entrants to the profession seven age groups have been used. An analysis of the results (Figure I) shows that there have been quite wide fluctuations in the age of entrants to the profession but that, on the whole, it is the youthful character of applicants that most clearly emerges. The group aged 50 and over which in the period 1930-34 represented 3·4 of the total of trained students finds no place in the period 1955-59 and the group 45-49 which in the period 1945-49 represented 7·2 of the total, represents only 3·2 in 1954-59. The lowest proportion for the group 22-29 is reached in the period 1945-49 (43 per cent), but in four out of five of the remaining periods it is over 50 per cent. Of particular interest from the point of view of the profession is the youngest of the age groups. This has always represented a significant proportion of successful students and the numbers in this group have increased steadily until the period 1950-54 when 33 students were in this age range. Altogether 127 students or 13·5 per cent of the total group have been in this age range. This proportion is significant in view of the fact that psychiatric social workers have often stressed 24 as the minimum age for acceptance. Psychiatric social work training is based as a rule on both previous qualification in the social sciences and previous experience in a social work job. Some in the group 22-24 have undoubtedly had the chance to acquire qualification and experience, but what of those who have not? It seems that approximately 45 students have qualified for psychiatric social work in this age range without previous experience in a specific social work job. Selection has, of course, been in the hands of the universities concerned and during the period studied there is some evidence at certain stages of a difference of opinion on the question of minimum age between the university and the professional body.

There seems to be little difference between the three courses in regard to age of qualification except that Edinburgh seems to accept a higher proportion than Manchester or London of the 20-24 group (29 per cent compared with 13·5 and 12·5 respectively), a lower proportion of the next age group and a slightly higher proportion in the 40-44 group. The figures for Liverpool are, of course, small, but four of the twenty successful students were under 24 on acceptance.

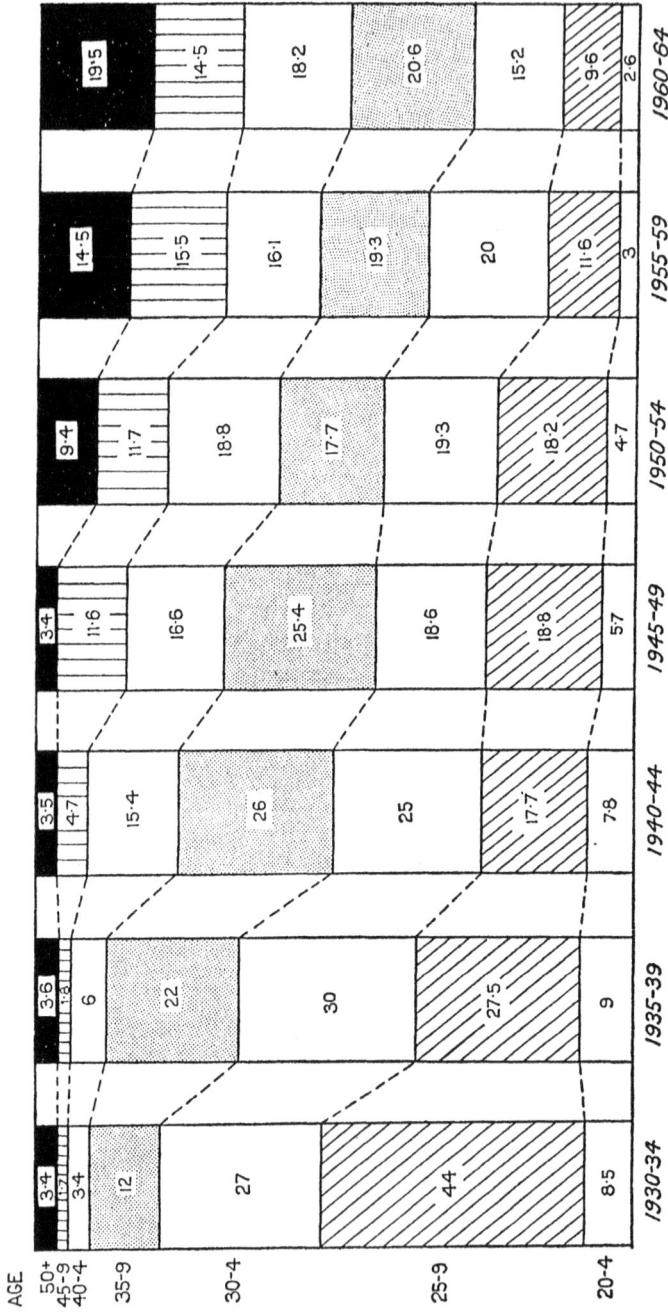

Figure II. All Successful Entrants—Cumulative Age Structure (Allowing for Retirements, Age 60. No Allowance for Deaths).

Figures for age of qualification, however, only show the age structure of new entrants to the profession. Figure II gives the Cumulative Age Structure allowing for retirement at the age of 60, but not for deaths. The figure shows how the youthful character of the profession has changed until by the quinquennium 1960-64 a more balanced age structure will, on the basis of recruitment at the level of the previous five-year period, be achieved.

A picture of marital status at time of completion of training shows that six per cent of the total trained have been single men, 76 single women, 3·8 married men, 12·6 married women, ·1 widowed, divorced or separated men and 1·5 women. Over the period there has been a general tendency for the proportion of married to increase and the single to fall. The greatest change occurs between single and married women; there is a general inverse relationship between these two groups. There is a slight tendency for the widowed and divorced to increase, but the figures for this group are, of course, minimal since facts of this kind may not always have been recorded at the Training Centres.

PREVIOUS ACADEMIC QUALIFICATION

Four categories have been used to sort information on the previous academic qualification of recruits, graduates without a social science diploma, those with such a diploma, students who had simply a social science diploma and those who have no university qualification. Of the total of psychiatric social work students

Table II: Distribution of Previous Academic Qualification on the Training Courses

Training Centre	Grads.	Degree & Dip.	S.S. Dip.	None
L.S.E.	20·5	17·5	52·5	9·5
Edinburgh	13	20	60·5	6·5
Manchester	29	9	52	10
Liverpool	30	10	50	10

successfully trained up to 1962, 21 per cent have been graduates without such a social science diploma, 17 have been graduates with such a diploma, 53·5 have been holders of a social science diploma alone and 8·5 have had no university qualification. A comparison of the training courses reveals some differences.

It is to be expected that L.S.E. students determine the characteristics of the total recruitment because of their considerable numerical superiority, but Manchester seems to have amongst its successful students a slightly higher proportion of those without university qualification, and Edinburgh a smaller proportion, than London. Manchester and Liverpool have the highest proportion of graduates but the lowest proportion of graduates who also hold social science diplomas. Edinburgh has the highest proportion of students with the simple social science diploma.

This is the picture of the total group, but there have, of course, been changes over the years. In the earlier period there were, as is to be expected with such small numbers, wide fluctuations. It seems that in the last ten years the number of successful students with no university qualification has remained fairly constant (about two each year) and this has also been the case with students holding degrees only. The major changes have occurred between those with social science diplomas and those with degrees and diplomas. In fact something like an inverse relationship is apparent. Since 1951, however, the number of graduates, whether they hold diplomas or not, has remained fairly constant, the average being 17 as compared with an average of seven in the period 1931-39.

One aspect of previous academic qualification that is of interest is the place at which the qualification was obtained. Before the institution of courses outside London not only were all psychiatric social workers trained at the same school, a significant proportion of them in the early years had had previous experience at L.S.E. The proportion ranges from about 50 per cent before 1935, goes down to somewhat less than a third in the late 1930's, rises somewhat above this average in the late 40's and has settled around slightly less than 25 per cent throughout the 1950's. In 1959, however, it rose to 34 per cent, but this may well be a short term change similar to fluctuations of similar size in the past. The proportion of Manchester students with previous experience at Manchester University is much smaller, being about 10 per cent for the period 1947-59. A higher proportion of 'home grown' recruits is recorded for Edinburgh, if the definition is widened to include all students with previous experience at a Scottish University. Adopting this definition just over 30 per cent can be included.

PREVIOUS EXPERIENCE

From what fields of work do psychiatric social workers come? To answer this question the careers of those who were successful on the training courses were analysed under two headings, previous experience and post on acceptance. In the first category the longest job held over nine months was counted. The overall average for all courses is as follows:

Table III: Previous Experience of Students

Previous Experience	Percentage of Students
Social Work (including voluntary work)	31·4
Secretarial and Clerical	20·7
Teaching	11·7
Forces	6·6
Health Visiting, Nursing	6·1
Industrial Welfare	1·9
Others	7·7
None	13·5

Some explanation of the categories 'none' and 'others' is required. The category 'none' is made up of those for whom no job has been recorded (five per cent) and those who seem by reason of their age, etc., not to have had previous work experience (8·5). 'Others' is an inevitable category in a profession that places considerable emphasis on qualities of personality and includes a weaver, a miner, stage dancer, documentary film maker, an industrial apprentice, a baker and so on. The highest proportion of students come with previous social work experience (31·4), and the next largest come from clerical administrative and secretarial occupations (20·7). Over a tenth of the students have had teaching experience. This means that nearly a third of psychiatric social workers begin their careers in non-social work fields. Some probably intended to take up social work but began teaching, for instance, to gain experience with children or because of a combination of family

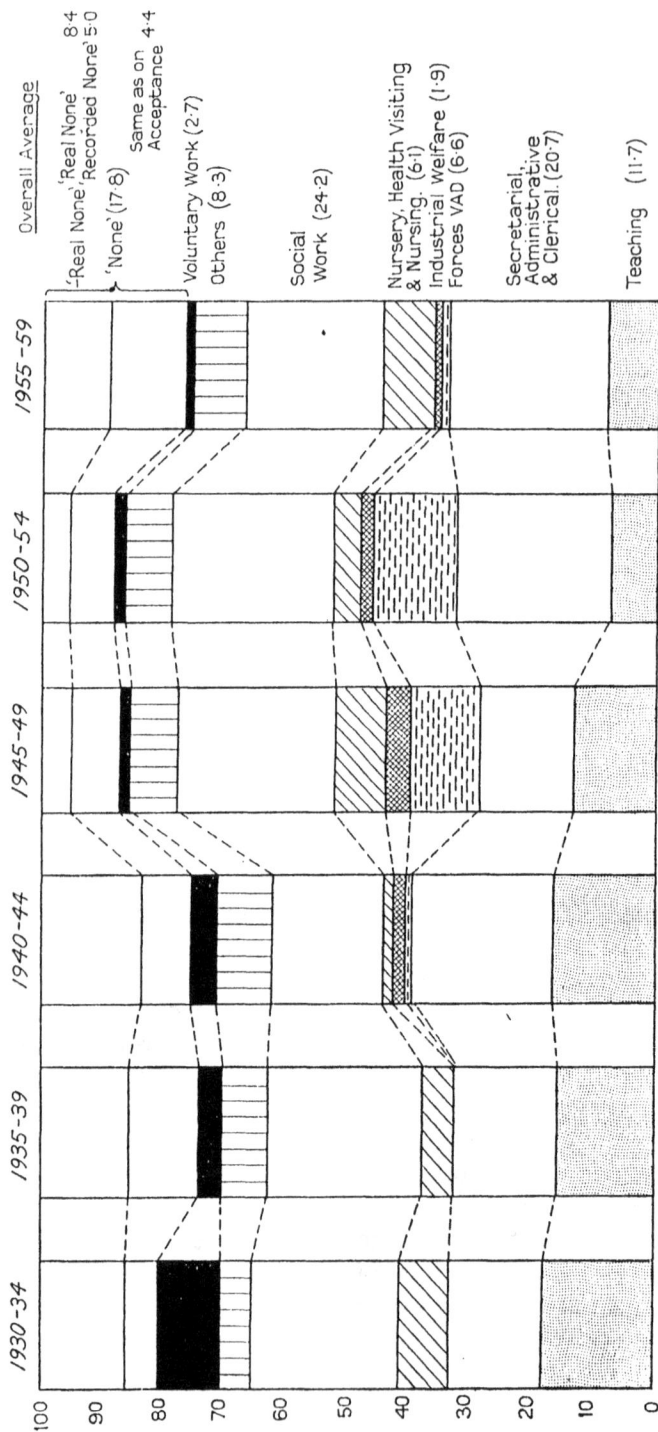

Figure III. All Courses—Previous Experience Other than Posts on Acceptance.

circumstances and job opportunity. Many, however, gave up their first choice of careers to come into psychiatric social work. A statistical study cannot say why they changed or what attracted them to this kind of social work, but these questions are implicit in the statistical material. They are important because, as we have seen, there is a considerable demand for social workers in this field.

Figure III shows the changes that have taken place in the proportions of students with different kinds of previous experience. From this it appears that teaching is a field of experience declining in importance; 18·5 of those qualifying in the period 1930-34 had had teaching experience compared to 7·7, 1950-54 and 8·3, 1955-59. On the other hand secretarial and administrative experience has increased (15 per cent in 1930-34, 25 and 26 per cent in 1950-54 and 1955-59 respectively.) Nursing fluctuates (8·4 in the first quinquennium, 4·7, 1950-54 and 8·3, 1955-59). Social work experience had been obtained by roughly a quarter of the students apart from those in the War years.

POSTS ON ACCEPTANCE

In analysing the posts held by students on acceptance for the Courses, an attempt was made to distinguish between several kinds of social work and between social work and other kinds of occupation. Non-social work jobs have been classified in the following section as 'Others'. The picture of the total proportions under each category for the three Courses is as shown in Table IV for the years 1930-62.

Just under a quarter of successful applicants are students for the diploma in social science or a degree when they are selected. Does this mean that they have in fact started on such courses with a view to applying for training as psychiatric social workers or is the notion of such training formulated during their course? If the latter, what makes the student turn to psychiatric social work? The data so far collected could not, of course, answer such questions, but since this group represents almost the highest proportion amongst all the 'occupational' groups these questions are important. The highest proportion, in fact, comes from social work in a psychiatric setting. Two figures are indicated in this

Table IV: *Proportions of Students in Training in Different Occupations*

Place of Training	Student %	Probation	Other Social Work	Residential	Nursing	Social work in a psyc. setting	Family Casework	Teaching	Almoners	None	Others
L.S.E.	22	3.8	14.4	3.6	2.2	18.6 + 3.1	4.9	4.6	7.3	6.4	9.2
Edinburgh	27	0.8	9.8	2.4	0.8	38.0 + 0.8	6.4	0.8	4.8	1.6	7.3
Manchester	29	1.8	0.9	4.5	1.8	44.0 + 0.9	3.6	6.3	—	1.8	5.4
Liverpool	20	—	35.0	5.0	—	—	—	—	—	—	—
For all Courses	23	3.1	12.0	3.6	2.0	24 + 2.5	5.0	4.3	6.1	5.3	8.6

column; the second indicates practice in a post of work with mentally defectives. The two figures can for many purposes be taken together (26·5 per cent). Social work in other settings produces a much smaller proportion of recruits. 'Other social work' accounts for the next highest proportion (12 per cent). This is perhaps not quite such a 'rag bag' as at first appears. By far the largest number in this group (102 out of 115) come from L.S.E. and almost a quarter of these are from the L.C.C. School Care Committees.

The overall figures are of some importance, but of particular significance are the changes that have occurred since 1930 in the proportions of different posts held at acceptance. The broad changes can be seen from Figure IV, which shows the Distribution of Posts for all courses during quinquennial periods from 1930. Comparing 1935-39, a period in which we might assume the course had stabilized after its beginning in 1930, with the period 1955-59 we can see some significant changes. The proportion of students had dropped from 28 to 15 per cent, but the proportion of social workers in psychiatric settings (which includes trainees—see chapter 9) has risen significantly from 13·2 to 40·9 per cent. This particular group of entrants seems of particular strategic importance in the development of the mental health services, since it accounts for nearly 40 per cent of senior career appointments. This increase has been made at the expense of students, those in other social work, those with no occupations and those with other non-social work occupations. There has been an increase in the proportion of those with family casework posts (8·6 compared to 5·7). Teaching and probation remain the same (2·8 and 4·6). Nursing, which includes nursery work, does not appear in the period 1935-39, but 1955-59 accounts for the same proportion as teaching.

This, then, is a picture of the expanding group of psychiatric social workers from 1930. The notion of a typical psychiatric social worker is perhaps misleading, since students qualify at different ages, and come from different backgrounds. However, we can say that most of them are women, but that men constitute an increasing proportion of the group. The majority of recruits are under 34. About a third of psychiatric social workers trained in England are graduates, and they are increasing numerically and proportionately. Psychiatric social workers have had previous

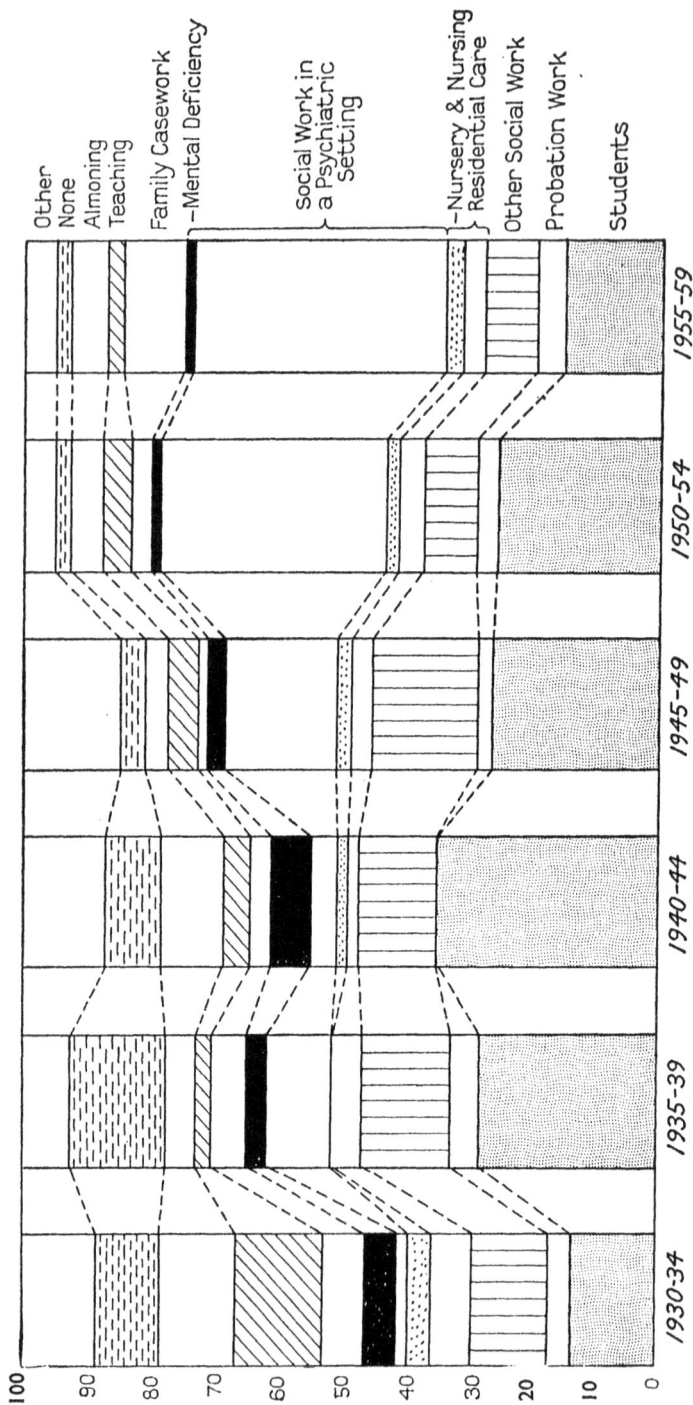

Figure IV. All Courses—Percentage Distribution of Posts on Acceptance.

experience in a variety of fields, industrial, commercial, teaching, nursing and social work. Some do not hold social work jobs when accepted on the courses, but the majority are working in some field of social work.

NOTES

[1] Basic information on sex, age, academic qualifications, etc. was recorded on schedules by the tutors of the Edinburgh and Manchester courses. I would like to acknowledge with gratitude the help of Miss Megan Browne, Miss M. Hamilton and Miss M. Irvine in this connection. Information on students at the London School of Economics and at Liverpool University was collected by the author with the kind permission of Mrs. K. McDougall and Miss J. Simpson, respectively.

[2] *Report of the Association of Psychiatric Social Workers for the years 1944-46*

[3] Krapf, E. E., and Moser, J., 'Changes of emphasis and accomplishments in mental health work, 1948-60.' *Mental Hygiene*, Vol. 46, No. 2, April 1962.

Chapter Four

THE CAREERS OF PSYCHIATRIC
SOCIAL WORKERS

IN this chapter we shall be concerned with the work history of psychiatric social workers, with the general question, what happens to such workers after they finish training. There are several different fields open to them after qualification both within and outside the field of mental health, and in view of the heavy demands made on the mental health services their actual distribution between these services is of considerable interest. Are psychiatric social workers responding equally to child guidance, the mental hospital and the local authority community care service or is one service receiving a much greater proportion than the others? Are the services 'deprived' by workers going into other fields of social work, into research, or university teaching other than the training of psychiatric workers? These questions are important from the point of view of the use made by society of its social work manpower. Equally important from the point of view of both psychiatric social workers and their clients is the question of mobility between fields of work and particular jobs within each field. Psychiatric social workers have continually stressed the insufficiency of a training of one year's duration. Irvine, for example, has recently drawn attention to 'such modest equipment of insight and skill as one can hope to acquire in one crowded year.'[1] It has been assumed that much of the experience on the Courses would be consolidated by continuous practice in one post, possibly with general help or actual supervision from a senior colleague. The Scottish Branch of the Association at one point recommended that a period of four years in a first job would probably be required before the full benefits of training were apparent. It is obviously difficult to state precisely the length of time required, but the problem of consolidation of the training is real and if there is considerable mobility in the years after training one solution is rendered useless.

For clients, too, mobility presents problems. If psychiatric social workers move fairly rapidly from one job to another, the consequent breaks in relationship, changes in personnel and possible resulting changes in policy are likely to cause harm or, at least, seriously to impede the process of help. The importance of continuity is perhaps particularly evident in the mental health field. For example, a psychiatric social worker describing her work with a small group of chronic schizophrenic patients, emphasized their 'need to be very sure that the therapist is going to stay with them, and is genuinely interested in them as individuals and able to bear with all their moods, before they are willing to engage in the treatment process.'[2] Here the continuity of the 'therapist' and her concern as a person for the patients are seen as the prerequisites of treatment at least for a particular diagnostic group. At a time when more patients are entering hospital and leaving after a comparatively short course of treatment, the therapeutic advantages of a reliable and continuing figure in the 'helping environment' are obvious for other groups also.

For the social worker, too, the detailed knowledge of a locality that comes only from fairly lengthy work or residence within its boundaries is a source of strength and increased helpfulness. In the task of rehabilitating mental hospital patients after their discharge and in trying to secure reasonable after-care, 'The social workers should know the neighbourhood, the factories and the social customs and most important the other social service agencies and what they will carry and what they will discard'.[3] The social worker who moves from area to area will in this important respect be at a disadvantage compared, for example, to the old relieving officer who not only tended to stay in one area for long periods of time, but was legally bound to reside within the area he served.

The career prospects of those qualifying as psychiatric social workers have changed radically in the last two decades. Those trained before the war must scarcely be able to recognize the demand for such workers and their increased prospects of promotion. Part of the change is due to the War which enabled psychiatric social workers to demonstrate their usefulness outside clinic and hospital; part is due to the new policies for mental health and the increased status of social workers generally in the 50's and 60's. In the 1930's psychiatric social workers were a struggling, pioneering group, labouring under a number of different handicaps. They were associated with psychiatry, they were part of the new mental health movement, their role in the mental hospital was by no means clear, and they had in many provincial areas to 'sell' not only themselves but child guidance also. In view of these pressures and uncertainties, few workers training in the 1930's could have been sure of their professional future. Ashdown and Brown recall that in 1936 the students nearing the end of their training were said to have applied in a body to the advertisement of one local authority. The present position is completely different. In 1956 the Association circulated 202 posts, of which 72 were new, but at the end of the year 116 posts of the total advertised remained unfilled including 46 new posts. In 1959, 248 posts were circulated and only 68 filled, though 27 of the 40 London posts were filled. The present demand for psychiatric social workers is considerable and remains unsatisfied, though there are some disadvantages in using demand at any one time as a measure of the *successful* growth of psychiatric social work. Demand, unless sustained over a period, may represent an unconsidered reaction to newly imposed pressures from above rather than a considered answer to problems that have been appreciated if not fully defined.

In the changing circumstances of psychiatric social service how have qualified workers been distributed both in social work generally and in the different fields of specialized psychiatric work? If we take the figures for the employment of psychiatric social workers certain broad and important facts emerge. Limitation of space prevents a detailed review of each year of the profession's history, and the years 1933, 1937, 1955 and 1961 have been selected for illustrative purposes.

In 1933, in the very early days of the profession, there was almost the same (small) number in child guidance as in the mental hospitals and nearly the same in general social work of a varied kind (Charity Organisation Society, Probation, Children's Care Committee, Residential Work and so on). The importance of this group of workers trained on the Mental Health Course, and working in fields other than the psychiatric, can be seen more clearly from the 1937 figures when there were the same number in these kinds of work as in child guidance (24). This parity with one of the main fields of psychiatric social work is rare, but there have always been a significant number trained as psychiatric social workers who are at any one time working in non-clinical fields. Since 1955, for example, each year has seen a hundred or so posts of this kind and in 1961 there were 155 compared to 65 posts in community care, 193 in mental hospitals and 219 in child guidance of various kinds. It would be inappropriate to interpret this figure in terms of wastage even from clinical work, since some of the posts will be directly concerned with schools for maladjusted children and with the training of psychiatric social workers. What is appropriate and important is the extent to which training in psychiatric social work is considered to be an adequate basis for a wide range of non-clinical positions. Take, for instance, the distribution of such posts in 1961. Of the total of 155, seven were in approved schools or schools for maladjusted children, 25 in almoning, child care or probation, 34 were teaching posts, mainly in universities and polytechnics, 22 were in research, 21 in voluntary social work agencies, 10 in the central government or local authority and 36 were in 'other posts'. In Chapter Nine we shall be concerned with some aspects of generic training which began in England in the 1950's but at this point it is important to remark on the fact that if 'generic' training means training in the basic elements of social work, the training in psychiatric social work can to a significant extent be described as 'generic' throughout most of its history. There is a good *prima facie* case for arguing that training in psychiatric social work has important elements which can be transferred to situations in many other kinds of social service, including work in institutions, and also to teaching and administrative responsibilities.

The other important aspect of the posts taken by psychiatric social workers concerns their distribution within the clinical fields of mental hospital work, child guidance and the local health authority. In 1933, as we have seen about the same numbers of workers were in posts in child guidance (18) as in mental hospitals, but by 1937 the position had changed in favour of the hospitals, where there were almost twice the number of workers (43) as in child guidance (24). This position of superiority has gradually been changed since the end of the war. In 1955, 182 psychiatric social workers were employed in mental hospitals, 138 in child guidance and 32 in local health authorities, but by 1961 the respective figures were 193, 219, and 65. These increases have not been steadily maintained over the period and the comparative position changed year by year, but the broad picture is clear. The child guidance, local health authority (and other posts) have increased their qualified personnel to a greater extent than the mental hospitals. Indeed there were less psychiatric social workers in mental hospitals in 1960 and 1961 than in 1956.

The factors which influence the choice of field are complex. Some workers seem to specialize in one kind of work, others are asked to take on pioneer jobs in different fields or the same field in different parts of the country. Certain general factors, however, seem to be influential. Public policy obviously determines the emphasis on any one field at a given time and creates opportunities for both employment and promotion. The increase in child guidance clinics since the end of the War has obviously created more opportunities in this field and this seems to be sustained in spite of fears expressed by some psychiatric social workers about the current emphasis on adult mental health. The Annual Report of the Association for 1961 remarked on the 'notable increase of posts advertised in child guidance clinics and hospital departments of child psychiatry'. It may be, however, that psychiatric social workers see experience in this field as crucial but temporary. Certainly, promotion prospects are better in the adult mental hospital and in community care. In 1960 approximately one sixteenth of child guidance posts were senior, compared to one eighth of these in mental hospitals and one third in the local authority. Of the 65 posts held in local authorities in 1961, 23 were senior appointments. Yet the figures so far given only show the employment position at certain times. They do not illustrate the working careers of psychiatric social workers, which have to be individually traced.

To pursue the matter further it was decided to investigate the employment records of the Association. These are kept in order to supply the office with current information and have been variably kept over the years, being most reliable for the last ten. They depend, too, on members reporting their changes of job and this method has produced many gaps in coverage. Consequently, the material evidence provided is not of a high standard. An analysis

was made of the average duration of service during three quinquennial periods, 1945-50, 1950-54, 1955-59. The evidence suggested that mobility increased somewhat in 1955-59 over the previous quinquennium, but was still considerably less than in the
five years following the War. This was probably to be expected;
the mobility of workers should on average decline over the years.
The profession is barely a generation old and hence has only just
begun to assume a balanced age structure. At each point in its
history to date there has been a successively higher proportion of
older people, principally people who have grown older in the
profession, and since it is common industrial experience that
labour mobility is much lower after two years in one employment,
it is arguable that an increasing level of professional experience
should entail a decreasing level of mobility. The evidence seemed
to bear this out, but two facts may be operating to offset this
expectation, the increase in number and kind of career openings
and an increased marriage rate in a predominantly female profession. On these questions the material could provide no evidence
and so it was decided to make a study of the careers of psychiatric
social workers who trained in certain selected years. The years
were 1947, 1948 and 1952, 1953. An examination of the careers of
students trained in these years will provide a picture of the work
history of two sets of students qualifying at two different points in
time. Nearly all of them are still potentially, if not actually in full
professional life. The analysis of their careers provides a good
view of current development in the profession in regard to
employment.

In the four years under review a total of 202 students qualified
as psychiatric social workers. Of these, 31 (15 per cent) are
definitely living overseas, and have been excluded from the study.
Of the remaining 171 psychiatric social workers, 161 (94 per cent)
were traced, and were sent a questionnaire asking for details of
work history, date of marriage and number and dates of birth of
any children. 135 forms were returned and this represents a return
of 78 per cent on all who might have been in the United Kingdom
at the time, and 84 per cent of those who were sent questionnaires.
This is an exceptionally good response for a postal enquiry, and
I would like to acknowledge with gratitude the willing co-operation of the psychiatric social workers who both completed the
questionnaire and wrote interesting and useful letters.

71

The response varied, of course, with the different training years (from 76 per cent for 1947 to 93 for 1952).

As might be expected the smaller response comes from the two earlier years when the chance of addresses being out of date was higher. Most of the addresses came from the Association's published list of members and of the sample of 202,159 (78 per cent) currently belonged to the Association. The sample obtained by answers to the questionnaire was found to be representative in terms of age and sex of the whole group of students trained in the years covered by the study.

1. *Mobility*

We have already seen the importance attached by psychiatric social workers to a period of consolidation in the first post after qualification. The analysis of the questionnaire began, therefore, with the attempt to discover the facts about the duration of first posts. Of the first group (those trained in 1947 and 1948) almost a quarter were in their first jobs for one year or under, but this applied to only 10 per cent in the second group (1952 and 1953). At the end of two years, however, practically 40 per cent of the

Table I: Number of Jobs Held by the Sample Groups

No. of Jobs*	% of P.S.W's	
	1947/8	1952/3
1	10 ⎫ 66	28 ⎫ 60
2	56 ⎭	32 ⎭
3	21	19
4	11 ⎫ 12	18 ⎫ 20
5	1 ⎭	2 ⎭

* All figures for the two groups relate to the position as it was on December 31st 1960. Three people who qualified as psychiatric social workers, but never worked as psychiatric social workers have been excluded from the study.

first group and 34 per cent of the second are no longer in their first job. Generalizing from this finding it would appear that a significant proportion of psychiatric social workers give themselves less than two years in which to consolidate the effects and reinforce the benefits of training.

Turning now to the number of separate paid appointments each informant held during the course of her career since qualifying. Table 1 summarizes the results.

It is immediately evident that there is higher labour mobility in the second group, since they have in less than two thirds of the time available to those qualifying earlier held on an average almost as many appointments. Furthermore, 12 per cent of the first group held four jobs or more, whereas the figure for the second is 20 per cent. The most mobile of the 1952-53 group has already had *more* jobs than the most mobile 20 per cent of those qualifying five years earlier.

How long, on an average, do psychiatric social workers stay in their jobs? The figure for the number of jobs held in the available qualified life does not at once provide the average duration of each appointment. 'Qualified life' is not the same as 'professional life' since any person is likely to forego a certain amount of professional service on account of illness, further study and so on. There will also be in time a number of permanent or semi-permanent withdrawals from the work, and in a largely female profession this will often be for marriage and for child bearing. Such loss of service from long term withdrawals will, of course, be cumulative as against steady level of lost time from temporary absence. Thus the longer standing group will have lost proportionately more service than the professionally younger one. In fact the proportions of 'lost service' are 24 per cent for the first group and 17 per cent for the second, giving an average 'professional life' of 9·9 years and 6·6 years respectively. The average duration of each appointment, then, is 4·2 for the first group and 2·9 for the second, counting both full- and part-time work.

This shortening of the average duration of jobs in the second group might be accounted for by a possible higher wastage rate, but at first sight, it would not account for the large number of jobs held in an equivalent space of time. Yet the 'wastage' rate might be an indirect answer to the question. Some who withdraw for marriage and child-rearing re-enter the profession later on a

73

part-time basis, and part-time jobs have usually a shorter duration than full-time. What are the facts when the training years are analysed with regard to sex and marital status?

Table II: Possible Service Realized and Average Duration of Post by Sex and Marital Status

	1947/8			1952/3		
	% of Group	% Poss. Service Realized	Avg. Duration of Post	% of Group	% Poss. Service Realized	Avg. Duration of Post
Men	12·5	77	4·1 yrs.	15	87	2·8 yrs.
Single Women	42	88	5·2 yrs.	40	90	3·1 yrs.
Women Married when Qualified	20	79	4·2 yrs.	15	81	5·2 yrs.
Women Married since Qualifying	25·5	45	2·3 yrs.	30	68	2 yrs.

Table II makes no distinction between full and part-time work, (defined as three days a week or less) so that in fact it gives a very generous allowance under the heading 'per cent of Possible Service Realized'. As we shall see this has benefited the married sector almost exclusively.

Those chiefly responsible for both wastage (i.e. having the lowest percentage of possible service realized) and for turnover (i.e. low average duration of post) are the considerable body of female psychiatric social workers who marry after qualifying. These represent 37 per cent in 1947/8 and 42 in 1952/3 of all single women who qualify. This group of between a quarter and a third of all successful students has served an average of less than six years in the profession, including part-time work (5·8 and 5·4 years). It is their withdrawal from paid work because of family duties that accounts for a very large part of all 'wastage' and much of the labour turnover.

Yet the effects of marriage cannot be considered without

reference to the birth of children and we should refer perhaps to 'infant care' rather than marriage wastage. This is important, for a considerable number of marriages, including those contracted before qualification, have so far been childless. Ten out of 28 marriages in the 1947/8 group (this excludes two women widowed before 1948 and one divorced after one year of marriage) and 14 out of 27 marriages in the 1952/3 group were childless at the end of 1960. Clearly there are likely to be more children born, especially to the later group, in the future. Even so the proportion of childless marriages is likely to remain high.

The wastage from the profession is related then not directly to the marriage level, but to the level of marriages with at least one child under ten. If we take full-and part-time work together we see that as the children of the married P.S.W's grow older there is a return to professional work. In the future we can then expect even more re-entrants, some probably on a full time basis after a period on part-time, and this expectation should modify some of our judgments on marriage wastage. It should also lead to a full review of the needs of these re-entrants in terms of 'refresher courses', supervision and other attempts to meet their specific requirements on re-entry into work after some years absence.

New marriages, then, and the care of young children are important factors in wastage and turnover, but there is little to suggest that this problem has increased substantially between the two groups under review. There was the same number of marriages in each group of women after training. The decrease in professional life for marrying women averaged only five months (making no distinction between full- and part-time work) and the average tenure of each appointment fell only by about four months. So while new marriages are the basis of most loss and turnover, there is no evidence that the second group has suffered substantially more from this cause than the earlier one.

The body of women who married before qualifying have in both instances had a remarkably stable professional history. In fact it appears to have become more stable in the second group, though Table II does not bring out the importance of part-time work in these wives' careers. But in the case of both single women and men workers there seems to have been a definite increase in mobility for the later group. A higher average tenure of appointment for the longer standing group is to be expected, but if the men in the 1952/3 group are ever to attain the average of 4·1 years in each job now held by the men of the earlier group, over a comparable period of service, no man in the later group will be able to leave his present job at any time throughout 1961, 1962 and 1963. Quite definitely the mobility of the male and unmarried female workers is significantly higher for the more recently qualified group, and this is clearly unconnected with wastage from the profession. We must postulate that there has been a significant increase in mobility within the profession, and the most likely explanation is a widening of the opportunities for psychiatric social workers.

Some idea of the nature of these opportunities can be obtained from the questionnaires. We must distinguish between vertical mobility, which involves promotion either within or outside the fields of psychiatric social work, and horizontal mobility involving movement between jobs but no promotion. In an area of potential employment as wide as that available to the trained psychiatric social worker the idea of promotion is not a simple matter of movement up one career ladder. For example, an appointment to a teaching post would generally be regarded by psychiatric social workers as promotion, as would an appointment as Children's Officer, and so on. It is in fact one of the major anomalies that promotion more often than not involves withdrawal from practice in the clinical fields and that success in clinical practice does not receive the status and reward to which it is entitled. With these reservations in mind it is possible to divide the mobility in the two groups studied into vertical and horizontal. In the first group approximately 10 per cent were still in their first jobs, and of these just under half had been promoted; in the second the figures were 20 per cent and one sixth, but of course the length of time since qualifying was shorter. Of the mobile remainder (the vast majority) movement in the first group was horizontal in 73 per cent of the cases, and in the second in 79 per cent of the cases. Thus, broadly speaking, we can perhaps identify three groups in connection with mobility, a minority that remains in the first job after training, a majority that moves within the field of first choice or between fields, and a minority whose movement is vertical. The reasons why any particular worker falls into any one group are naturally complex. One worker will have to move to another area because her husband changes his job and work in the new area may be found only in a different field. Another worker moves to gain more experience, or to work under a particular psychiatrist and so on. Yet the possibility cannot be ruled out that each of the three groups represents a different type of personality. The relationship between career and personality still requires investigation, but any lead that might throw light on the question of mobility should be followed.

Finally, in this section attention will be given briefly to the amount of part-time work carried out. This amounted to 9 per cent of the total years of professional service for the 1947/8 group, and just over 10 per cent for the 1952/3 group. The overall significance of such work is not, therefore, great, but it is greater for some groups than for others. Part-time work is almost completely confined to married women. No man in either group ever worked any period of over two months solely engaged on part-time work in the profession. Nor did any unmarried woman in the earlier group, and only two in the later group, contributing only two and a half per cent of the total unmarried female service. Part-time work accounted for just over 30 per cent of the service of those who married after qualifying in 1947/8 but only 11·5 for their counterparts in the 1952/3 group, which suggests that part-time work is a feature of later married life. This last suggestion is supported by the fact that part-time work accounted for 21 per cent of the service given by those women who had married before qualifying in the first group, and 41 per cent for those in the second (being largely older women, some of the earlier group have now retired).

2. Fields of Service

So far we have considered simply number and duration of the jobs held by psychiatric social workers, but we need also to identify these jobs if we wish to see how these workers are distributed within the available employment openings. For the purposes of analysis psychiatric social work was divided into six fields of service: Child Guidance, Hospital Psychiatric Work, Community Care (mostly Local Authority Health Dept. posts, but including some posts with voluntary bodies like N.A.M.H.), Research, University and Mental Deficiency. There is an arbitrary element in this division, since some posts make an exclusive definition of the field served difficult. However, it was possible to categorize each of the respondents' jobs according to what seemed to be its principal character.

Table III shows the percentage distribution of total years of service over the six fields of work.

Table III: % Distribution of Total Years of Service
in Six Fields of Work

	1947/8	1952/3
Training	8	3
Child Guidance	39	34
Hospital Work	33·5	44
Community Care	11	13
Research	5·5	5·5
Mental Deficiency	2	1

(All figures are percentages of total years of service in each group)

Child Guidance and Hospital Psychiatric work obviously dominate the profession as they did in the figures given for earlier years. Over 70 per cent of the service contributed by the first group, and almost 80 per cent of the second were in these two fields. The two fields are roughly equal in work/years, though their relative positions are reversed between the two groups. Community Care follows a poor third in each group, about 12 per cent in both cases, and Research in both groups is about half as strong. Mental Deficiency work was the chief occupation of only four people at any time in their careers. Training is a field that seems to have fallen off in the second group, but this may not be significant since few posts are involved.

Part-time P.S.W.'s are virtually confined within the three largest fields, among which they are fairly evenly distributed in terms of work/years. However, this part-time contribution naturally represents a far higher proportion of Community Care work, which is so much smaller in total work/years than the other two. For both groups of workers about 7 or 8 per cent of Child Guidance and Hospital employment was carried out by part-time P.S.W.'s, and about 15 to 20 per cent of Community Care. The figures in this paragraph, however, do not properly indicate the amount of each field of work which is performed on a part-time basis, but only the importance of the respective fields as employment outlets for these who would otherwise not be professionally occupied, and the extent to which these fields depend on such workers.

We know the rate at which P.S.W.'s in both groups have changed their jobs, but what is the extent to which they change their fields of work. Of those qualifying in 1947 and 1948 42 per cent worked in one field only, 50 per cent in two fields and 7 per cent in three. The figures for the second group are respectively 52, 35 and 12 per cent. These figures may very generally be compared with those of a previous study of 50 students qualifying between 1934 and 1939 whose careers were traced to 1949.[4] Of these 36 per cent had worked in one field, 40 per cent in two fields and 24 per cent in three or more. The data thus available suggests that a high proportion of psychiatric social workers change their field of service. In my own sample the average number of fields is almost the same for each group, 1·65 for the earlier and 1·55 for the later. And again, not only has each of the second group on average served in almost as many fields as each of the longer qualified, but the most mobile element, those who have served in three fields is already proportionately larger than in the other group.

The average duration in any one field is higher for the first group (6 years) than the second (4·3 years) and there seems to be a tendency in each group for the child guidance clinic field to show more 'stability' than the mental hospital. The difference, however, largely disappears when the average length of service is considered.

Table IV shows the average duration of a worker for each group in each of our six fields. This average includes all service in a field, whether continuous or not, and both full- and part-time work.

The highest averages in both cases are in the two dominant fields of Child Guidance and Hospital Work. The number of work/years in these fields is to a certain extent the result of long

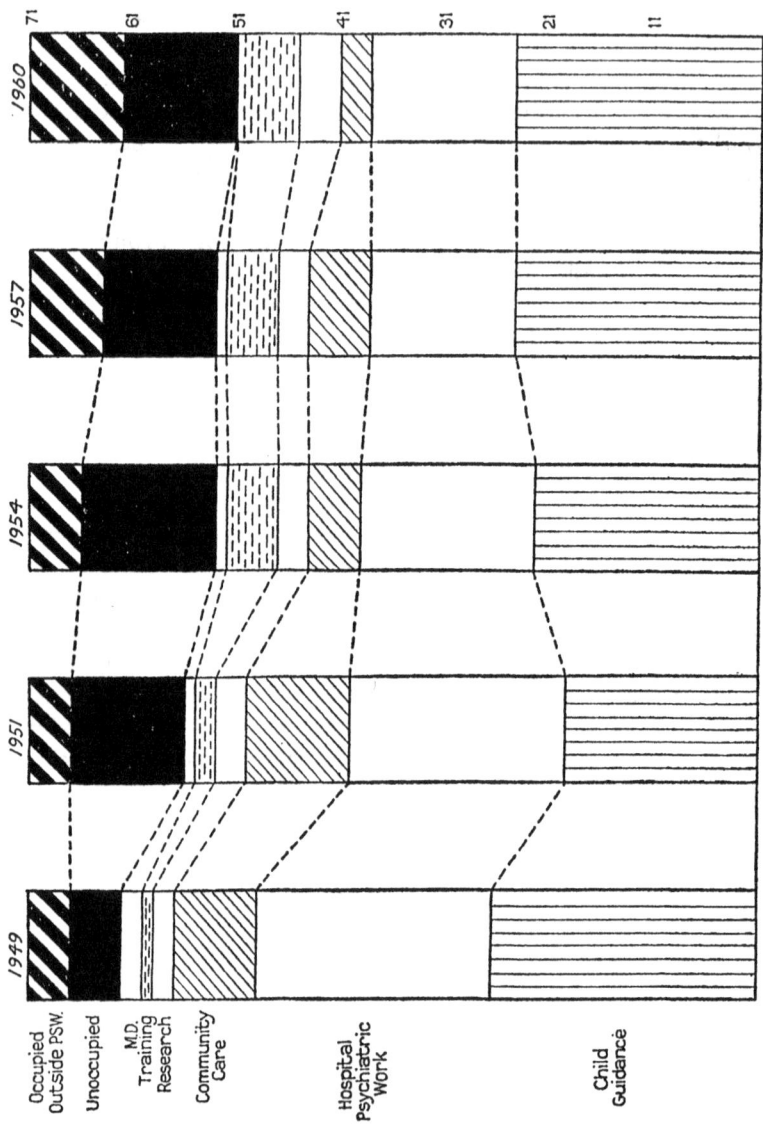

Figure I. P.S.W. Work Experience—Employment Distribution of Persons Qualified 1947–8, at Various Dates (Employment as at 31st December in Each Given Year).

The Careers of Psychiatric Social Workers

Table IV: *Average Length of Service per P.S.W.*
by Fields of Work

	Average length of Service per P.S.W. (Yrs.)	
	1947/8	1952/3
Training	5·7	3
Child Guidance	6·4	4·1
Mental Hospital	6·2	4·9
Community Care	4·6	3·7
Research	5·4	2·5
Mental Deficiency	5	4
Average	6 years	4·3 years

service in the fields by certain individuals. The two dominant fields have an advantage in this respect over research and training, for their low figure for work/years is partly because people usually enter these fields after some other form of psychiatric social work. On the other hand, the low figure of work/years, and the low average duration of service, in Community Care and Mental Deficiency work are probably at least in part the result of a drift away from these fields in the course of professional life.

So far we have examined the position at a particular point in time. Figures I and II attempt to show the position at regular intervals, to provide, as it were, some kind of running commentary.

Figure I should be self-explanatory. It supports most of the conclusions about the course of service in different fields. The only feature which is perhaps unexpected is the recovery of workers to the Child Guidance field after an initial loss, whereas Hospital Work and Community Care show a continuous 'wastage'. Nearly all the loss to the major fields of service at the earlier dates was to the 'unoccupied' sector (that is chiefly due to marriage), as against a certain loss later on to Training and Research. Later on there is in

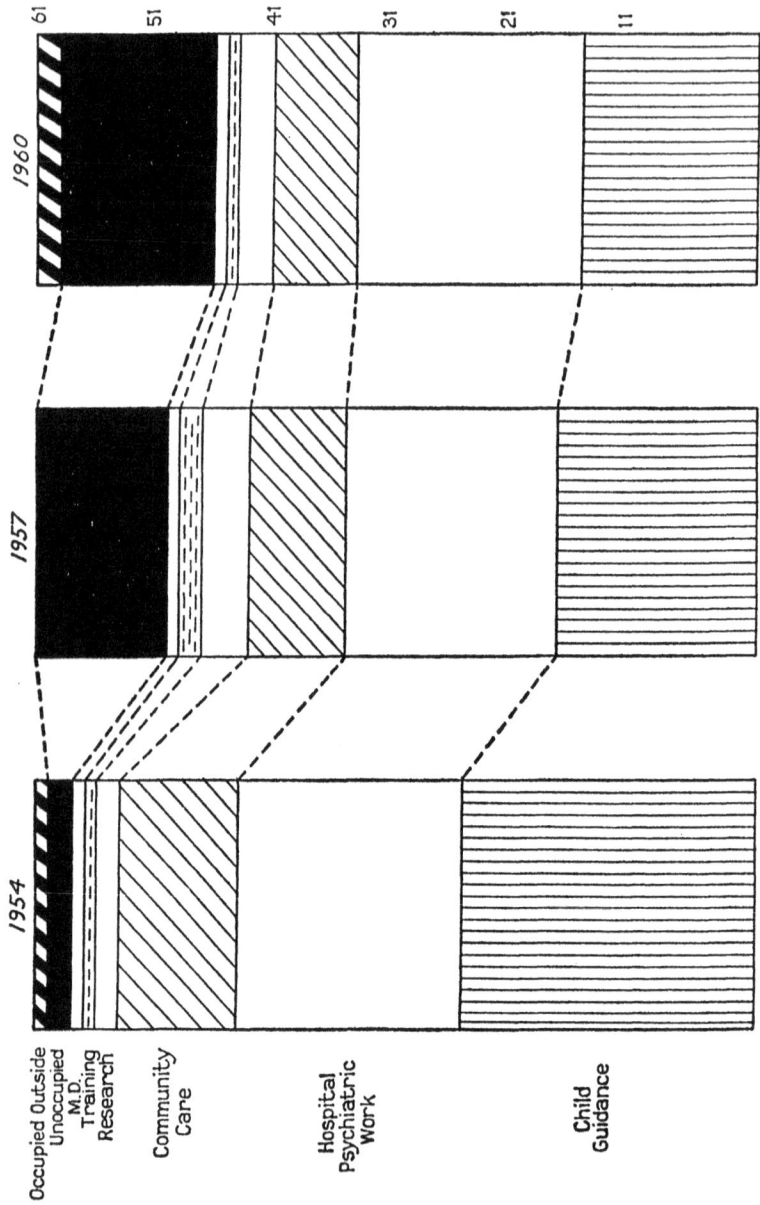

Figure II. P.S.W. Work Experience—Employment Distribution of Persons Qualified 1952–3, at Various Dates (Employment as at 31st December in Each Given Year).

fact some recovery of persons from the unoccupied sector, as married women take on part-time work. Presumably Child Guidance benefited sufficiently from this source to show an increase in numbers at the later dates. Against this theory we have to admit that as large a proportion of Hospital Work as Child Guidance was carried out on part-time P.S.W's service.

Figure II does not show this same trend with regard to Child Guidance, and in fact it is Hospital Work which has recovered numbers slightly by 1960. Both Child Guidance and Hospital Work do, as we have established, employ re-entrants from the 'unoccupied' sector, but an apparent preference for Child Guidance work by the re-entrants in the first is not so obvious in the later qualified group.

3. The locality of work

An important aspect of employment concerns geographical distribution which is shown clearly in the two maps showing the employment of practising members of the Association in 1940 and 1959. A simple contrast of the two maps shows two facts of importance. Today psychiatric social workers are more widely distributed over the British Isles. Northern Ireland had no psychiatric social workers in 1940, but had seven in 1959; (largely owing to the action of the Regional Hospital Board). Wales had three in 1940 and seven in 1959. The South West of England and East Anglia were not represented at all on the earlier map, but showed some psychiatric social workers in 1959. Yet the distribution is very uneven. In spite of a wider distribution over the British Isles, there has been no change in the predominance of the London area. The proportion working within a thirty mile radius of Charing Cross is over 50 per cent both for 1940 and for 1959. The majority of practising members of the Association are to be found in London and the South.

The predominance of these areas is, of course, a feature of professional social work as a whole. In child care, for example, it has been estimated that 60 per cent of qualified staff were employed in London and the South and South East. Among almoners employed in the hospital service about 50 per cent were employed in the four Metropolitan Hospital Regions in 1952 and in 1959. The proportion of almoners working for local authorities in

83

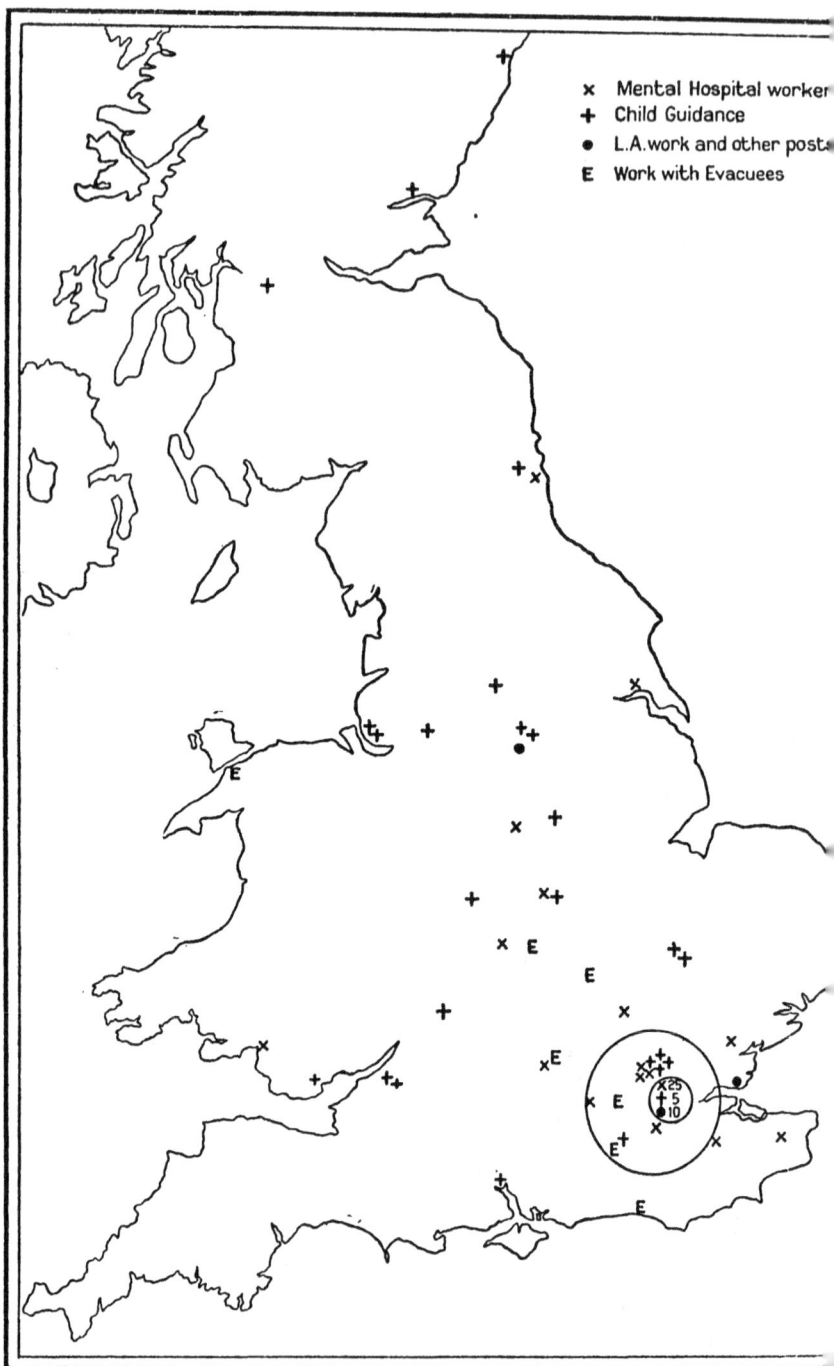

Legend:

- **x** Mental Hospital worker
- **+** Child Guidance
- **●** L.A. work and other posts
- **E** Work with Evacuees

Inset circle:
x 25
+ 5
● 10

Distribution of Practising Members of the APSW, 1940.

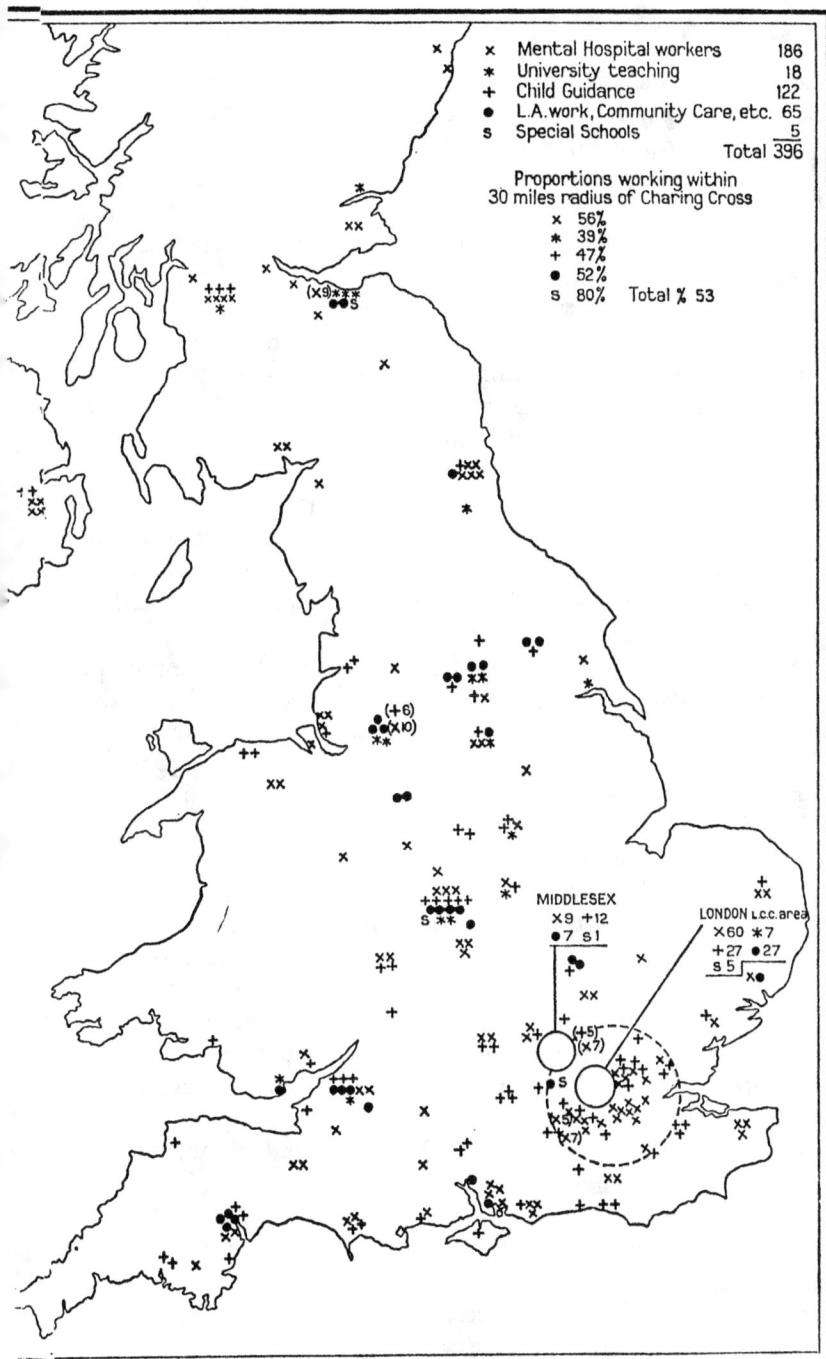

x	Mental Hospital workers	186
✱	University teaching	18
+	Child Guidance	122
●	L.A.work, Community Care, etc.	65
s	Special Schools	5
		Total 396

Proportions working within
30 miles radius of Charing Cross

x	56%	
✱	39%	
+	47%	
●	52%	
s	80%	Total % 53

MIDDLESEX
X9 +12
●7 s1

LONDON L.C.C.area
X60 ✱7
+27 ●27
s5

(+5)
(X7)

Distribution of Practising Members of the APSW, 1959.

London and the surrounding counties runs even higher. On the other hand, psychiatric social workers in local authorities seem to be less concentrated in one part of the country.

What is the attraction of the South, and especially of London, for psychiatric social workers? Clearly this attraction is shared with other professions, but there are also particular reasons why psychiatric social workers are distributed as they are. As we have already seen, the majority of psychiatric social workers are trained in London and in the two groups studied the majority of those working in London both immediately, and over ten years, after training are from the London School of Economics. London and the South possess a considerable proportion of the available psychiatric resources of the country and psychiatric social workers will find more support from colleagues and attractive possibilities for service. It is probably true to say that most psychoanalysts are to be found in the London area, and this again is an incentive for those workers who feel the necessity of an analysis for personal or professional reasons.

Some employing bodies who have unsuccessfully attempted to attract psychiatric social workers have referred critically to the desire of such workers to go where they can receive the support of colleagues. 'Undoubtedly it is pleasanter', states one psychiatric social worker, 'for the trained caseworker to work in an area where her contribution is appreciated and her methods understood.'[5] Yet to talk exclusively in these terms is to miss an important feature of the role of the psychiatric social worker. Much of her work is of its nature private and unobserved, but it is also exacting work in which results are difficult to assess. In this, as in other forms of personal service, it is difficult to continue without some confirmation of success, and without some measure whereby success or failure can be checked. Teachers are much less unobserved and have some kind of measurement of success in examination results. Doctors in general practice are more unobserved, but their success or failure in curing is much more evident. All professional service in which a considerable part of the worker's personality is invested requires some kind of observability of role performance. In psychiatric social work this is largely attained through contact between psychiatric social workers or with the teams of certain established and well-known clinics and hospitals.

The Careers of Psychiatric Social Workers

The time span between 1940 and 1959 is, of course, considerable and the simple contrast between the two maps hides the large amount of geographical mobility within the profession. Maps were prepared illustrating this for the two groups of workers studied at various points after qualification, but limitation of space prevents their full reproduction. However, some examples can be used to illustrate the changes. Of the 1952/3 group four trained in Scotland are working in Northern Ireland in 1954, but by 1960 they have all left. Of the 1947/8 group, three are working in hospital psychiatric work around Bristol, but by 1954 they have moved away to other areas. All areas, including London and the South, are subject to this geographical mobility, but the areas around the training centres seem more likely to attract replacements or to retain psychiatric social workers for longer periods. Geographical mobility has, of course, implications for manpower policy, but it must also affect adversely the kind of social service given. Such service needs to be based, partly at least, on a good acquaintance with local custom and conditions and on reasonable working relationships with the personnel of other social and local services. Knowledge and working relationships of this kind take time to foster, and can be easily squandered if a successor is not appointed.

In this chapter we have described certain important aspects of the working careers of psychiatric social workers: the movement between posts and different fields of work, marriage and child care as factors in mobility and turnover, the geographical distribution of workers. Perhaps the most important aspect is the mobility between posts and fields of service. Indeed the situation now seems similar to that of American psychiatric social workers described much earlier by French. In that study of workers in 1933 and 1938 it was found that: 'not only do psychiatric social workers in general stay for brief periods in any one job, but also they move freely from one type of agency to another . . . the whole picture is one of continuous shifting, both within and without the clinic and hospital field.'[6] The speed of movement in Great Britain is probably the outcome of many forces. In part it is the result of new policies in mental health, a new emphasis on consultation, and the opening of new career prospects.

The Younghusband Report recommended that psychiatric social workers with 'sufficient experience' should, together with

87

other professionally trained social workers, 'act as advisers or consultants to other social workers in a range of services, and as supervisors (in the sense of teaching and guidance) of newly qualified or appointed social workers, and to assist with in-service training'.[7] In addition such workers are to specialize in initial interviews with difficult cases, and to provide casework for those needing 'the most skilled help'. These recommendations raise important questions concerning the roles and training of the psychiatric social worker, but what is of interest in the present context is the implicit danger in the combination of high expectation and high mobility. 'As a demand for support and consultation grows, inexperienced psychiatric social workers may be expected to undertake these functions too soon. We must not suppose that one year of specialized training can equip us to support all and sundry. We need time to take root in our own field, to become secure in our skills, before we let colleagues lean on us to any extent.'[8] At present the danger is only implicit. An analysis in July 1962 of the 71 workers in senior career positions as psychiatric social workers shows that the great majority of these appointments are held by experienced workers, with the range of experience extending from 7 to 30 years, after training, with the average around 10. A small proportion (about four per cent) receive swift promotion within a year or two of training, though this may be a regular feature of each year's successful candidates. Present trends favour the chronologically younger worker and in these circumstances the dangers of the situation may become explicit.

NOTES

[1] Irvine, E. E., Introduction to *Ventures in Professional Co-operation.* The Association of Psychiatric Social Workers, 1960.

[2] Sheppard, M. L., 'Psychotherapy with a Small Group of Chronic Schizophrenic Patients'. *British Journal of Psychiatric Social Work*, Vol. V, No. 4, 1960.

[3] McDougall, K., 'The Psychiatric Social Worker in the Mental Hospital', *Case Conference* June 1958.

[4] Ashdown, M., and Brown, Clement, *op. cit.* p. 127.

[5] Brown, M. A., 'Reform and Therapy' in (ed.) Halmos P. *Moral Issues in the Training of Teachers and Social Workers* Sociological Review Monograph No. 3 1960.

[6] French, L. M. *Psychiatric Social Work* New York Commonwealth Fund 1940 p. 93.

[7] *Report of the Working Party on Social Workers in the Local Authority Health and Welfare Services* S.600.

[8] Irvine, E. E. *Ventures in Professional Co-operation* op. cit. p. 99.

Chapter Five

THE WORK OF THE PSYCHIATRIC
SOCIAL WORKER—THE CHILD
GUIDANCE CLINIC

WE have seen the varied backgrounds from which psychiatric
social workers come and the wide range of jobs into which they
go after they have been trained. It is clearly impossible to follow
them into each kind of work they undertake, but the main fields
of activity can be studied. In this and the following chapter the
work of the psychiatric social worker will be discussed under
the headings of child guidance, the mental hospital and the
local health authority. This discussion will be concerned with an
historical account of the development of the work in each of
the settings and a review of its main problems.

A. CHILD GUIDANCE

Between 1930 and 1939 child guidance clinics developed spor-
adically and unevenly over the country. Most of the early
clinics were under voluntary auspices, like the East London Clinic
established by the Jewish Board of Guardians in 1926 and the
London Child Guidance Clinic started by the Commonwealth
Fund in 1929. In some areas clinics were established under the
Local Education Authorities; in Birmingham, for example, a
clinic was established through the pressure of local demand and
the co-operation of the Child Guidance Council. By 1935, 18 child
guidance clinics had been recognized by the Council and two
years later the number was 46. The Council's policy was to recognize fully-staffed and well administerd clinics, but in fact quite a
high proportion of the clinics recognized (18 out of 46) were

described in a survey of the work of the Council as 'part staffed', having a medical director and/or psychologist or social worker. The Second World War at first produced a substantial dis-organization of the developing child guidance service, but gradually the psychological needs of a large number of children separated from their homes became apparent. Child guidance personnel unable to work in their accustomed centres were spread throughout the country to help such children. For psychiatric social workers this involved two important developments. They were brought into direct contact with the children and also with the staff of residential hostels set up as an attempt to meet the emotional problems of some disturbed children. This gave psychiatric social workers new administrative responsibilities and also encouraged them to develop skills in helping other staff to help children.[1] The interest and knowledge gained in this field made a significant contribution to the development of the new training for the child care service that was established in 1948.

A further significant stage in the growth of services for the disturbed child was reached with the Education Act of 1944. The Act imposed obligations on the local education authority in connection with certain categories of pupils requiring educational treatment and in the 1945 Regulations the six categories included, maladjusted pupils. Finally, in 1950 a Committee of Enquiry was appointed 'to enquire into and report upon the medical, educational and social problems relating to maladjusted children, with reference to their treatment within the educational system.' This Committee (the Underwood Committee) reported in 1956. Their first recommendation accepted by the Minister indicates the extent to which the ideas of child guidance have become accepted: 'There should be a comprehensive child guidance service available for the area of every local education authority . . .'[2] In the space of twenty to twenty-five years child guidance clinics have changed their position in society in a remarkable way. From being a few pioneering institutions run by voluntary societies they have become an accustomed part of the social services provided by statutory bodies, attempting to meet heavy demands on their existing facilities and continual demands for the expansion of their work.

Yet, in spite of the acceptance of the ideas of child guidance, the provision of services remains critically inadequate. The Underwood Report suggested that the service required the full-time equivalent of 140 psychiatrists, 280 psychologists, and 420 psychiatric social workers. What in fact is the manpower situation? Between 1950 and 1960 the total number of clinics provided by local education authorities increased from 162 to 271, the number of full-time equivalent psychiatrists from 51 to 83, psychologists from 101 to 197 and psychiatric social workers from 93 to 124.[3] Of the three groups it is psychiatric social workers who have shown the smallest percentage increase. Clearly the total number of psychiatric social workers at present working in child guidance clinics is approximately a quarter of the number required according to the Underwood Report.

What, within the framework of these broad changes, has been the work of the psychiatric social worker in the child guidance clinic?

From the beginning of the child guidance movement the psychiatric social worker had a recognized place in the team composed of psychiatrist, psychologist and social worker. The importance of the combination of the three disciplines was recognized by the sponsoring bodies. In the beginning, too, the roles of the three members of the team were fairly clearly defined; the psychiatrist treated the children, the psychologist tested children and gave remedial tuition, and the psychiatric social worker saw the parents (usually the mother). Her aim in doing this was firstly to obtain for diagnostic purposes a history of the child's development. The findings of all members of the team would ideally be discussed and combined in a case conference; if it was then decided to take the child into treatment at the clinic, the psychiatric social worker would interview the mother while the psychiatrist treated the child in a series of regular sessions.

This is a brief account of the classical view of the child guidance team, but in actual experience the model was often disregarded or altered. This was partly due to local conditions. In some clinics the psychiatric social worker might be the only full-time member of the team and would therefore become responsible for much of the administration of the clinic. Other clinics had a psychologist as director rather than the psychiatrist and this situation would affect the roles of the other members of the team. However, ambiguity in the model was also responsible for much variation in practice. This ambiguity mainly centred on the psychiatric social worker and the justification of her place in the team. If the team was seen as the means of co-operation between three disciplines or three kinds of knowledge or of skill, the psychiatric social worker was obviously the odd man out. Her discipline was uncertain in nature, her knowledge vague and unformed and the special aspect of her skill by no means obvious. If, for instance, the psychiatrist suggested that she should aim at becoming a specialist in the social aspects of maladjustment and mental illness, what could the psychiatric social worker reply? According to Ashdown and Brown she could say that this was indeed the basis of her skill, the underlying feature of the profession of social work in which she was a specialist. 'The social worker with special training for psychiatric social service brings to her new calling something corresponding to the physician's perceptiveness, by reason of the fact that she has been accustomed to think and act in relation to the 'body social', as he in relation to the human organism, body and mind, However far the reality falls short of the ideal, there exists among experienced social workers, besides actual knowledge about the structure, functioning and ills of society which it is the part of the social sciences to study and formulate, a perceptiveness in relation to the 'body social' which may be regarded as characteristic of their profession.'[4] This is a large claim, but it is expressed with sufficient 'mysticism' to obscure its precise nature. Such claims can, however, be viewed less as pretensions to knowledge and skill and more as a defensive measure to deal with problems arising from the fact that psychiatric social workers have to form close working relationships with members of higher-status professions. A comparatively recent study of the mental health professions in America showed that psychiatric social workers 'value psychiatry more than their own profession and many wish they were psychiatrists rather than social workers.'[5] The identity of the psychiatric social worker is not as clear-cut as that of psychiatrist or psychologist and her work easily overlaps with theirs. In such a situation, the psychiatric social worker is led to claim skill and knowledge which are uniquely hers. Such claims are difficult to substantiate when the psychiatric social worker is learning about her own work through comparing it in some ways with that of the psychiatrist or analyst. This comparison is likely to result in the undervaluation of the work of the psychiatric social worker as a kind of miniature of the psychiatrist's.[6]

Perhaps the most important developments in the child guidance role of the psychiatric social worker arose from the different interpretations that came to be placed on her function in working with mothers of children being treated at the clinic and from the different policies adapted by clinics to deal with the fact that the demand for their services far exceeded their resources of time and personnel. A more detailed exposition of these two developments is clearly required.

One of the difficulties in attempting to describe developments in the work of the psychiatric social worker in child guidance is that so much of what may appear as new is to be found either implicitly or explicitly in early practice. This is particularly true of developments in the treatment of mothers in the child guidance clinic, since this work contained from the beginning some important ambiguities and questions. What was the objective of the worker's interviews with the mother? Could it be said that the worker 'treated' the mothers? If so, which aspects of the mother's problem were the object of treatment and what might be the effects of such an objective on the other aspects of the work, such as the compilation of the social history. Presumably the treatment envisaged would be some kind of therapy in which a professional relationship was established and used. If the relationship of social worker and client thus came to have pre-eminent importance what should the worker do when the demands of history taking seemed to conflict with the demands of a beginning relationship? These and similar questions soon pressed for answers, and were certainly discussed on the training courses from 1935 onwards.

One important objective of the contact of psychiatric social worker and parent which was recognized at an early stage, was that of explaining and representing the clinic to the parents. The psychiatric social worker was usually the first member of the team to meet the parent. The most significant development in this aspect of the work has probably been the change from fairly straightforward explanations of the way the clinic functioned to the attempt to discover what the parents had heard and imagined about the clinic so that the kind of explanation was related more specifically to their particular fears and wishes. The problem is seen, in other words, not so much as an isolated one of ignorance, but as part of the parents feeling about receiving help for their child. Two extracts from the writings of psychiatric social workers at different periods of time may illustrate some of this development.

(1945) 'The next step is for the social worker to give some explanation of the methods employed. Unless this is done early in the treatment, and even repeated from time to time, most parents begin to feel that they are wasting their time in bringing their children to a clinic where they apparently do nothing but play. The relation of play to phantasy life, and its use in diagnosis and treatment, are not easy matters to explain to those who are unaccustomed to such ideas. Fortunately it is usually only the more intelligent who demand a theoretical exposition.'[7]

(1950) 'In this original contact she must be able to understand something of the situation behind the application for help, to bear this in mind when interpreting to the parents the part that they must play in the treatment of their child. For example, sometimes the reassurance that it is good, responsible parents who come to the clinic may be sufficient to remove initial apology and apprehension; sometimes the parent reveals hostility to anyone trying to help which must be met appropriately if the child needing treatment is to continue to attend.'[8]

Turning to the objectives of the psychiatric social worker's interview with the mother once the child was in treatment, the functions of the psychiatric social worker were at first conceived as effecting some change in the child's environment and ensuring that the child came for treatment. Once again there was ambiguity in the task, what *was* the child's environment? Surely, the parents were the most important part of it. In the early years it would seem that psychiatric social workers concentrated on changing the mother's handling of the child by advice and by explanation of his behaviour. The earliest published case of psychiatric social work in this country shows the worker attempting to explain the child's symptoms to the mother. We find the worker in the first interview discussing educational methods and giving 'instances of children, who, perhaps as a result of early deprivations, felt an exaggerated need to be in the limelight even when the consequences were always painful. Restlessness was instanced as drawing a great deal of attention, and the worker even went so far as to ask whether Jimmy did not get more attention through his restlessness than for anything else.'[9]

The explanations that psychiatric social workers gave, and the advice that, for example, sex information should be given or sand and waterplay be improvised in the home gave the worker the role of an expert or 'authority' in the situation. This can be seen explicitly in the following quotation from a comparatively early standard work of English child guidance:

'We have considered the social worker's part in adjusting the environment as an adjunct to therapy. It remains to say something of what she can do to ensure that the work of the clinic is not wasted through backsliding . . . In such cases the social worker visits the home from time to time, and, if the need arises, sees that the child is brought back to the clinic.'[10] The authoritarian implications in this quotation are partly contained in such words as 'backsliding' and also, if less obviously, in the idea of the worker as 'adjusting the environment'.

Some psychiatric social workers faced with the task of altering the child's environment, began to doubt the value of attempts to convince mothers of the wisdom of changing their minds. The treatment of mothers began to be envisaged.

The issue of treatment has been discussed by child guidance workers from the beginnings of child guidance in this country. At the first Inter-Clinic Conference in 1933[11] it was suggested that two extreme views on the place of the psychiatric social worker were possible '(1) the restriction of the social worker's activities to mere observation of the home situation and relationships, (2) her part as an active agent in the treatment of a case.' There was some discussion of the importance of considering the temperament of each worker before she was selected for 'treatment in the home' and of the desirability of an effective relationship between the social worker and the parent. 'It was generally conceded that such a relationship was necessary in order to get the information required. A trained social worker's attitude ought to be objective and such relationships controlled by her.' The relationship between worker and client did not receive much detailed examination apart from these aspects of control and it was agreed 'that the function of the social worker is to assist the psychiatrist to get the best possible results from whatever method of treatment is adopted.'

At the Second Inter-Clinic Conference, however, in 1935, Hardcastle, a psychiatric social worker, firmly presented the importance of the relationship between client and worker as something other than a necessary and perhaps relatively painless way of extracting information. 'We have learnt more and more', she told the Conference, 'that psychiatric social work is something other than social work carried out by a worker with a psychiatric background. We have come to realize the factor of relationship and as increasingly we realize this factor, we see that we have a very specialized job to do. We get our histories, we carry out the plan which our psychiatrists have formulated, but in doing this we have come to see that we are of necessity doing therapy ourselves. Every contact with a patient implies a relationship whether we desire it or not, because all therapy is based *a priori* upon relationship. Through this controlled relationship with the worker the anxious mother is enabled to see her problems and work through them.'[12]

In these statements we can see clearly some of the main problems and attractions for the psychiatric social worker in claiming to undertake therapy. In making this claim the worker can obviously declare her difference from a mere social worker—psychiatric social work is not simply social work by someone with some knowledge of psychiatry and the mental health services. In the 1930's the differentiation of psychiatric social work from non-psychiatric social work was made, in one sense, easier by the undifferentiated state of the latter which could with some justice be described as 'general social work' rather than social work in a probation setting, in a child care setting and so on. Secondly, in claiming a therapeutic function, the psychiatric social worker was obviously stressing a major element in all social work when she drew attention to the relationship between the client and worker. However, there was always the danger that 'therapy' and the worker's function of co-operative work with the psychiatrist would be split off from each other, so that the 'therapy' would not be seen as largely a product of the way in which the psychiatric social worker carried out her clinical function.

The theme of 'treatment' was taken up again at the Tenth Conference in 1939 when the first session was directed to The Treatment of Parents.[13] Miss Addis began her talk by stating: 'For the Social Worker at a Child Guidance Clinic the question is not whether to give treatment to parents or not, but how? Just listening to what the mother or father has to say about the child's problem involves you willy-nilly in treatment. The parent coming to ask for help, and the Clinic worker being ready to give it, create the therapeutic situation, and from the first the way in which the material is accepted or explored begins the treatment.' Finally, the speaker suggested that 'if in Child Guidance work a social worker's approach differs from the psychiatrist's, it seems . . . once more a question of degree. Perhaps she works more from the conscious to the unconscious and not the other way round. While being as aware as possible of unconscious factors, sensitive to indications of what is going on under the surface, ready to deal with unconscious material as it comes up (and dreams are often presented unasked) prepared to interpret, suggest, give an apt question, yet we begin with what the parent knows.' In this contribution the ideas of treatment are taken a stage further. It is now claimed that psychiatric social workers are in a treatment situation whether they acknowledge it or not, a treatment situation, moreover, which is very like that of the psychiatrist. It is, however, defined so broadly that it includes both diagnostic procedures (listening) and also courteous attention to requests for help. Similarly, Ashdown and Thomas in the same year wrote of a case carried by a psychiatric social worker in a mental hospital that 'With him, the fact that someone wrote to invite his co-operation and asked him to suggest a time convenient to himself for the interview was therapeutic, and it seems to us that the mere expression of these attitudes and grievances constitutes a means of catharsis which is of real sociological value.'[14] Here, the long-term implications of 'therapeutic' colour what should be regarded as a by-product of simple courtesy. Because the psychiatric social worker began to display an attitude that might be helpful and because the outlines of a therapeutic situation might be present, it is inappropriate to claim that therapy or treatment have begun. In much of the discussion of the work of the psychiatric social worker the necessary conditions for therapy are taken to constitute also its sufficient conditions.

The view of psychiatric social work as therapy appealed to one part of the profession and seemed unacceptable to the rest. It raised issues of considerable importance both for the life of the Association and for the theoretical formulation of the ends and methods of psychiatric social work. These issues will be considered in later chapters. At this point it is sufficient to state that the practice of psychiatric social workers varied considerably in their interviews with parents (predominantly, the mothers). The basic problems and issues involved in claiming to 'treat' mothers had all been stated in the first decade of the profession's history— was the focus of treatment the mother's problems as an individual or as a mother? How could such treatment be differentiated from that given by the psychiatrist and so on? Psychiatric social workers chose their individual solutions and the problems are still basically unresolved. Take, for example, the issue of the aim of 'treatment interviews'. In the latest publication of the Association Barnes has said that 'I know many psychiatric social workers do not agree that their function (in child guidance) is to deal with whatever the parents bring. They feel their work should be focused on the child's difficulties and in helping the mother to help the child.'[15] Obviously it is not necessary for all psychiatric social workers to agree on a single way of working in a child guidance clinic, but the implications of the two different approaches need to be explored.

In the first instance the psychiatric social worker is defined as someone who deals with the material her 'patient' produces whatever its nature. In the later instance the worker does not launch on the seas of unchartered psychotherapy, but relies on the focus provided by the function of her agency (helping disturbed children) by concentrating on the difficulties the mother has in her role as the mother of a disturbed child. This provides a joint focus for both client and worker.

Some of the differences between psychiatric social workers on the issue of 'treatment' were at one time expressed in terms of the difference between clinics. Some clinics were thought of as 'intensive' and some as 'superficial' or in the more polite psychological terminology of Ashdown and Brown, as 'introverted' and 'extro-verted'.[16] These terms referred to two of the possible answers to the question what policy should the clinic adopt in the face of excessive demand for service? Some clinics nourished their roots in the local community, maintained contact with local doctors, schools and social work agencies and undertook a considerable amount of diagnostic work. Campbell, for example, at the Sixth Biennial Child Guidance Inter-clinic Conference,[17] emphasized the 'social work' elements in psychiatric social work: 'as social workers, we are inevitably concerned with other social services. They are the tools with which we have to work, and it is part of our job to know how to use them, to find them, to establish links, to avoid overlapping and to define the boundaries—in fact, everything that is implied by that much abused word "co-operation".' Here the 'tools' of the psychiatric social worker's trade are seen not as 'relationships' or personalities, but as the social services. Others worked intensively on a smaller number of cases, concentrating their resources on long-term treatment rather than on diagnostic and advisory services to the local community. This difference has to a considerable extent now broken down and with the present emphasis on the clinic as a centre for consultation the two aspects of treatment and community service are now seen as complementary. Again it is important to observe caution in regard to developments labelled as new.

The Maudsley Child Guidance Clinic, used for student training, has always emphasized some kind of consultative service and provincial clinics have nearly always been concerned with serving the local community. Hutchinson in an early issue of the Journal referred to the passing of 'the days of cloistered calm when the clinic stood apart, and possibly aloof, from the often red-tape-entangled machinery of local government,'[18] but in many areas such days existed more in the imagination than in reality. Nonetheless there is about the present emphasis on the consultative role of clinic and psychiatric social worker a sense of purpose and direction which is certainly new. This can be seen in the latest publication of the Association, *Ventures in Professional Co-operation*, which is concerned with inter-professional collaboration and the relationship between the psychiatric social worker and the social services.

These, then, are the most important general changes in psychiatric social work in child guidance. Firstly a movement towards more sustained work with parents and towards viewing the other aspects of the worker's role (e.g. explaining the clinic) in the light of the specific difficulties parents have in perceiving and accepting the clinic and themselves as helpful. Secondly, an approach to a more effective diagnostic and consultative service to others working in the community. These two developments have contributed to and benefited from an increased flexibility in the assignment of roles in the clinic. Sometimes, for example, the diagnostic interview of mother and child will be conducted jointly by psychiatrist and psychiatric social worker. Sometimes the psychiatric social worker will try to help mother and child together or take on the child while the psychiatrist treats the mother. Many different combinations of this kind are possible and they indicate a change in the work as exciting if not as profound or extensive as present changes in the field of mental hospital work.

Before leaving the field of child guidance, however, some reference should be made to a significant extension of this work that has been pioneered largely by psychiatric social workers. This is the development of psychiatric social work in the maternity and child welfare centre. The Child Guidance Council had shown some interest in 'preventive' work in these centres; in 1938, for instance, two psychiatrists with experience in child guidance work had acted as consultants to selected maternity and child welfare centres for an experimental period. However, intensive pioneering in this field was a feature of the development of psychiatric social work after the War. It has taken two forms. The first, chronologically, was some direct experimental work undertaken by the worker seeing the mothers of children under five for short-term but intensive help. This kind of work has been well described by Joseph in a paper with implications much wider than its title suggests.[19] The second development was the inauguration of a form of consultative-educational service for the staffs of certain centres with the object of improving their skills in recognizing and dealing with incipient mental health problems in their own work.[20]

So far, however, developments have been discussed in general terms and it would be difficult to extract from such an approach any detailed idea of what social workers actually do in child guidance. An attempt is made in this study to begin to fill some of the gaps in our knowledge of the job of the psychiatric social worker in this field. A previous attempt by Ashdown and Brown approached the subject by interviewing a group of psychiatric social workers and asking them questions about their practice. The present study attempts to analyse the case records of the psychiatric social workers in a provincial child guidance clinic from 1936 to 1957. A comprehensive picture of what a worker does will probably emerge only when one can study her interviews fully recorded on tapes, and interview both worker and client after the interview. However, the present study offers new material on what workers do from an analysis of their records of interviews with clients.

During the years under review (1936-57) the clinic saw 6,849 cases. From this total group a random sample was collected by choosing every twenty-fifth case. In this way a group of 274 cases was selected for study.

Of the group of 274 cases studied 39 were excluded because they involved no contact between a psychiatric social worker and a parent. In some of these cases the parent did not come to the clinic; in other instances the work was undertaken by someone other than a trained psychiatric social worker. Any complete account of the work of the clinic would obviously include such cases, but from the point of view of studying the psychiatric social worker they are clearly irrelevant. Of the remaining 235 cases 70 (41 mothers and 29 fathers) or about 30 per cent were seen by the psychiatric social worker once only. Many of these were cases in which a report was required by the juvenile court; some were, of course, cases in which the parent did not continue contact. The high proportion of single interviews whether intentionally so or not raises important points especially in view of what follows in connection with short-term contact in the mental hospital field. First, if contact is intentionally short, have we examined with sufficient thoroughness ways in which this can be made more helpful to the short-term client? Secondly, if contact is broken by the client, what aspects of the first interview contribute to this failure and what policy should be adopted in regard to following-up such interviews? Is the problem primarily due to a failure in communication based on the fact that clients initially define the contact with the clinic (and social worker) as transitory and its outcome is seen largely in terms of advice, while the social worker thinks in terms of a long process of exploration and 'working-through' various relationship problems?

Of the parents interviewed more than once (i.e. of 165 cases) the average number of interviews was approximately five per case, but this is misleading since 14 of the cases had 16 interviews or over. A more accurate representation is to take the modal value for the number of interviews which is two.

It is frequently remarked that child guidance clinics seem to show some reluctance in seeing and treating fathers. One of the early trained psychiatric social workers has pointed out that 'Although work with parents is usually considered to be one of the special features of child guidance, in actual fact there are clinics in which only one parent—usually the mother—plays any active part, either in contributing to the social history or in the general plan of treatment.'[21] In the total group of 235 cases the mother alone was seen in 214 cases. This figure requires interpretation. It is, for example, not always a possible matter for choice where the mother alone is seen. Some fathers were dead, had deserted or were in the forces. As far as could be ascertained this was so in 15 per cent of the total group of cases and in 22 per cent of those cases where the mother alone was seen. This, of course, qualifies the general picture, but the mother-centred focus of the psychiatric social workers remains, on the whole, true. It remains true no matter what the age of the child or his problem. Of a total of 1049 interviews and home visits 56 were with fathers.

This is a finding of some importance and suggests that the decision about which member of the family to work with is to an important extent governed by a general attitude on the part of psychiatric social workers. This is not, of course, to suggest that the decision is determined by this attitude. Other factors also exert an influence: generally speaking, mothers are more easily available and are expected to escort children to other kinds of clinics. Obviously, at certain ages mothers are much more important to their children than fathers, but it is also true that at other ages fathers are equally if not more important. Yet, psychiatric social workers (and other social and medical workers also) seem reluctant to make the necessary special arrangements to see and work with fathers and indeed other family members and appear tied to a model of family interaction (the predominance of the mother-child relationship) which might well be preventing them seeing and grasping other therapeutic opportunities.

Studies in America have suggested that social class factors exercise a considerable influence on the extent to which help is given in cases of mental illness and on the kind of help and the length of time for which it is held available.[22] In the present study an attempt was made to investigate the operation of such factors in the caseload of the clinic studied. All the cases involving more than one interview were analysed in terms of the Registrar General's Classification of Social Class. In approximately one fifth of the cases no classification was possible either because father's occupation had not been recorded or its recording was too vague. Of the remainder approximately nine per cent were in Social Classes I and II, 63 per cent in Class III and 28 per cent in Classes IV and V. It is difficult to assess this finding since the small amount of work that has been done on follow-up studies scarcely ever gives information about the social class composition of child guidance clinic patients. The spread appears to be much less even than that in the one relevant study so far published.[23] Clearly in my study the majority of parents for whom a classification could be made were in Class III, but a significant proportion were in the two lower classes. Much, of course, will depend on the class distribution of the area covered by the clinic. It is extremely difficult to obtain a picture of this over a period of time and all that can be said is that data on present distribution suggests some under-representation of the two upper and the two lower classes and some over-representation of Class III. It is not possible to identify over time the various factors in the complex system of referral of cases, but this does not appear to operate in favour of the upper and professional classes.

What, however, happens once cases have been successfully referred? Is particular favour shown to any one social group as measured by the number of interviews? The answer is in the negative. Of the interviews given to parents whose social class could be obtained (132 cases) there seems to have been an equal sharing of the numbers of interviews, with some preference being given to those in Class III. The point at which social class becomes influential is when a decision about home visiting is made. The majority of interviews over the whole period were conducted in the clinic but home visiting was undertaken at some point in about 30 per cent of the cases. The chances of a home visit increase as one descends the social scale.

On the evidence of this study it would seem that American findings in regard to the influence of social class do not apply to the same extent in Great Britain. Clearly more research is required into different clinics in different parts of the country, but as far as this study goes it does not appear to be the case that psychiatric social workers are exclusively concerned with one social class or that they show preference in terms of the number of interviews given. Yet preference can be shown in other ways. For example, certain techniques could be reserved for clients in one social group. Again, the study shows that techniques in so far as they could be isolated were used over the whole range of social class.

To talk of techniques, however, takes us beyond such comparatively simple matters as the class distribution of clients and the number of interviews. What *does* the psychiatric social worker do when she interviews a client (parent) in a child guidance clinic? Obviously the records cannot convey a picture of the total inter-action of client and worker, but an analyis of the 165 cases (with more than one interview) reveals certain important features. Firstly, the worker is concerned with encouraging the client to give information concerning a number of important topics. In nearly all cases (whether of one interview or more) the psychiatric social worker has taken a social history, but during treatment the records indicate that the worker encourages the giving of further information. It is rare, however, for such information to be used as the basis for any re-assessment of diagnosis (in so far as this would be recorded). In most interviews the parent gives informa-tion about the current position in regard to the child referred to the clinic. In approximately 68 per cent of the interviews this seems to be the main basis of the interaction between client and worker; in 14 per cent the basis is discussion of the mother, in 7 per cent the father and in 3 per cent the marital relationship.

The psychiatric social worker is, however, more than a recipient of information. What other activities does she pursue besides encouraging the client to report on the child's progress and current situation? It seems that these can be analysed under the following headings—discussion of function, explanation, advice, interpretation, encouragement and reassurance. A definition of these terms is necessary. Discussion of function refers to the worker's giving information directly connected with the clinic's function (including her own). Thus, in a case in 1941 the worker recorded that she 'discussed alternatives in connection with the boy's placement'. Or the action of the worker in a case in 1942 was again classified as 'discussion of function' when the worker recorded that she 'discussed the clinic's findings'. Explanation has as its objective the attempt to help the parent grasp some aspect of behaviour intellectually. To put it formally, explanation completes for the parent an equation which has on the other side a piece of behaviour or an attitude usually of the patient or his parents. For example, in a case in 1943 the worker 'discussed masturbation. The mother had never seen patient masturbate and thought she probably did not. The worker explained that patient might have done this in the past, and felt guilty and her present behaviour was the equivalent.' In 1952 the worker recorded that she 'discussed self-drive, the release of tension through the expression of feeling compared to the bottling up and getting on with the job in hand.' This also was classified as an explanation. Advice was defined as the recommendation of a particular action or policy; its objective is to try to get the client to do something. Examples of this in the records are: (1937), the worker 'talked with the mother about how she might manage patient by giving him more credit for the things he could do and by taking less notice of his tempers, particularly stressing the fact that if she wanted him to go away later on she must stop now threatening to send him away'; (1940), 'mother complained that patient copied his brother and now played in the water in spite of her scolding. The worker suggested that they should be provided with old clothes and given plenty of opportunity to play with water and mud. The mother said that patient pencilled on the walls and she punished him severely for this. The worker suggested giving him large sheets of old paper on which he could scribble. Mother seemed to accept the ideas and the worker's explanation of play.' (In the second extract two pieces of advice have been recorded and also an explanation). Interpretation has been defined for the purpose of this study as the attempt to help the client accept a new way of seeing behaviour by drawing attention to feelings that are implicit in the situation. A distinction has been made between what may be termed an historical interpretation (now you have particular feelings or a particular purpose because you had these feelings (or purpose) in the past) and an interpretation of feeling (or purpose) that belongs explicitly to one object in the present, but actually belongs to another object in the present. Some examples will clarify this distinction:

(1936) 'Mother began with an outburst against daylight saving, which, she claimed, made it all the more difficult for parents to get children to bed. The worker suggested that mother thought it was very easy for the clinic to sit and give advice when she had to deal with the child';

(1950) 'The step-father blamed the worker for having told mother that she had no self-discipline. The worker asked if he was quite sure that he had not used discussion about the clinic to slip in this criticism of mother';

(1942) 'Mother eventually agreed that she had projected all her mother's criticism and disapproval on to her son and she eventually discovered how much she was wanting the perfect mother';

(1951) 'Mother cannot see her aggression towards me, which I tried to point out. She admitted that she used to put herself out to come to the clinic, but does not do so anymore.'

Encouragement is defined as the attempt to confirm the client in an attitude or action; its objective is the continuation of an attitude or action. For example, in a case in 1940 the worker 'told mother that she could see it was difficult for her to stop herself doing things for Raymond (aged six), but that it would help him if she encouraged him to be more independent.' Finally, reassurance has been used to indicate relief of fear or anxiety by words of comfort; if successful it is likely to lead to a change in action. For example, in a case in 1936 the worker was trying to help a mother continue to tolerate the aggression of her child. The mother described her anxiety about fighting; she was nearly sick at the sight of her boy quarrelling with his friend. The worker suggested a link between this and her fears in connection with the open quarrels of her own parents. She reassured mother that no great harm would befall her if she tolerated her son's aggression.' In this case an interpretation is followed by re-assurance.

These, then, are the categories used to analyse the activities of the psychiatric social workers, (five were concerned in the cases studied)—discussion of function, explanation, advice, interpretation, encouragement and reassurance. The cases were studied in detail and every recorded instance of any activity was noted. In this way it is possible to arrive at some idea of the distribution of each activity in the total verbal intervention of the workers. The activities seem to fall into two main groups; advice, discussion of function and explanation account for 25 per cent, 25 per cent and 22 per cent of the total recorded verbal intervention respectively, with interpretation (15 per cent,), encouragement (four per cent) and reassurance (nine per cent) forming the second group. If the activities are examined over the period it appears that the use of reassurance is most constant and that there has been a marked increase in discussion of function and in explanation and a decrease in advice giving. Interpretation seems to be the category whose use varies most over the years and it is perhaps the activity which most differentiates the work of one psychiatric social worker from another. Finally, it is worth observing that it is usual for all activities to find a place in the treatment process, though interpretation tends to be reserved for the longer case (with an average of about 24 interviews).

What conclusion can be drawn, albeit tentatively from this data? It seems that the psychiatric social workers in this provincial clinic maintained a flexible approach to their clients, with no one method apparently preferred. They gave direct advice with reasonable liberality, in spite of much heart searching in the profession on this question.[24] They discussed their function and that of the clinic with sufficient frequency at least to question the view that what they were doing was captive psychotherapy, and they were often engaged in some kind of educational role in helping parents to accept explanations of behaviour. Sometimes there were direct attempts to help parents accept interpretations of behaviour, but explicit verbal reference to the relationship between the worker and the client was rare. The case (1943) in which the worker recorded that 'she had to interpret a little to the mother her feelings towards me; she was getting upset at my going and was not prepared to accept the artificial,' (limitations of her relationship with the clinic) is by no means typical. This is not, of course, to deny the importance of the relationships that undoubtedly existed without any comment being made upon them. Obviously, we need more (and fuller) descriptions of what psychiatric social workers do in child guidance clinics and other fields, but the present study goes some way to increase our understanding of their activities.

NOTES

[1] See e.g. Winnicott D. W., and Britton C., 'Residential Management as Treatment for Difficult Children', *Human Relations*, Vol. 1, No. 1, June 1947, for an account in one county of the development of a wartime hostel scheme in which the psychiatric social worker acted as the central pivot.

[2] *Report of the Committee on Maladjusted Children* (Underwood) H.M.S.O. 1955, p. 144.

[3] Figures taken from *Education in 1959, Education in 1960*, H.M.S.O.

[4] Ashdown and Brown, *op. cit.*, p. 11/12.

[5] Zander A., *et al.*, *Role Relations in the Mental Health Professions*, 1957 (Research Centre for Group Dynamics), p. 41.

[6] In 1949 a psychiatric social worker suggested that many patients projected authority images on to the psychiatrist and it was his task to interpret these to the patient. She then stated that psychiatric social workers should also do this 'if in our clinical work a *faint shadow* (my italics) of this authoritarian greatness is projected upon us because of our association with the

doctor'. Hunnybun N., 'The meaning of the word "social" in Psychiatric Social Work', *British Journal of Psychiatric Social Work*, Number 3, November 1949.

[7] Burbury M., Balint E., and Yapp B., *An Introduction to Child Guidance*, 1946, p. 159.

[8] Lewis K., The Role of the Psychiatric Social Worker, *British Journal of Psychiatric Social Work*, No. 4, 1950.

[9] Illustrative Material to pamphlet by the A.P.S.W. (1932). *Psychiatric Social Work and the Family*.

[10] Burbury *et al.*, *op. cit.* p. 176.

[11] *Proceedings of First Inter-Clinic Conference*, duplicated N.A.M.H.

[12] *Proceedings of the Second Inter-Clinic Conference*, Child Guidance Council 1935.

[13] *Proceedings of the Child Guidance Inter-Clinic Conference*, Child Guidance Council 1939.

[14] Ashdown M., and Thomas E. L., *Psychiatric Social Work in a Mental Hospital*, Mental Welfare, Vol. XX, No. 2., April 1939.

[15] Barnes M., 'Collaboration within the Therapeutic Team', in (ed.) Irvine E. E., *Ventures in Professional Co-operation, op. cit.* p. 36.

[16] *Op. cit. pp.* 130/32.

[17] *Proceedings of the Sixth Biennial Child Guidance Inter-Clinic Conference*, 1943.

[18] Hutchinson D. M., 'Clinic and Community—Psychiatric Social Worker's Role in Preventive Child Guidance Work'. *British Journal of Psychiatric Social Work*, No. 2, 1948.

[19] Joseph B., 'A Psychiatric Social Worker in a Maternity and Child Welfare Clinic', *British Journal of Psychiatric Social Work*, No. 2, August 1948.

[20] See e.g. Irvine E. E., 'Opportunities for Guidance in the Early Years', *Royal Society of Health Journal*, Vol. 75, No. 9. September 1955.

[21] Hunnybun N., 'A Short Communication on the Place of Father in Child Guidance', *British Journal of Psychiatric Social Work*, No. 2, 1948.

[22] See e.g., Gursslin *et al.*, 'Social Class, Mental Hygiene, and Psychiatric Practice', *Social Service Review*, Vol. XXXIII, No. 3, September 1959.

[23] See follow-up study of Bromley Child Guidance Clinic, in *Proceedings of the Ninth Child Guidance Inter-Clinic Conference*, 1951.

[24] See, for example, the discussion on advice in Ashdown and Brown, *op. cit.*, pp. 151–3.

Chapter Six

THE WORK OF THE PSYCHIATRIC SOCIAL WORKER—MENTAL HOSPITAL AND COMMUNITY CARE

B. MENTAL HOSPITAL

ANY attempt to describe the kind of work undertaken by psychiatric social workers in the mental hospital encounters several difficulties, which deserve some attention since they represent important aspects of the professional situation of the social workers we are studying. Workers in the mental hospital field have often been reluctant to describe their work because they felt it was somehow inferior to that of their colleagues in child guidance.

Such feelings seem to have derived—in the immediate past, at any rate—from several sources. Workers in mental hospitals were often dealing with those rejected by their families, workmates etc., and by a process of identification they may have themselves felt rejected and undervalued. They had difficulty in defining their role in the hospital, and frequently met amongst their colleagues the idea that their work was mere social work, whereas those in a child guidance clinic were engaged in therapy or at any rate psycho-therapeutic casework. Jones and Hammond refer to these questions in their article on training. 'Faced by so overwhelming an amount of incurable illness, and without, perhaps, knowing quite where her place lay in the services offered by the hospital or in its hierarchy, it is hardly surprising she was tempted to accept the defensive superiority of some of her Child Guidance colleagues.'[1] Psychiatric social workers were an essential part of the original conception of the child guidance clinic, but mental hospitals had been in existence for a century or more when the first worker was trained in England and the kind of work they might undertake in the hospital was by no means clear. The new psychiatric social worker was assured of a welcome in the child guidance clinic and to be part of a new movement was in itself encouraging. In the mental hospital, workers had to create their own role, to find their function and their place. In these circumstances the work spread slowly; by 1937 there were only eight psychiatric social workers in mental hospitals outside London.

If psychiatric social workers could complain with justification of a lukewarm welcome to the mental hospital field, the Board of Control did all it could to encourage their appointment. The annual reports of the Board in the 1930's nearly always contain some reference to the benefits to be obtained from appointing such workers. In the report for 1932 a circular letter from the Child Guidance Council was quoted in which the purpose of the new Mental Health Course was stated: 'to equip social workers with sufficient knowledge and practical skill to enable them to work with the psychiatrist and assist him by obtaining histories of their patients and their families and by carrying out any necessary re-adjustments in the home of the patients.'[2] The Report stated that 'We know of no psychiatrist who, after having experienced the benefits of the service, would be without it.' The Board in pursuing a policy of encouraging the use of psychiatric social workers soon found itself in some difficulty. In order 'to sell' them to the hospitals it was necessary to stress their usefulness in saving the doctor's time, though in fact, as Ashdown and Thomas correctly observed, their appointment would 'increase rather than lessen the burden of the psychiatrist, for the approach from the social side, by emphasizing the multiplicity of causation of the illness, will indicate the necessity of treatment from more than one angle, thus extending the scope of the hospital.'[3] Yet the Board of Control had to attempt some description of the work which would satisfy the psychiatric social worker without threatening the medical superintendent. Were psychiatric social workers indispensable because they had specialist knowledge (therapy is implicitly ruled out in the Report for 1936) or because they had a unique skill in obtaining information or because they saved the doctor's time? The last two possibilities were expressed almost simultaneously in the Report for 1935: 'The value of social workers is becoming more generally recognized every year, but there are still committees who forget how uneconomical it is to allow doctors to spend time doing work which is within the competence of social workers. Indeed, the doctor cannot obtain by questioning the patient, or by correspondence, anything like such a complete picture of the patient's home conditions, as the report of a good social worker will give him ... In fact there are so many ways in which social workers can help the medical superintendent that it is safe to say that no one who has had experience of this value would ever again be content to be without one.'[4] The Reports of the Board in this decade form a good illustration of the problems of initiating a new service into an already existing organization with strong hierarchical tendencies. In the particular situation some form of distortion of the function of the psychiatric social worker as she herself understood it (distortion which showed her part as a medical auxiliary collecting information for doctors) was perhaps inevitable.

The role of the psychiatric social worker in the mental hospital developed in response to the individual demands of each particular institution. This lack of uniformity is evident in American psychiatric social work also. Berkman's study of the practice of social workers in psychiatric hospitals and clinics found little similarity of practice, but that the kind of social service given was in large part determined by and sometimes prescribed by the psychiatrist.[5] This determinant would seem to apply in Britain. It would be inaccurate to imagine that variation of role between staff members is not possible in the child guidance clinic, but the psychiatrist (unlike the superintendent of a mental hospital) is rarely full-time, and this must affect the relationship of his activities to those of the psychiatric social worker. There is also in the mental hospital a wider range of possible work than in the child guidance clinic, and perhaps a greater difference of opinion amongst psychiatrists as to the role of the psychiatric social worker.

Take, for example, the meeting of the Psychological Section of the B.M.A. on 'The Role of the Psychiatric Social Worker' in July 1950.[6] Dr. J. B. S. Lewis appeared to give full recognition to the psychiatric social worker. 'She should', a report of the meeting states, 'of course, work in close conjunction with a psychiatrist; but it must be remembered that she had a skill of her own, and he could learn from her as she from him. Her duties were multifarious. She had to explain to the patient, his relatives, employers, etc. what the hospital or clinic was doing; to take a social history; to follow-up and help discharged patients; to co-operate with other social services; to help in administration and in therapeutic work and in research; and, in fact, to carry out many *other chores.*' The fairly high status accorded to the psychiatric social worker is somewhat diminished by the ambivalent comment in (my) italics. Of more significance, however, are the comments during discussion from two professors of psychiatry who were emphatic that it was the responsibility of the psychiatrist as physician to take the social history. This has usually been assumed to be one of the main responsibilities of the psychiatric social worker, but here the argument was that the psychiatrist could not under any circumstances rely on second-hand information.

There was, then, considerable variation in the expectations that psychiatrists held of the psychiatric social worker, and this results in a variety of role in the mental hospital. Sometimes this left the psychiatric social worker considerable freedom within which to experiment. There has recently been some pressure towards greater uniformity in so far as mental hospitals have taken up with some enthusiasm the new policies of community care outside their walls and of the therapeutic community within. For the first time mental hospitals can share in a new movement akin to the early ventures in mental health which proved such an encouragement to the child guidance team. Yet the new policies only complicate the problem of description and could easily increase the actual anxiety of social workers trying to put them into practice. As Hayward has commented: 'Now they (the psychiatric social workers) are seen as members of a team with close inter-relationship between the nursing staff, doctors and the administration. Within this team, roles are not clearly defined, but are worked out by mutual adaptation, according to what each person does best.'⁷ This kind of approach means that the role of the psychiatric social worker in this setting will again vary considerably from one hospital to another. The fact that each worker may have to work out anew her role in each hospital certainly places a considerable strain upon her and her colleagues, particularly in view of the fairly rapid turnover of hospital staff, including, as we have seen, psychiatric social workers.

The present time is one of considerable change in the mental hospital field, and it is still not possible even to describe general trends in psychiatric social work in this area. We can, however, describe some general features of this work in an historical perspective.

At first, workers had gradually to evolve their function in each hospital setting. In general, however, they were responsible for taking social histories, sometimes as a routine procedure on all new admissions. They worked with relatives at the time of admission, enlisting their confidence, explaining hospital procedure and possibly the kind of treatment that might be given. From then until the time of the patient's discharge it was unlikely that they would have further contact with the relatives: 'as a rule, although exceptional cases or homes may have to be psychiatrically nursed by the worker, no further active work is undertaken in the home until the time for the patient's discharge approaches.'[8] At this time the work of after-care would begin. These functions represent the three main items of early psychiatric social work in the mental hospital field and there was, of course, considerable variation between different hospitals and at different times, the emphasis changing from one theme to another. Basically, however, the work changed very little before the Second World War. McDougall has suggested that in this first period 'The psychiatric social worker developed her skills in mental hospital social work, finding a place in the hospital, getting accepted.'[9]

Since the Second World War, however, there have been considerable changes in the mental hospital itself, which have inevitably affected psychiatric social work. One of the most important has been the increase in the turnover of patients due to the developments of chemotherapy and a different attitude towards discharge. McDougall has pointed out that this has meant more interesting work for doctors and nurses, but this is limited to some extent by the capacity of the hospital. 'From the social worker's point of view these changes have not necessarily had quite the same results. The number of her clients, or what she should do for them—nothing or how much—is not so governed by bed numbers or floor space, or whether the patient is in hospital, and one of the biggest changes remarked on by all social workers is the increased pressure of work, the rapid turnover and short contacts with patients and relatives.'[10] The psychiatric social worker is now being spread to cover a much larger number of people in need of help, and the workers are faced with considerable problems in deciding how best to use their scarce resources. There seems to be little agreed policy within most hospitals, or the health service or even within the social worker's own professional group. McDougall reports from a small pilot survey that the psychiatric social worker seems to manage between three and five interviews with any one case referred to her. If this is true for psychiatric social work in general in the field,[11] then, again the worker is left with little support. On the training course emphasis is placed on long-term treatment. Such cases provide indispensable learning opportunities, but, they may not have direct relevance for the conditions of actual practice. There has been, moreover, surprisingly little study of the special aspects of short-term casework.[12]

Another change in psychiatric social work has been in the greater amount of contact with patients themselves. This development has been the result of a number of factors and their operation is a good illustration of the various forces at work in shaping psychiatric social work. To some extent the increased amount of contact was a simple outcome of the psychiatric social worker's presence on the staff. Professional ambition was also operative, since direct work with patients was of higher status in the hospital than work with relatives. This development was reinforced indirectly by the decision of the Ministry of Health in 1950 not to classify psychiatric social workers as mental health officers on the grounds that they did not work directly with patients and did not, therefore, qualify for some of the benefits given to mental health officers (e.g. earlier retirement). This decision encouraged psychiatric social workers to stress this aspect of their work. More recently changes in attitudes towards the mentally ill and in mental health service policy have emphasized direct work with patients. These now tend to be less ill when they come into hospital and the development of after-care in the local authority (embryonic though it is in many areas) has encouraged the hospital psychiatric social worker to think more of her distinctive contribution within the hospital.

The amount of time psychiatric social workers actually spent with patients was not, however, apparent even within the profession until 1954 when a small study was undertaken in fifteen different hospitals. The immediate impetus for this came as a result of the request from the Ministry of Health for statistics on the work of the psychiatric social worker. These statistics were to record such work excluding visits outside the hospital. The Association was of the opinion that such an exclusion could result only in an inadequate picture of the work and psychiatric social workers in fifteen hospitals were asked to keep records in May, June, and July 1954. Twelve were mental hospitals in London, Manchester, Leeds, Plymouth, Oxford, Berkshire, Macclesfield, Shrewsbury, Somerset, Sheffield, Surrey and Sussex, and three were teaching hospitals in London and Liverpool. The results of this study which covered different kinds of hospital and rural and urban areas came as something of a surprise to the profession, especially in regard to the question of contact with patients. Considering, first, in-patient work, the percentage of all the psychiatric social worker's visits and interviews concerned with patients themselves ranged from 36 to 85 per cent with an average of 56 per cent.[13] In connection with out-patients the average was only slightly less, 54 per cent. The amount of home-visiting varied considerably but the average for in-patients was 35 per cent in mental hospitals and 8 per cent in the teaching hospitals and for out-patients 26 and 5 per cent respectively.

One of the most important developments in recent years has been the growth of group work in psychiatric settings, particularly in the mental hospital. The first signs of an interest in this method are to be found in the second half of the 1940's, but the last few years have seen a considerable expansion in the range of groups now organized. A study by Hutten[14] identified four main kinds of groups in which psychiatric social workers were currently involved: therapeutic groups in which adults or children, patients or relatives were treated; administrative groups in which patients and staff participated in the more democratic organization of the hospital, educational groups for in-service training, consultation or the enlightenment of public opinion; and finally, therapeutic social clubs. The growing importance of work in and with groups emphasizes the need for teaching in these areas to be included on the training courses.

Work in groups also has implications for the role of the psychiatric social worker. Some of these implications can be seen in one of the earliest articles by a psychiatric social worker on group psycho-therapy.[15] In this article the worker's contribution to group therapy was summarized in the following way: '(a) she is particularly concerned with structure and cohesion of the groups as a whole (the psychiatrist tends to concentrate on the treatment of the individual in the group); (b) she is responsible jointly with the psychiatrist for the creation of social roles for the patient which offer release, satisfaction, and a feeling of achievement; (c) as an auxiliary to the psychiatrist her task consists in breaking down resistance as another lay member of the group in discussion, psychodrama and sociodrama; (d) she presents the possibility of an alternative transference . . . (e) she assists in creating a permissive family atmosphere, the background essential for therapeutic groups; (f) in the guiding of discussions on social adjustment her social knowledge is used.'

In work in groups with a psychiatrist the main role problems in the relationship between psychiatrist and psychiatric social worker can be clearly seen. Is the work of the psychiatric social worker auxiliary to that of the psychiatrist or does she follow an approach or possess some knowledge or skill (e.g. (a), (f)) that is different from the psychiatrist's? She may be described as 'assisting' him and as carrying joint responsibility with him. Perhaps she carries all these functions together, but the relationship between them creates difficulties both for theoretical analysis and for the day-to-day work of psychiatry and psychiatric social worker.

How far do the changes so far outlined mean an alteration in what might be considered the traditional functions of the psychiatric social worker which used to revolve around the processes of admission, discharge and after-care? A considerable number of referrals by psychiatrists are still requests for a social history, and a considerable amount of time is spent by psychiatric social workers in carrying out such requests. It is possible that the purpose and method of taking the social history have changed, since psychiatric social workers now think they are called on not so much for a detailed exposition of family history but for an assessment of the present situation or a clarification of particular aspects of that situation. Work with or in connection with new patients seems to occupy varying amounts of time in different hospitals. In the study of fifteen hospitals previously mentioned the proportion of time spent in this way ranged from 14 to 68 per cent, with an average of 34 per cent.

Work with or in connection with patients on discharge also

remains one of the chief areas of concern for the psychiatric social worker, though referrals from psychiatrists may not always come sufficiently early to allow for reasonable planning. Arrangements for after-care vary considerably. Some patients are given out-patient clinic appointments and the task of the psychiatric social worker is to support the family; after a period the psychiatric worker will carry the case on her own. Others are not given appointments but the psychiatric social worker keeps in touch with the patient and his family and the patient's general practitioner is informed. It is quite common for psychiatric social workers to continue supervision of a patient long after the psychiatrist has left the area. These are some of the administrative arrangements for after-care carried out by the staff of mental hospitals, but the efficacy of such care is another matter. As the Association of Psychiatric Social Workers stated in their evidence to the Younghusband Working Party: '. . . whether after-care is carried out by local authority workers or hospital staff, it is clear from the replies received (from members) that with the present rapid turnover of patients in mental hospitals, social workers in most areas have so far been unable to tackle the after-care of the patients in a systematic way and the problem of providing adequate social and medical after-care remains largely unsolved.'

It would seem that there are many uncertainties and many unanswered, perhaps barely formulated, questions facing the psychiatric social worker in the mental hospital field. The mental hospital itself is undergoing something of a revolution and the psychiatric social worker is being encouraged to become a full member of the treatment team in what is coming to be considered as a therapeutic community. This in itself creates a need for considerable readjustment and for many will pose the further question, will the worker who becomes part of the treatment team still be able to carry out the essential function of representing the 'outside' within the hospital? Within the traditional functions of the psychiatric social worker the challenge of increased demand and a decrease in the time available for each client must be faced. We need in this respect much more study of the short-term contact and the kind of demands made by this approach on casework skill. Finally, after-care in this field as in the whole of social work must be considered and studied. Here we need to consider especially the kinds of patient that should be selected for after-care. The

Association has suggested that there are four groups for whom at present after-care is requested: the patient who, although he has made a successful recovery, still needs help in his adjustment to his social environment; the partially recovered patient who may be enabled to remain in the community; the patient who has discharged himself against advice and the one whose personality has undergone change through radical forms of treatment. We must consider not simply the kind of patient but also the sort of family to which he returns, and we should make use of research findings in the formulation of after-care policy.[16]

C. COMMUNITY CARE

Present policy for mental health gives considerable emphasis to 'community care'. The term, which is itself not without ambiguity or undertones of wishful thinking, refers to the attempt to care for mentally ill people in the normal community and it clearly has implications of some importance for psychiatric social work. If care for such people is to be attempted within the community then both patients and their families will need a considerable amount of help from social workers. Empirical studies are beginning to support such a commonsensical observation, but the supply of psychiatric social workers in this field falls far short of the number necessary to make the policy a working reality. There have been several attempts to estimate the number of psychiatric social workers required in this field and each new estimate finds earlier ones too low. Blacker estimated that 100 psychiatric social workers were needed to help 'the Medical Officers of Mental Health' (assuming the post would exist and would include 'the disposal of psychiatric emergencies and the community care of mental defectives').[17] The Macintosh Report doubled Blacker's estimate, and the Younghusband Report, whilst accepting 200 as immediately useful suggested that the aim over the next ten years should be something like one psychiatric social worker to every authority with a population under 100,000 and two to each of the larger authorities (i.e. about 300 psychiatric social workers). These estimates are, of course, blind guesses which attempt to make highly complex calculations on the basis of several unknown factors—what is the 'need' for such workers, how are they to be used, how will present policy actually work out? Yet some esti-

119

mate must be made and if we compare any of the estimates to the actual position the general seriousness of the present situation is clear. In 1951 there were eight psychiatric social workers in full-time posts in local authorities and by 1959 there were 26. This represents a considerable increase though Professor Titmuss calculated[18] that it would take more than 50 years, at the present rate of increase, before each of the 145 local authorities had just one psychiatric social worker. However, between 1958 and 1961 the number of psychiatric social workers doubled and there seems every indication that the rate of increase will not remain static.

'Community Care' is often referred to as a new field, particularly for psychiatric social workers, but they have been working for local authorities almost from the beginnings of their training in this country. Most of the hospitals for which they worked were, before 1948, local authority institutions and the war saw a considerable development in local authority social work. By the end of 1942, local authorities, largely due to the encouragement of the Mental Health Emergency Committee, had appointed 32 psychiatric social workers. It was in fact the War which led directly to experiments in community care as it is envisaged today. The story of these experiments is of importance for the development both of psychiatric social work and of mental health policy and it has not so far been told.[19]

Before the Second World War mental health work in the community was confined to the supervision of mental defectives and to limited after-care for patients who had been in mental hospitals. Work with mental defectives had attracted very few psychiatric social workers and after-care had still 'only begun to receive the attention which it deserves.'[20] The possibility of an after-care scheme for service psychiatric casualties was discussed soon after war had begun, but it was three or more years before any scheme materialized. There seem to have been two main difficulties, the question of financial responsibility and the weight of medical opinion that a psychiatric social service should be directly under medical control (i.e. discharged patients should be referred by hospital doctors to psychiatric out-patients or panel doctors who would call in the help of specialized social agencies when necessary). Evidence of the need for such a service, however, began to accumulate. Of special importance was the project at St. Andrew's Hospital, Northampton, which led in December 1941 to a request that the regional workers of the Mental Health Emergency Committee should help with A.T.S. and W.A.A.F. cases in the hospital. It was arranged that a psychiatric social worker should visit the hospital at regular intervals, when the doctor in charge would give her a list of patients for whom help was required. Requests were mainly for home visits, either to obtain a social history or to discover if the patient could return home on discharge. As confidence in the visiting psychiatric social worker grew she was allowed to see those female patients awaiting discharge who asked to see her. She was thus able to hand on to the social worker in the patient's home area some idea of the patient's social problems as well as the psychiatric recommendations. The social workers in the home areas were the regional representatives of the Mental Health Emergency Committee and some psychiatric and other social workers whose employers allowed them to participate in the project on the understanding that ordinary duties were not neglected. During the first 15 months 114 cases were referred to the visiting psychiatric social worker, of which 68 were requests for a social history and 38 were referred for after-care. The scheme was financed by the Mental Health Emergency Committee, with unofficial support from the War Office and the Air Ministry. In 1943, the Board of Control, having asked for and received a report of this project, requested the Provisional National Council for Mental Health to organize a more general service of after-care for men and women discharged from Service Psychiatric Hospitals.

As a result of this request experienced psychiatric social workers were appointed to each of the 12 civil defence regions. It was rare for more than one trained psychiatric social worker to be appointed, because of the severe shortage of such personnel, and assistants (trained social workers without the Mental Health Certificate) were appointed to work under their supervision. The staff consisted of 18 psychiatric social workers (10 part-time) and 45 social workers (10 part-time). The demands made on the scheme were heavy and by the end of 1946 some 10,000 cases had been dealt with. The service was at first financed by the Board of Control for the benefit of service personnel, but since the service was operated through a voluntary agency it was not possible to exclude civilian clients from the help available and eventually the

National Council was authorized to spend money on their behalf. The problem of the relationship of this kind of social service to the psychiatrist was solved by compromise. Initially a Medical Advisory Committee was established by the Board of Control, consisting of five psychiatrists who were to hold a watching brief. Six monthly statistical reports were submitted to them by the regional workers, and they advised the Board of Control on future policy. Psychiatric consultants were to be appointed in each region, but it did not prove possible to begin such appointments until 1946, when a psychiatrist was made medical director of the scheme.

This scheme of after-care has been described in some detail because of its significance for the development of mental health policy and of psychiatric social work. For the first time a community service on a national scale had been provided for a selected group of psychiatrically ill people. A demonstration had been made of the need for such a service and of its value. The scheme served in several areas as a model of the inauguration after the National Health Service of a local authority community care service. For psychiatric social workers it presented a challenge to accustomed ways of thinking and acting. It brought them much more closely into touch with other social workers, and played an important part in the adaptation of their ways of thought and action to the problems of social workers in a non-clinical setting. This process of adaptation can be seen in the following quotation from a paper by one of the psychiatric social workers in the after-care scheme: 'I think we have all been amazed to learn how material and practical aid given psychiatrically, that is to say, at the right moment, within the framework of a treatment plan, can contribute to social adjustment.'[21] This would not, of course, cause 'amazement' now, but at the time amazement was the result of the fusion of clinical ideas and experience and non-clinical problems in the setting of a community-orientated service.

The after-care scheme was also important for the status of psychiatric social work. It marked a significant recognition by the Government of the value of psychiatric social workers, which was to be seen also in the appointment of such workers to help in the selection of personnel for the women's forces. Within the scheme they were given powers to enter the service mental hospital in their area, and some found themselves ranked almost on the level of the medical staff. In each area the regional psychiatric social worker developed a service to some extent in keeping with her own interests. In one, for example, the emphasis was on mental health education, in another on casework service. In all, however, there was an impressive demonstration of the psychiatric social worker in the community. Since the end of the war interest in community care has developed both inside and outside the profession, and some of the difficulties and advantages of such a service are beginning to emerge more clearly.

In work in the community the psychiatric social worker is not part of her usual team, even if the word 'team' has been used defensively in mental hospital work to cover up a wide range of expectation on the part of psychiatrists and psychiatric social workers. In the community the psychiatric social worker has very often to work with only very limited consultation from a psychiatrist. Some community workers have seen this not as a liability, but a positive asset. Goldberg, for example, stated in an early study of this field, that 'It is precisely because we are "free-floating" in the community, with wide contacts . . ., and not chained to clinic or hospital, that we come across problems of instability and maladjustment which will never reach a clinic without intermediary help.'[22] Others have attempted to re-create the team, either in the group of psychiatric social workers or among the other social workers in the area. One psychiatric social worker, for example, has recently stated that she has 'felt part of a different team, composed of health visitors, the Children's Department, the Mental Welfare Officers, the Almoners of the local General Hospital; my identification was finally crystallized in being a community worker, as all these others also are.'[23] It seems that in one way or another the psychiatric social worker, trained to work in a team, has to deal when she enters the field of community care with the problems of isolation. In dealing with these problems since the beginnings of Community Care she has expanded her sympathies and tested her skill over a wide range of problems, including that of offering consultative service to other social workers.

Another development in psychiatric social work in this field concerns the setting. As we have seen, psychiatric social workers have been employed by local authorities almost from the start of the profession, but they are now more closely involved in the administrative structure of the local authority particularly since several psychiatric social workers hold senior appointments. This represents a challenge for workers trained in the largely therapeutic atmosphere of hospitals and clinics.

Perhaps the most important challenge of the After-Care Scheme and of its offspring, Community Care, is contained in the range of problems dealt with and the range of sources of referral. 'After-Care' is, of course, more specific than 'Community Care', but as the quotation from Goldberg indicates, there are several widely different groups of patients treated under the scheme. Her article in fact concluded with a statement of four categories of work which extended the psychiatric social worker far beyond the care of patients once discharged from hospital. She suggests that 'The field that could be covered by the psychiatric social worker in the community may be summarized as follows:

(a) preventative work; spotting minor difficulties of adjustment by making her services freely available to all types of social agencies, and particularly to panel doctors;
(b) preliminary work with potential patients and their families to pave the way towards treatment;
(c) After-Care and rehabilitation of the ex-hospital patient and participation in the social re-education of the chronic patient not suitable for clinic or hospital treatment;
(d) educational work and research.'[24]

Actual developments in community care have been characterized by considerable flexibility and variation according to the interests of individual workers and the needs of particular localities. Some workers emphasize their functions of after-care and possibly pre-care, and deal with patients discharged from the mental hospital, or act as a channel along which patients may reach psychiatric help. Others find the terms 'after-care' and 'pre-care' restrictive; this description of their work 'inevitably establishes certain limits, with a focus on the local mental hospital and those patients who have been treated there, or may need to be referred to it.'[25] Such workers emphasize their general functions of giving direct help to the emotionally disturbed and of offering indirect help in the form of a consultative service to other social workers who carry such cases themselves. Whichever emphasis is chosen it is becoming clear that extremely varied groups of clients are being referred to the Community Care Worker and this is a consequence both of the statute under which such workers are appointed and of the need for a service that is consultative for other social workers and residual for certain kinds of client who can live in the community only with the help of social workers over a long period of time. Section 28 of the National Health Service Act (1946) gave local authorities power to 'make arrangements for the purpose of the prevention of illness, the care of persons suffering from illness or mental defectiveness, or the after-care of such persons.' Such terms of reference are highly general in themselves, but also as local services have become established there has been an increase both in the sources of referral and in the diversity of the problems referred.

The situation in Community Care is, then, varied and changing; the lines of future development cannot be clearly seen, and the pioneering nature of the work is obvious. Its challenge is, however, obvious and the enthusiasm of workers sometimes contagious. But what are the difficulties in this branch of the work, what may be some of its dangers? Does it have complete parity with the older fields of the mental hospital and the child guidance clinic?

The main characteristics of community care work seem to be threefold. Firstly, social work is carried on without the support of a clinical setting and with differing amounts of collaboration from psychiatrists. Secondly, the clientele of the service suffer from every kind of illness and maladjustment. Thirdly, workers not only carry cases themselves, but also provide a consultative service for their colleagues in other social services. The first two characteristics presuppose a good training in differential diagnosis (reinforced by clinical experience) so that different mental illnesses can be recognized and appropriate help given. This is also presupposed in the provision of a consultative service insofar as this is seen as consultation in problems of psychopathy rather than simply casework problems. Thus, community care work seems to rely to a considerable extent on knowledge already consolidated in mental hospital social work.

Yet, it could be argued, the worker in community care faces problems in taking his or her service to many different kinds of clientele that workers in the mental hospital or in child guidance clinics do not encounter. Many of the people referred for help are not eager to acknowledge that they have problems and help has to be actively and persistently offered, sometimes for long periods, before it is made acceptable to the client. This special problem has perhaps not been faced to the same extent in child guidance clinics where long waiting lists encourage clinic staff to concentrate scarce treatment resources on the willing families. Mental hospitals have, of course, many resistive patients, but the social worker may be working with the relatives and has in any case the support of the hospital in facing such problems. Community care workers alone in psychiatric social work face this problem largely on their own.

Work in this field requires, therefore, perseverence, flexibility and ingenuity, but these are not in themselves original or basic activities, they are variations on established themes. Thus, a worker is flexible or ingenious in the varied application of already established principles and procedures of help.

The work of community care is frequently described by those who practise it as 'unorthodox'. Such a description refers to standards, more imagined than real, within the professional group of psychiatric social workers. It is a rather defiant expression of a defensiveness often felt by community workers viz-a-viz their colleagues in child guidance and mental hospital. This defensiveness may in fact lead to exaggerated claims on the part of the community care worker and a desire for 'independence' may result in an exaggeration of the differences between this and the other fields of psychiatric social work. It has, for example, recently been claimed that the field of community care should become one of the fields in which experience is given on the training courses. In fact, as I have just argued, the field of community care is one in which the experience and learning in the mental hospital is applied. It is perhaps worth observing that community care has attracted a comparatively high proportion of male psychiatric social workers. This is, of course, partly connected with the higher grades of salary available, but it may also be an expression of resentment on the part of the male workers at their presence in a predominantly female profession and a challenge to the controlling status of the psychiatrist. It is certainly important in any discussion of the content of any field of psychiatric social work or of any possible changes in training policy to distinguish clearly between 'the differences which we like to attribute to setting but which are actually the result of feelings about ourselves and our professional role, and those objective ones which demand some modification in training policy.'[26]

NOTES

[1] Jones I., and Hammond, P. 'The Boundaries of Training', *British Journal of Psychiatric Social Work*, Vol. V, No. 4, 1960.

[2] *19th Annual Report of the Board of Control, 1932, Part I*, p. 43.

[3] Ashdown M. and Thomas E., *op. cit.*

[4] *22nd Annual Report of the Board of Control, 1935, Part I*, pp. 3/4.

[5] Berkman T., *Practice of Social Workers in Psychiatric Hospitals and Clinics*, American Association of Psychiatric Social Workers, 1954.

[6] *British Medical Journal*, July 28th, 1950.

[7] Hayward S. T., 'The Changing Function of Professional Staff in the Mental Hospital' in (ed.) Irvine E. E., *Ventures in Professional Co-operation*, *op. cit.*, p. 42.

[8] Kimber W. J., 'Social Values in Mental Hospital Practice', *Journal of Mental Science*, Vol. LXXXV, No. 354, January 1939.

[9] McDougall, K., 'The Psychiatric Social Worker in the Mental Hospital', *op. cit.*

[10] *Ibid.*

[11] The short-term nature of the contact between patients and the psychiatric social worker is stressed in Woodward's recent account of American practice. See his 'Changing Roles of Psychiatric Social Workers in Outpatient Clinics in U.S.A.' *Case Conference*, Vol. 8, No. 8, February 1962.

[12] I can trace only two short articles devoted specifically to this topic: Hay-Shaw, C., 'The Short-Contact Interview', *British Journal of Psychiatric Social Work*, No. 4, October 1950, Swann M. B., 'Short-Term Case Work', *British Journal of Psychiatric Social Work*, No. 8, November 1953.

[13] A later study of 50 psychiatric social work posts showed that the majority of psychiatric social workers spent over half their time with patients. See McDougal K., *The Psychiatric Social Worker in the Mental Hospital, op. cit.*

[14] Hutten J., 'Varieties of Group Work in Psychiatric Settings', *Case Conference*, Vol. 5, No. 5, October 1958.

[15] Chance, E., 'Group Psycho-Therapy and the Psychiatric Social Worker', *Mental Health*, Vol. VIII, No. 1, August 1948.

[16] See e.g., Simmons O. G., and Freeman H. E., 'Familial Expectations and Post-hospital Performance of Mental Patients', *Human Relations*, Vol. XII, No. 3, August 1959. This study shows that tolerance on the part of family members is a key factor in the continuation of community life for former patients. Parental families appeared more tolerant of deviance than conjugal ones.

[17] Blacker C. P., *Neurosis and the Mental Health Services*, 1946, p. 94.

[18] Calculation made by Professor Titmuss in an address to the N.A.M.H. Conference in March 1961.

[19] The history of the after-care scheme is based in general outline on an unpublished account by M. Bavin made available by the National Association for Mental Health.

[20] These words from the *Royal Commission on Lunacy and Mental Disorder* (*1926*), p. 28 applied also to the period before the Second World War and are still applicable today.

[21] Goldberg E. M., paper read to the Social Psychiatry Section of the R.M.P.A. in 1947.

[22] Goldberg E. M., 'The Psychiatric Social Worker in the Community' *British Journal of Psychiatric Social Work*, Vol. IV, No. 2, 1957.

[23] Hunèeus E., 'Some Aspects of Community Care', *British Journal of Psychiatric Social Work*, Vol. V, No. 4, 1960.

[24] Goldberg E. M., 'The Psychiatric Social Worker in the Community', *op. cit.*

[25] Hunècus E., *op. cit.*

[26] Jones and Hammond, *op. cit.*

Chapter Seven

THE PSYCHIATRIC SOCIAL WORKER'S
CONTRIBUTION TO THE WRITINGS
AND RESEARCH OF SOCIAL WORK

SOCIAL WORK WRITING

THE social worker has nearly always been a reluctant writer. It was until recently a common complaint amongst social workers that their colleagues seldom described their work or formulated their problems and theories in print. Now it seems that some of those outside the profession are voicing firm and indignant complaint, but about the content of what social workers have managed to publish, not its rarity. Such criticism would have been more positive had it taken into account some of the difficulties facing workers who might, for example, be trying to describe aspects of their work. These difficulties arise from the social workers' view of themselves, from certain aspects of their training and from their position in society.

In the first place social workers have seen themselves as characteristically in action. 'Social workers, as their title implies, have a practical function. Called into existence because of human needs, the urgency of these needs has always made a first claim upon their time and skill ... Their methods have been evolved from daily practice ...'[1] Yet this activity has been emphasized at the expense of the improvement of the activity and of the formulation of principle and practice for the education of those already in the profession and of new entrants. To be in a continual state of unappraised activity is a well-known defensive strategy in individuals, which it seems is also used by professional groups. Yet why should it be necessary? What is the problem the group does not want to face? The answer to these questions is to be found in the ill-defined position of social work in present-day society. Social workers are most frequently employed in agencies which have objectives different from, often wider than, those of social work. They are thus generally speaking in subordinate positions. Yet they also claim knowledge, expertise and objectives that are specific to social work. Their claims are firmly made, but their position in agencies is often unclear or ambiguous. In such a situation to describe one's work in detail is to abandon the defence of the mystery of human relationships and to risk challenge, criticism, and denial of the position that social work has some unique contribution to make to human welfare. For an evolving profession, still seeking to persuade all kinds of authority of its value, this is not an easy challenge to accept.

Social work is often concerned with aspects of human relationships and these have been subjects for writers, poets and philosophers through the ages. To describe human relationships and to attempt some generalizations about them is, therefore, to risk humiliating comparisons. Sometimes, however, social workers have complicated the task for themselves by misunderstandings which have served a defensive purpose.

It has, for example, been suggested that the attempt to describe the 'dynamic' interaction between people is doomed to failure, simply because it is changing. Such defeatism is fundamentally based on the obvious fallacy that if one tried to describe a dynamic situation the terms of the description must themselves somehow be dynamic. In facing difficulties of this kind, social workers have until very recently received no help from their training. Training courses still pay far too little attention to the objective of developing a theory of the practice of social work, and workers have had little help from any kind of gradually evolving theoretical framework. There has thus been no check on the changing fashions in social work practice and writing, and no emerging criteria against which to appraise the ideas of the moment or the grandiose definitions and objectives for social work proclaimed by those outside the profession who have adopted its cause.

Granted that the position of the writer in social work is difficult, this chapter is concerned both with the quantity and quality of the writings of psychiatric social workers.

They have certainly made a comparatively large numerical contribution to the as yet unanalysed, unassorted, collection of social work writing. As complete a bibliography as possible of these writings up to 1960 was compiled, and from an analysis of the authors it would appear that about 16 per cent of the profession have been articulate in print. Of this group somewhat over half have contributed only single articles. About 20 people had produced by 1960 over five articles or the approximate equivalent in book or pamphlet form. Two questions can obviously be asked about this contribution to social work writing: how does it compare with that of other groups of social workers (e.g. almoners, probation officers etc.) and do the psychiatric social workers who write possess any identifiable features as a group?

To answer the first question an analysis has been made of the authors of articles in the two main social work journals, *Social Work*, and *Case Conference*,[2] for the years 1939-60 and 1954-60 respectively. From this analysis it emerged that the two journals attracted a different group of writers. The largest group of contributors to *Social Work* was a very heterogeneous collection of writers from overseas, administrators, doctors, solicitors, health visitors etc. Whereas the largest group of contributors to *Case Conference* was university teachers. If we examine the distribution of authors amongst the different professional groups in social work, it is found that in *Case Conference* psychiatric social workers represent 29 per cent of the authors, while in *Social Work* the proportion is 22 per cent. In *Case Conference* this represents the highest contribution with the exception of the university teachers (38 per cent). In *Social Work* psychiatric social workers contribute more than university teachers, but a lower proportion than family caseworkers (36 per cent). The contribution of other professional social work groupings is in fact extremely small. Almoners, for example, represent 10 per cent of the authors in *Social Work* and 1 per cent in *Case Conference*; probation officers represent 1 per cent and 7 per cent respectively, and child care officers 3 per cent in each journal.

It would appear, then, that psychiatric social workers make a contribution to the writings on social work which, compared to other groups within social work, is significant. Only a certain proportion of psychiatric social workers, however, as we have seen, contribute to such writings. Is this a group marked by any observable, objective characteristic?

A simple comparison between the more and the less prolific

would be misleading, since in so young a profession the proportion of recently qualified members is quite high and such workers have obviously less time to produce written work as psychiatric social workers than their professional elders. Consequently, the years 1954-58 were taken as a five year sample period, and note was taken of work published in that period by those who had been qualified at least a year before its commencement. In this way it is hoped like has been compared with like and all writers are 'competing' on equal terms.

The result of this analysis showed that psychiatric social workers who write are somewhat older than others in the profession and the more prolific writers are somewhat older still. Those who qualified in the five years before the war were the most inclined to write of the generations of successful students, but since the end of the war an increasing proportion of students have been coming out of training wanting to write. Age seems to be a more important factor than length of professional service in determining who is likely to produce published work.

When analysed according to formal qualifications, not a great deal emerges. The only group whose written productivity is more than a few decimal points from the average are those with both degrees and Social Science Diplomas. This is the smallest group, and when all graduates are reckoned together, the result lies very close to the overall mean. The writers with degree and diploma on average are about half an article ahead of any others.

It would seem that an analysis in terms of age, academic qualification and qualifying date produces some material, but of strictly limited interest. The sort of information that would be of greater interest lies in the personal ambitions and motives of writers and in such institutional factors as the high value placed on publication when promotion is considered in the universities. This kind of information could be obtained only by intensive study of the personalities and situations of psychiatric social workers.

RESEARCH AND STUDY

Social workers have been slow to contribute to research. From time to time in the development of the profession reference has been made to the vast quantities of valuable data locked away in the records of social workers, but little or no attempt has been made by social workers to exploit their strategic position as observers of behaviour and as agents of change. In this at least psychiatric social workers have followed tradition. For some, it is true, research is a term of honourable status, but for many others it is an activity both inferior and unrelated to casework with individual families. Some see it as the object of legitimate ambition, others as an escape. We are concerned with some of the determinants of the complex of fantasy and real expectation that seems to surround the subject.

It can be assumed that most students apply for training because they are concerned with some aspects of their social work practice; they wish to finish the course better equipped to help people in various kinds of distress. Ashdown and Brown found in their study of students trained 1935-39 that 'Of all the statements in the list of motives given to subjects at their study interview the one most often marked ran: "I wanted to gain more understanding of the problems I was already meeting in my own work".'[3] Too exclusive an emphasis on such idealistic motivation would obscure the real value of professional qualification in the career structure in social work, but it remains true that the student comes to the courses concerned about her practice and for individuals and their families. This has at least two important results: helping people directly is given first importance, and the emphasis on understanding particular clients produces a reluctance to generalize. Amongst the psychiatric social workers studied by Ashdown and Brown, some showed signs of a definite repudiation of research, whilst others expressed some attraction to it 'provided that it grew naturally out of casework and could be carried on without detriment to it'.[4]

This, however, is not as simple as it sounds. As one psychiatric social worker has said, '. . . we must realize that we are in a new role as investigators, and that we can no longer pretend that it is the same as the one we take up when acting as therapists. Once we become more certain about the components in the investigator's role and about our aims, we will represent something more real and convincing to our subjects. At present we seem to hover uneasily between our customary therapeutic clinical role and our new role as investigators.'[5] That this role seems so new is explained partly by the personal preferences of many workers for direct helping activity, but also by the neglect of the training courses to give any grounding in research method. Moreover, the emphasis in training is on help and change, and to achieve such objectives it is permissible to use many kinds of concept and theory. As Wisdom has remarked, '. . . it is legitimate (in clinical practice) to draw on anything or to think that one is drawing on something that helps one, provided one achieves one's goal; but this in no way justifies the supports or gives them the status of theory or science.'[5] There is, thus, some opposition (ultimately resolvable) between research and the question being asked on the training courses, not is this true, but does it produce beneficial results?

Casework draws on many branches of knowledge and this hinders the development of a theoretical basis for research. Casework is also subject to fairly swift changes of fashion and, as Arsenian has stated of research in psychiatric social work in America, 'multiple and shifting conceptual preferences produce eras of adoption, assertion, faction and dogmatism rather than continuous lines of enquiry.'[7] These, then, are some of the factors in the training itself that hinder the development of research interests.

Conditions of work also hamper research. There is a shortage of time, and the dependent relationship with psychiatrists may often hinder the development of initiative. Ashdown and Brown have remarked that 'in some investigations, loosely termed research, where psychiatric social workers follow up certain groups of patients discharged from mental hospitals . . ., their part seems to have been confined to one or more home visits, with little share in the planning of the inquiry or responsibility for interpreting their own findings.'[8] Arsenian in a small study of psychiatric social work research in America found that all the workers she investigated were engaged in collaborative research. In England most of the contributions to research have been made in collaboration, mainly with medical writers.[9]

We should ask also what are the factors in the new role of investigator that might create difficulty for the psychiatric social worker. These have received some discussion in the writings of Goldberg and of Morris. Both comment on the difficulties for a social worker of situations in which she can give little and has to take much. Goldberg comments that her own role 'became even more uncertain and unfamiliar when working with those families and patients who had to be followed up rather insistently in order to maintain contact. This kind of pursuit is the reverse of the situation in which people come to us for help, and it has always produced in me uneasy feelings and a good deal of anxiety.'[5] This uneasiness arises, of course, from the misleading ideal that casework should be carried on only when the client comes to the agency. It would now be recognized that much casework has in fact to be taken to people and offered 'rather insistently'. Morris refers to logical and technical differences in the organization of skills for research and for therapy: 'In the research situation, the psychiatric social worker is employing observational techniques for the objective evaluation of family behaviour, whereas in the clinical situation her observation tends to be both less systematic and more subjectively oriented, in so far as she is seeking, not an overall picture, but likely foundations upon which to build an emerging casework relationship.'[10]

It is worth observing that social workers, as a whole, are frequently deprived of what might be an important incentive to research. I refer to the low visibility of the failures and successes of social work. Social workers, partly because of the partial and episodic contact with families encouraged by the present organization of the social services, are often unaware of the future development of cases and are thus deprived of the opportunity of seeing long-term success or failure. This factor is, of course, emphasized by the mobility of clients and social workers and we have seen already the high mobility of psychiatric social workers.

Some of the difficulties of engaging in research can be illustrated from the history of the Association of Psychiatric Social Workers amongst whose original objects was, in the words of the constitution:

'To contribute towards the general progress of mental hygiene
(a) by affording opportunities for the sharing of ideas and experience,
(b) by promoting and facilitating research.'

The history of research within the Association is one of temporary enthusiasms separated by long periods of silence. In August 1934, an anthropologist who had addressed a General Meeting of the Association met the Chairman and Secretary to discuss the possibility of joint research, and headings were drawn up for later discussion, but the fate of this undertaking is obscure. In

135

January 1941 a founder member of the Association reported that she had been in touch with a psychoanalyst over the possibility of help being given to members interested in recording the effect of war on individuals. In the May bulletin of the same year Dr. (now Sir) Aubrey Lewis suggested that members were not taking this question of recording seriously. In the same issue a member reported that two general meetings on research had been held and 40 members had expressed interest. Yet once again what (if anything) materialized is uncertain, save that the group interested in such matters changed their name from 'research' to 'study' group.

An interesting development in research came with the establishment of the Parents Group. In November 1945 this group reported the intention of conducting research on the psychology of mothers in pregnancy, various aspects of childbirth, puerperal psychosis; separation anxieties, feeding difficulties and their intention was rendered more ambitious by the addition of 'etc., etc.' This is, of course, too grand a series of projects, but a useful attempt nonetheless to use the reflective experience of the group. Two papers emerged from the Parent Group, but the general response to their first questionnaires was very disappointing.

In November 1948 the Home Office asked the Association's opinion on the subject of Children and the Cinema. The Association held a General Meeting on the subject and wisely decided that it would be inadvisable to give an opinion on the subject unless 'some careful research had been made'. A small committee was established to investigate the matter. In May 1949 this reported that two members of the committee had been invited to the Home Office to discuss a scheme of research submitted by the Association in February. At this same meeting of the Association, one member suggested that psychiatric social workers be asked to record reactions to the film 'Snake Pit'. 'It was agreed to do this with the proviso that no questions be asked and, if possible the exact words be noted'. Nothing further is heard of the project.

So far the Association seems to have squandered whatever interest in research existed over a miscellany of subjects. Sometimes the aims of research are set impossibly high or described so vaguely that nothing concrete could be attempted. Some change in this attitude seems to have come in 1950 when a Training

Research Committee was established. It looked as if here at last was a problem of a fairly concrete kind well within the scope and experience of many members. Unfortunately, the committee ended its life in February 1952 without having achieved a clear definition of the objectives of its existence. It testified by its existence to the importance of the idea that training was a proper object for research, and by its confused end to the apparently inherent difficulties of the enterprise. The interest of members in research revived again quite recently and the Annual Report for 1959 stated that 'eighteen members indicated that they would like to join a Special Interest Group, and it is hoped to call a meeting early in 1960.' The Report for 1960 records no Interest Group in Research.

This discussion has stressed the difficulties for the psychiatric social worker in research. Yet even if these and other difficulties exist some psychiatric social workers are able to overcome them and a small number of studies by individuals are being published.[11] Publication by individuals should not, of course, be taken as the final goal and measure of work, but in a profession where dependency plays a large part, it is both a welcome and an important sign. There are also indications that more psychiatric social workers are taking up specific research appointments. In 1962, 90 psychiatric social workers held such posts. It is of some interest to note that in certain respects they were as a group not representative of the general profession, having a higher proportion of those with a social science diploma and a background more often of teaching, and social work in the mental health field. All but one had been trained at the London School of Economics and half of the group had qualified within the last ten years.

So far we have been considering research as some kind of contribution to empirical knowledge. A broader view of 'research and study', however, shows a different picture. If we look at the 'theorizing' and writing on social casework undertaken by psychiatric social workers in this country we find that they are in a dominant position. Ignore the contribution of psychiatric social workers to casework writing from 1930 to 1960 and little of importance remains. From a very small beginning with two pamphlets in 1932 the Association has gradually developed its publishing activities. The first important stage was reached in

1947 when the journal was first published and the second in 1956, when the Association published *The Boundaries of Casework*, its first book.

Originally the journal was intended primarily as a domestic publication. The first editorial stated that 'contributions from psychiatric social workers will be of greatest value if they are in the nature of communications between members of the profession, and are not written with an eye on a larger public.' The sphere of operation was also defined by the beginning of the issue of pamphlets 'directed towards a wider public, which cannot be assumed to share a common professional experience or understand a common professional language.'[12] In fact, however, the journal has changed in character from a purely domestic publication to one aimed at a wider audience, though the articles have always come predominantly from psychiatric social workers.

An analysis of the articles published between 1947 and 1962 shows that the profession has had certain preoccupations. It has been concerned with the definition of its role, with theorizing about casework in general, with social work in the mental hospital, the child guidance clinic and in the community care programme. It has also shown some interest in training, groups and work with institutions. Policy in regard to mental health services and work with mental defectives have figured in only a small number of articles. Articles categorized as 'research and study' have appeared fairly regularly, but with the exception of two follow-up investigations in 1953,[13] a research critique in 1954[14] and an interesting small-scale investigation of the effect of leucotomy on family life in 1956,[15] most of the articles have been descriptive studies. The analysis proved useful in showing the kinds of subjects about which psychiatric social workers wrote, but it could not be used to trace historical changes in predominant interests. Some of the articles, for example, reflect the planning of the Association's Professional Development Sub-Committee, while others have been due to feelings of obligation on the part of members of the Editorial Board. Institutional and accidental factors combine in a way that makes a study of trends in writing practically impossible.

I wish now to consider the content of these articles, to think, in other words, not of the industry but of the achievement of the psychiatric social worker as a writer. This is of interest because social work writing requires at the present time some cumulative analysis, so that an assessment can be made of the present situation. So far social work writing has grown through piecemeal additions rather than a considered attempt to develop any systematized body of knowledge and viewpoint. To consider the content of the articles in the journal, the three headings of theorizing, knowledge and treatment will be used.

I. THEORIZING

This refers to general talk about a subject rather than discussion of subject matter. In other words my reference is to a level of abstraction above that contained in such questions as, is casework psychotherapy? There has in fact been very little discussion of this kind in the journal; references until very recently have been spasmodic and incidental and all concerned with the science-art aspects of casework. In fact discussion has been hampered partly by the hidden assumption that casework can be exclusively discussed, at this level, in terms of science or art. Casework it is assumed must simply be either an art or a science. A hindrance to discussion in these terms has been the failure to be clear about what being 'scientific' means. By some writers it is simply contrasted with intuition,[16] or interpreted as an obligation to be clear and accurate,[17] or skilful in attaining objectives. Few writers accept the full challenge of these terms, art and science. One suggests that '. . . we have both to respect the uniqueness of this man, and to guard against the mistake of over-veneration of his singularity. In addition to its therapeutic value, this attitude enables us to realize the satisfaction of other scientists whose discovery of the single instance is made exciting because of their understanding of its relation to other objects and processes.'[18] This statement is partly true, partly misleading. In discussing the caseworker as 'scientist' one of the central issues revolves around 'uniqueness'. It would perhaps be true to say that the caseworker is interested in the unique individual and the scientist in instances of general statements. The caseworker uses 'knowledge', some of it capable of testing, but it would not be fruitful to suppose that the caseworker is a scientist interested in extending the frontiers of knowledge by means of her social work. She uses general statements (e.g. about the relationship between frustration and aggression) to understand individuals; she sees whether these statements apply in particular cases, but she is not usually concerned to see how the individual case affects the generalization. She is concerned with understanding rather than explanation.

A more rewarding approach is to avoid this unreal dilemma of art or science, and try to form some idea of what caseworkers do. In the first place, they use varying kinds of knowledge.

2. KNOWLEDGE

A broad distinction can be made between 'sociological' and psychoanalytic knowledge.

(i) 'Sociological' Knowledge
The importance of this seems to have been a more popular theme at the beginning than the end of the period we are studying. It is mentioned in two out of six articles in 1947, one in 1948, two in 1949 and two in 1950, but not again until 1955. In spite of recent interest in the importance of knowledge of this kind which comes from critics within and without the profession we have no major contribution on the theme, and only two references in the Journal 1957-60. However, a change has come about in the kind of knowledge to which we refer by using the term 'sociological'. In the beginning it was knowledge of social conditions. Some of the early references, for example, are to knowledge of the neighbourhood, of 'normality' and so on. Later, those outside the profession (and a few inside) look to the psychiatric social worker's knowledge of the social services as a basis from which she can participate in the role of social reformer. It is clear that the issues of the Journal convey very little about such a role. Castle, in 1950, calls attention to the psychiatric social worker's role of social scientist 'which might be said to rest upon the principle of endeavouring to establish a healthy individual in a healthy society',[19] but later speaks of 'treating' society, not reforming it.

There is, however, a third important kind of knowledge which can more properly be called sociological i.e. general statements that employ sociological terms. Some writers have suggested that we have departed from an earlier and fruitful use of such knowledge. Goldberg, for example, argues that an emphasis on psychoanalysis has 'led to a temporary neglect of an important former source of knowledge, the social sciences.'[20] She mentions the notion of group equilibrium and the influence of socio-cultural forces. It seems true that some of the theories and concepts of sociology could be of considerable use to the psychiatric social worker. Considerable emphasis is at present being placed, for example, on the concept of 'role'. Yet most of the exploration of the specific place of sociological knowledge remains to be done. The social sciences helped social workers in the past not by providing theoretical ideas, but by presenting information about the condition of society. Social work now needs both kinds of help.

(ii) *Psychoanalytic Knowledge*

This is the body of theory that receives most mention in the literature of psychiatric social work. In view of the differing ideas of the function of psychiatric social work in the profession, and of the complex and changing situation of psychoanalysis itself, it is hardly surprising that only fairly narrowly selected aspects of the subject are discussed in the journal. The piecemeal nature of the borrowing from psychoanalysis has at least two important aspects, one historical, the other theoretical. Historically, there has been a development in the use psychiatric social workers have made of psychoanalytic knowledge. In the beginning, as we have seen, they used some of the central concepts (such as ego and libido) in a rather crude attempt to classify behaviour. Fairly soon some of the theories were used to understand behaviour (e.g. the Oedipus complex). Yet in both these phases workers were often carrying out treatment in terms of the traditional social work means of advice, explanation, and control of the environment. Perhaps the most important change came when psychiatric social workers began to think of their work in terms of 'transference' in the psychoanalytic sense. This was important not because of the technical usefulness of such a borrowing, but because it turned the psychiatric social worker's attention to the ways in which the client was using his relationship with the worker. More will be said about this aspect later, but this very brief mention of the main developments in the use of psychoanalysis demonstrates some of the modifications that should be made in the view that psychoanalysis *dominated* casework in the 1930's and the following decades.

The theoretical aspects of this piecemeal borrowing have received some attention in the journal. Beedell, a psychologist, has stated that 'psychiatric social workers hold to a rag bag of assorted psychodynamics. Their theoretical framework seems to be derived from analytical or other special settings, and as the psychiatric social worker has to deal with the patient's everyday life on a more direct level the validity of application of these ideas is doubtful.'[21] The author suggests that in any attempt to extend their theory and communicate their use of human relationships 'they suffer . . . from the lack of a defined academic field whence they can draw theoretical constructs; nor are they experienced in using a body of theory.' The implications of this for research and writing have already been discussed. Mason has drawn attention to some of the possible motivations behind the selective use of psychoanalytic theory. In discussing transference, for example, she suggests that 'Perhaps as psychiatric social workers we are at times carried away by a fantasy of transference in which we become both larger and more important than we actually are in the lives of our clients, and also less personally responsible than in our daily relationships.'[22] Some will certainly be of the opinion that selective use of theories is comparatively unimportant. What, they would argue, does it matter if psychiatric social workers use theories of the ego derived from Anna Freud or a concept of therapy as a corrective of early faulty experiences which Abrahams introduced as long as we obtain satisfactory results? Such views oversimplify the relationship between fact, theory and evaluation and underestimate the importance of systematic theory for training and practice.

What are the aspects of psychoanalysis most stressed in the writings of psychiatric social workers? In the first place the theorists most used appear to be Freud and Klein. The work of Jung and Adler is hardly represented in the professional literature (though see footnote 37). An important project of study for the future would be an examination of the theoretical positions of psychiatric social workers, and of the difference such viewpoints make to their understanding and treatment of clients.

The main emphasis in the writing seems to have been on three areas: the importance of experience in infancy and childhood for the future development of the personality, the mechanisms of defence and certain concepts about human feelings, and the psychoanalytic technique of transference interpretation. The last is dealt with under treatment.

In the writings of psychiatric social workers the experiences of infancy and childhood are seen as crucial. Thus, one worker sees past relationships as a model for present relationships. Discussing the case of Mrs. J. she writes: 'Mrs. J. was very much on her guard, and it will surprise nobody to learn that her relationship to her own mother had been very bad indeed. I soon became for her a bad mother-figure who could not or would not give in to her demands for special consideration . . .'[23] Another worker stresses the values in past relationships (good or bad). In discussing 'why people have such difficulties in relationships as to seek specialized help', she suggests as a general reason 'the lack in early life of the kind of relationships which could remain predominantly good while permitting the integration within it of the hostile and destructive impulses which every child must experience in relation to his love-objects.'[24] Others see the past as creating the beginning of a cycle of response unless there is some therapeutic intervention. Thus, one psychiatric social worker writes of a mother: 'She was very much a deserted, destitute, destroyed child still, who in her turn was about to destroy her own children, in particular the little girl.'[25] Or childhood is seen as a period in which certain tasks have to be accomplished and failure to accomplish them produces a disabled personality. One client is described as 'an immature young married woman who never managed to become independent of her mother. In her turn she cannot let go of her children, and she is only slowly becoming aware of her resentment of her mother, who had always preferred her two sons to this daughter.'[25] These issues are all expressions of the basic idea that attitudes learned in childhood tend to be systematically reflected in adult life and that unresolved problems in parent child relationships can be resolved through a later symbolic re-creation of such relationships.

There has been no extensive discussion of the importance of the mechanism of defence, though in view of the beginnings of emphasis on ego psychology, the need for such discussion assumes some importance. In the literature of psychiatric social work there has been a tendency to use the idea of defence in a general way to describe the total reaction of clients at any one time. Thus, one worker talks of a mother with a 'defensive shell' of aggression and fierceness behind which she hid sensitivity and insecurity, while another speaks of an interview in which 'all the defences came down', of clients who talk defensively and so on. The idea of the defence mechanism could, however, be used more specifically to describe particular ways (e.g. projection, denial) of dealing with particular anxieties. This kind of approach perhaps removes some of the unnecessarily negative undertones implicit in the general use of the term. Defences or ways of dealing with anxiety are essential aspects of the personality and it is important that we try to understand a client's characteristic ways of dealing with stress.

The feelings of clients have received emphasis in the literature of psychiatric social work. Psychoanalysis has been used to understand the dual nature of feeling (positive and negative intertwined together) and the value of the expression of feeling within a therapeutic situation. Irvine illustrates the importance of the idea of ambivalence when she states that 'serious difficulties in relationships are always expressions of inability to tolerate and integrate ambivalent feelings.' This view led her to consider the value of allowing or indeed encouraging the client 'to bring all his feelings, negative as well as positive, into the relationship with the worker, to demonstrate in one's own person the ability to accept hostility without fear, and to resist demands without anger.'[24] The value of the expression of feeling in casework has been stressed in much of the writing. One worker described the 'basic aim' of her work with the client as 'restoring his faith in the capacity of others to tolerate his aggression and hostility without hitting back savagely on the one hand, or being hurt or damaged on the other.'[25] Another suggested that we help clients 'to become aware not only of their positive feelings for us but also of their defences and unresolved hostilities in relation to ourselves';[26] another regrets that in her work she is unable to give the hostility she meets in mothers 'its full significance'.[27] The recognition of the existence and meaning of hostility and hatred was an important step forward in social work even though there was perhaps an over-concern with eliciting hostile, negative feelings. What began as a necessary and important corrective to an earlier and easier acceptance of the client's positive feelings came to support an over-valuation of one kind of feeling against another. It is interesting to observe the results of a recent study of case descriptions by the three members of the clinical team (psychiatric social workers, psychologists and psychiatrists).[28] It was found that psychiatric social workers saw their clients as being more concerned with what were classified as negative-active relations (i.e. bossing, rebelling, competing etc.) and less with positive-active relations (i.e. giving help, love etc.) than members of the other two disciplines.

The literature shows that there have been a number of different objectives behind this emphasis on negative feelings. Sometimes the mere expression of feeling is taken to be the therapeutic aim, sometimes what is considered important is the reassuring effect of expressing negative feeling in the presence of a second person who remains undamaged and who still continues to offer help. At other times the expression of hostility towards the worker is considered to deflect some of the feeling that might otherwise have been expressed against those more vulnerable in the client's environment.

(iii) *Treatment*

'To attempt any precise formulation of the processes involved in psychiatric social treatment is too difficult and is perhaps valueless'.[29] This rather pessimistic reluctance was at one time a reaction of many social workers, psychiatric and other, to the question, what do you try to do when you work with your clients? To accept it as a final statement on the question is, however, to fall back on a combination of intuition and vagueness which provides neither comfort nor justification. In fact some of the essentials of treatment can be found in the writings of psychiatric social workers and several of the crucial issues involved. This takes us at least part of the way towards more precise formulations.

The aspects of 'treatment' that have received emphasis in the literature are all concerned basically with the relationship between client and worker. Within this broad interest writers have discussed their behaviour towards the client, their general activities (e.g. giving advice or reassurance) and the meaning and use of their relationship with the client. A very small amount of attention has been given to the objectives of treatment and to the selection of particular methods of help for certain kinds of client. These themes have not been pursued cumulatively apart from important articles by Goldberg[26] and by Irvine,[30] and the subject of treatment, as far as the literature is concerned, remains in an unsatisfactory condition.

There are perhaps two main reasons for this. Firstly, psychiatric social workers have of necessity to work on assumptions, on untested theories, on general ideas and so forth. Uncertainty is at the basis of most social work. The worker does not, often cannot, have scientific evidence for his appraisal of a situation, but he has nonetheless to act; he cannot await the results of the sort of tests that would establish many of his generalizations on a firm basis. This is, on the whole, not a comfortable position in which to find oneself, particularly from the viewpoint of the critic from outside the profession. The result is that many workers adopt a defensive position such as that outlined in the quotation at the head of this section. Scientific knowledge, clear formulation and the like, it is argued, cannot have a place in this activity which is artistic, individualistic and (fortunately) indescribable in any detail.

The second reason is more simple. The subject of treatment is made more vague by the failure to be clear about the meaning of terms and consistent in their use. Two examples will illustrate this statement. The two terms are 'interpretation' and 'transference'. Interpretation is used to refer to a skilful description of the work of the clinic to other social workers;[31] to an explanation to a client of 'the particular psychological approach which is to be made to the problem';[32] to a description given to the psychiatrist of the social problems leading to the situation facing the client;[32] to an explanation suited to the ability of someone to bear it (e.g. giving relatives some idea of the reasons for the patient's behaviour). Sometimes the term refers to helping doctors use other social services, sometimes to an explanation to the client of what he feels underneath behaviour which seems to him to demand no explanation. Finally, the term is used in the technical psychoanalytic sense of making explicit feelings, fantasies and purposes which may or may not be unconscious, but have been implicitly expressed, of showing the client that he is transferring on to the worker feelings and attitudes that 'belong' to his early relationship with his parents, and siblings. Thus, there is considerable variation in the content of 'interpretation', in the purposes for which it is used and the kinds of people to whom it is addressed. Its use over such a range of phenomena suggests that the status associated with the technical, psychoanalytic, use of the term has been generalized to cover other aspects of the work which could have been described in more traditional terms.

The second confusion in the use of terms concerns the question of transference interpretation. This has been used in two main ways. Firstly, to refer to a transference of feeling from early experience to the present relationship with the worker (e.g. you felt your mother was punishing you when she gave attention to your younger brother and you feel now that I am punishing you because I see other clients). Secondly, to draw the client's attention to feelings that are being expressed indirectly towards the worker in the present without reference to an ealier situation. This can take two forms at least. The worker may suggest that when the mother says at the first treatment interview 'My son is feeling very apprehensive about coming' she herself is wondering what will happen. Alternatively, the worker may call the client's attention to the implications of the terms she uses. For example, a mother told a male psychiatric social worker that her husband was coming to 'demand satisfaction'. The implications of her term indicates some of the feeling that is being indirectly expressed. The two main uses of 'transference interpretation' are apparently quite clear, but the term is nonetheless used indiscriminately and important distinctions are obscured. To speak of transference in social work is to refer not to the whole relationship between client and worker, but to only part of it.

(a) *The Psychiatric Social Worker's Behaviour.* One of the difficulties involved in a description of 'treatment' undertaken by psychiatric social workers is that for many workers it can best be described in terms of the establishment and nurturing of a relationship rather than of a series of separate techniques applied one by one. This point of view can be summarized in the statement by Waldron in the second issue of the journal: 'Our field of study is our contemporary man living his life. Our craft is our mode of behaviour towards him.'[18] It is, however, possible to describe such behaviour and certain aspects have received mention in the literature.

The psychiatric social worker is expected to 'accept' the client, to be, in the words of one writer, 'someone who could accept him and believe in him.'[33] Several questions immediately arise, some of which have received differing answers in the literature. What does the worker accept? Answers to this questions vary between the client's personality, his badness and even his neurosis.[31] What precisely is involved in 'acceptance'? How does the client know that he or particular aspects of his personality have been accepted? Questions of this kind have received little attention. The impression given by some writers certainly is that 'acceptance' simply means letting people talk. In such circumstances how can clients feel 'accepted' rather than 'tolerated'? On the other hand, several answers have been given to the question, what does acceptance accomplish. In the first place the acceptance of hostility was seen as bringing a measure of relief to the client. 'If', stated Irvine, 'we show that we are not unaware of his hostility, that our friendliness and lack of fear is not based on ignorance of his feelings, and that we understand something of the reason for them in terms of the present situation and perhaps also of the past, then he is apt to be considerably relieved.'[24] But, treatment is not seen as a mere sum of relieving incidents since Irvine envisages 'the basic aim of our work with the client in terms of restoring his faith in the capacity of others to tolerate his aggression and hostility without hitting back savagely on the one hand, or being hurt and damaged on the other.' In other words the cumulative effect of a series of 'acceptances' is to be found in some modification of the client's images of himself and of others.

Another view of the objective of acceptance sees it primarily in terms of learning. One worker writes of a client that 'as she found security and acceptance in her relationship with me, she also became more accepting of the children, and it seemed as if she were learning from me how to handle, and almost how to love a child.'[23] Irvine has written of the worker acting out 'the part of an accepting and tolerant mother; the client then, partly by identification, became able to be similarly accepting and tolerant with herself and her child . . .'[30] Others seem to speak of the process more vaguely. What all writers share, however, is the assumption that from the acceptance of the worker the client receives an experience or a lesson that both corrects earlier experiences or lessons and serves as the basis of generalization to other situations. These are important claims which merit more clear formulation and testing.

But acceptance and a passivity on the part of the worker that seemed often to accompany acceptance have been questioned by other writers. Is it possible to talk of acceptance when faced with certain kinds of clients or certain problems?

In the literature it has been suggested that some clients need much more than simple acceptance, and that 'psychiatric social workers should not be afraid of playing a more active part, of setting the stage and shifting the scenery.'[34] Again, another writer argues that some difficult reality situations can be boldly and directly tackled provided the worker knows the meaning of the situation. It is difficult to differentiate the clients who are considered to be in need of this more active approach from those with more 'insight', but Tilley has asked specifically of the anti-social client, 'Should the worker take a moralistic line, or should she be entirely tolerant and permissive?'[35] She argues that it is 'essential with the anti-social client to convey somehow or other that right and wrong matter; but without appearing to pass judgment upon him as a total person.' This argument is based upon the assertion that 'the client sees the worker to a certain extent as representing law-abiding society, and it will confuse and shock him if this representative seems just as muddled as he is about right and wrong.' It may be that clients see the worker in this way and it would be worth establishing this as fact, but it seems that the argument confuses legality with questions of right and wrong and suggests that because of a perception on the part of the client of what *is* the worker *ought* to act in certain ways. The subject of the place of the worker's own values is of importance and also of considerable complexity and needs further consideration by social workers. It seems that acceptance itself is an elusive concept but that (whatever its nature) it is thought to achieve four results:

(1) relief of feeling, (2) learning by imitation or identification from the worker, (3) improved attitudes towards others, (4) a conveyance to the client of the worker's non-condemnatory attitude. Observing these distinctions may assist in the clarification of the meaning of acceptance and of the place of the worker's own values.

It is not, however, only the values of the worker that present a problem. What is the place of the worker's feelings? Their importance has certainly been emphasized in the literature. Williams and Castle suggest that 'the best work is done when genuine feelings of sympathy and interest have been aroused in the worker either by the personality of the parent or the nature of the problem, and the poorest work when a case seems dull or when fatigue or unconscious hostility have inhibited her own spontaneous response.'[36] If the worker's untutored response is so crucial what can be done to help the worker enlarge the range of her sympathies and what use can she make of her reactions to the client's personality and problem? Tilley has suggested that the feelings aroused in the worker by the client are important diagnostic indications of the client's capacity to relate to others, while Lederman[37] has questioned the view that the psychiatric social worker should observe 'strict neutrality and detachment', on the ground that the way to psychological growth is not through the detached interpretation of attitudes. Rather it is through allowing the client to 'experience his own personality, including his neurotic attitudes. This cannot be done unless we provide him with the opportunity of relating himself to another human being, who meets him both with understanding and with feeling. This can happen only if we behave in our therapeutic relationships as real people, and do not act as screens'. The greatest safeguard to the many dangers involved in this approach is to be found in 'the deepening of our insight and the development of our self-awareness.' The notion of behaviour as 'real' people is important and will be taken up in discussion of the relationship between client and worker. But it is clear from the foregoing discussion that the relationship between the workers' own feelings and moral values are considerably more complex than most social workers allow.

So far we have been examining the sort of behaviour psychiatric social workers have been expected to show to their clients. In general it may be summarized in Ashdown and Brown's view that the psychiatric social worker 'will see her own role as one of giving courage for the adventure (of self-discovery), not through persuasion and externally applied reassurance, but through the building up of a relationship between herself and the client within which he will feel confident and free enough to make his own discoveries.'[38] This is a slightly mystical, highly generalized description of what psychiatric social work is about and it is not surprising that some psychiatric social workers were often vague about their objectives and that others preferred to emphasize the more concrete aspects of the task.

The P.S.W's Contribution to Writings and Research

(b) *Activities of the Psychiatric Social Worker.* The title of this section does not entail the view that acceptance or even passivity are not activities, but it is used to draw attention to writing on the more concrete aspects of psychiatric social work. Attention will be paid to the social history and to the giving of advice and reassurance.

That the compilation of a social history was an essential part of the psychiatric social worker's role was recognized by workers and psychiatrists from the beginning of their work together. The main developments have been the growing recognition of the importance of observing the expression of feeling as well as recording facts and a blurring of any rigid distinction between investigation and help. 'Some psychiatrists' stated Castle and Williams, 'think that every history should be based on a solid framework of factual evidence and regard certain chronological facts as being psychologically important in every personality development. This may lead them to regard the psychiatric social worker as a collector of factual data on which they will put their own interpretation. From past experience, we would say that the entirely factual history, divorced from all specific emotional reactions of the individuals concerned, is apt to be as misleading as circumstantial evidence in law.'[36] The movement away from the 'factual' kind of history is due to the assertion by the psychiatric social worker of her function as something more than a collector of facts for the psychiatrists.

Such an assertion seems evident in Ashdown's earlier advice that psychiatric social workers should regard with some suspicion their own eagerness to produce a 'good' social history.[39] What workers were claiming was a measure of therapeutic autonomy, the right to allow their history taking, for example, to be influenced by the claims and needs of their own developing professional relationship with the client. Thus, Lewis states that 'we think that the formation and maintenance of a good relationship with the parents is more important than obtaining factual information, although quite often this is a therapeutic process in itself. The parent may feel that it is part of his contribution towards the solution of the difficulty. This is the beginning of the process of social diagnosis, which I think is complementary to the psychiatrist's diagnosis of the child's difficulties.'[32]

Advice is not an activity that has received a very favourable press amongst psychiatric social workers. 'On other occasions one

151

may be tempted to offer direct advice, only to find that though this may have been what was requested it was not what was wanted. Our own needs to be good mothers or siblings may thereby be fulfilled, but to what purpose?'[23] Another worker writes that 'if I find myself primarily giving intellectual, factual advice, I usually discover that the case is one where I do not really feel that I can help, and that I am giving the advice to assure myself that I have done all I can . . .'[40] What is required is some differentiation of topics about which advice might be given and investigation of the actual effects of advice giving. More recently it has been suggested that 'it is better to admit that even the psychiatric social worker may have clients who not only need advice, but also the experience of contact with someone who is prepared to give unpalatable advice and to take full responsibility for it.'[30] This represents a more open attitude to the question, but this means only that advice giving has become a respectable activity, not that we are very much clearer about how, when, why or to whom it should be given.

Reassurance also figures in the literature as one of the activities of psychiatric social workers. It has been pointed out that the administration of reassurance can prevent the worker recognizing with the client some of his negative feelings about himself or other people. Other workers have described cases in which they gave no reassurance or considered none was needed. Others have argued that emphasis should be given to the beneficial effects of reassurance. Bree has suggested that to think of reassurance as if it were a concrete thing in itself is confusing. She holds the opinion 'that any service, any activity, or deliberate and appropriate passivity can convey reassurance, but not unless the service itself has some value proper to the situation.'[41] This is a point of view that has important implications for any general view of the psychiatric social worker's activity. How far can separate techniques, such as reassurance, advice-giving and so on be separated from the total service given to the client by the worker? If they can, then it should be possible to describe and study the form and objectives of such techniques. If they cannot, then, it would be much more profitable to begin exploring the work from the point of view of developing role-relationships.

(c) *The Relationship*. We have already seen (in the discussion of acceptance) some of the views of psychiatric social workers on their relationships with clients. No comprehensive study has been made of this relationship, but it seems to be a medium through which workers attempt to help clients either by the support of sympathy, reassurance and advice or by showing the client some of his unacknowledged purposes and wishes that are affecting his present situation. A broad distinction can be observed in the writings of psychiatric social workers between these two main methods of working, the development of 'insight' on the one hand, and, on the other, supportive help to maintain a situation, prevent deterioration and encourage psycho-social growth. The first approach was certainly given more prestige in the literature. This was regarded as something very like the activity of the psychotherapist and some workers spoke and wrote about their 'patients'. This method is considered more highly even when it is allowed that some clients are unable to face the 'adventure of self-discovery'. In such cases, argue Ashdown and Brown, for example, 'the psychiatric social worker is not justified in refusing, because she has a *preferred* method',[42] other kinds of help (my italics).

The two main approaches to treatment were distinguished only slowly and with little attention to the precise characterization of either. The first issue that became clear in the development of these two approaches was the general question, do psychiatric social workers 'treat' their clients? This question raised considerable controversy in the profession and is mentioned in half the articles published in the Journal between 1948 and 1950 (inclusive). Sometimes the argument seems to be a simple request to use the word 'treatment' in a particular way. At other times the issue is expressed in the form of the question: is casework psychotherapy? Discussion of such questions was obscured, however, by a failure to see that it was impossible to cover all of the main activities of psychiatric social workers by using the one category. In the 1930's some psychiatric social workers were anxious to press their claims to be 'treating' parents and in so doing they argued that though the work varied from the intensive to more casual interviews it was of the same therapeutic kind.

However, as some distinctions began to be made regarding what workers did with their clients, it became necessary to ask what one was attempting with the clients who were *not* 'treated'.

To some the answer could be found in some form of split between the two parts of the worker's title: the social work aspect referred to 'practical social work', and the psychiatric to 'psychological understanding'. One part of the work was thought of as 'chores' and the other as therapy. Others regretted such a division. Waldron, for example, wrote in 1949 that 'It would be unfortunate ... if we identified (our ability to make use of all available social resources) with our social worker character, and our skill in relationship with our psychiatric character.'[18] The most sustained and useful attempt to distinguish the 'social work' from the 'therapeutic' aspects of the work is to be found in Bree's article in 1952.[41] She maintained that in her setting (a clinic for neuro-syphilis) there were 'so many concrete factors, bad in themselves and alterable, that I would be making a situation worse by consciously building a relationship first. I do what it seems best to do in the actual situation and the relationship between the relative and myself appears to take care of itself.' There have been two main attempts in the literature to heal the split between the two views of psychiatric social work as primarily 'social work' or 'therapy'. Goldberg and Irvine have both published important articles on this problem.

Goldberg, in 1953, argued that even if in some settings workers have, for example, 'to take immediate action dictated by dire emergencies' workers are nonetheless important to their clients. 'Is it not possible that, if we but care to look, our old friend, the transference is there in many guises? . . . I am inclined to think that, if we work with a patient, we have to accept that *the whole* of him is involved in the relationship with us, however much we may have to limit our function. It is therefore still important to understand our relationship with him and this in no way excludes the possibility of doing a great many 'chores'. The performance of these 'chores' is then not only dictated by the demands of the reality situation, but also takes into account the patient's inner problems and the use he is making of his relationship with us.'[26] In this account the relationship of the client and psychiatric social worker is made central to any intervention, and is seen largely in terms of transference (loosely defined). The assertion that the client's 'whole' man is involved in his relationship with the worker makes a very large claim. How could it be, one is prompted to ask, and yet how could it be shown not to be? The assertion could perhaps be usefully seen not as a semi-metaphysical statement, but as a technical principle in the form of an instruction to the worker to be as alive as he can to the different aspects of personality that may be displayed at different times.

Before describing Irvine's attempt to characterize the range of the psychiatric social worker's intervention, it is necessary to explain the development of ideas about the use of the transference in psychiatric social work. The word is a technical term taken from psychoanalytic therapy: it refers to the process by which feelings and attitudes built up in early relationships in the family are transferred persistently onto the analyst. The term was used by psychiatric social workers quite early in the history of the profession. At the Second Inter-Clinic Conference, for instance, the term was used in discussions in the Social Workers' Section. Developments have occurred in the use of the 'transference' and in the realization of the varied ways in which the term itself could be used.

Some psychiatric social workers seem to have thought of transference phenomena as something to be dealt with before getting down to the 'real' work. One worker, for instance, stated that 'it is essential that the worker should be aware of the transference so that she can deal with it before attempting to modify the mother's attitude to the child.'[43] Others have expressed the view that great skill and tact were required in dealing with the transference, but gave no description of their methods.[44] Their view can perhaps be summed up in the words of the central character in de Vries' novel, *Comfort Me with Apples*: 'This must be what they call "transference",' I said in an unsteady tone, casting an anxious eye at the open door. 'It's a stage a patient goes through, and our object will be to get you through it as fast as possible.' (p. 194). Others stressed that the transference situation should be avoided or controlled. 'We do not necessarily seek to avoid the "transference" situation, but if as social workers we consider we are not equipped to deal with the psychological mechanisms released by it, we must increase our awareness of how we avoid it . . . If we do accept our role in a "transference" situation there is still need to examine it, for the course of a patient's growth from dependence on his social worker is probably different from that which he develops from his "transference" to his doctor.'[18] Still others based their work firmly on an exploration and interpretation of the transference between the client and the social worker. This point of view can perhaps be best illustrated by Hunnybun's paper at the Eleventh Inter-Clinic Conference (1955).

Meanwhile, however, some necessary distinctions were being drawn between different meanings of the term. Irvine in 1952 drew attention to the ambiguities involved. 'It has perhaps created some confusion in this country that the term transference has come to be used not only in the narrow specialized sense . . . (now distinguished by the term "transference neurosis") but also in a broader sense which denotes the total emotional situation between worker and client . . . It is perhaps in this broader sense that a psychiatric social worker can be said "to use the transference".'[24] Mason made a similar point when she reported her 'impression that there is a tendency for psychiatric social workers to think that the transference situation with which we meet has the same intensity and potentiality for influencing behaviour as the transference neurosis.'[22]

Returning now to Irvine's important article,[30] which attempted 'to construct a frame of reference within which we can formulate an account, consonant with Freudian theory, of the variety of ways in which we try to promote or facilitate emotional growth and development in clients, or to modify their attitudes and behaviour.' This, of course, assumes that these are the objectives of casework and obviously the promotion of emotional growth requires careful definition. Accepting, however, that more attention must be given to the clarification of casework objectives, Irvine's attempt at a general description of the ways of achieving them is still important. She sees two main kinds of work that can be attempted, acting out a parent-child relationship between the worker and his client, and attempting to develop insight, partly by interpreting to the client his unreal perceptions of, and reactions to, the worker. In work of the first kind, the worker's own emotional response, her presentation of herself as a 'real' person, her ways of controlling the development of the transference are the essential ingredients. In the second kind of work the experience with the worker of a new and helpful relationship remains of great importance, though attention is also paid to developing the client's insight. In this kind of work it is suggested that 'If the transference is interpreted . . . the aim will usually be not so much to explore the inner world which is projected in the transference as to remove the veil of distortion and enable the client once more to experience the reality of the relationship.' What require more detailed formulation are answers to such questions as—what are the main factors in a good parent-child relationship at different ages; what exactly is helpful about gaining insight and so on.

The preceding description of the ways in which psychiatric social workers have written of their work allows a number of conclusions. Firstly, in spite of the difficulties of describing inter-action between worker and client, an important beginning has been made in formulating some theoretical ideas about its content. Of these perhaps the most important is the recognition of the reality of both love and hate. Secondly, the extent of theorizing so far attempted makes considerable claims for the effects of relationships of certain kinds and these must be tested. Thirdly, the differentiation of methods and objectives has been insufficiently developed. Is the relationship the necessary but not the sufficient condition of success, for example? Without a re-lationship work may well fail, but is a relationship sufficient to ensure success, or is it simply a necessary medium within which the problem-solving work of client and caseworker is transacted? Can the objectives of casework be seen clearly for different kinds of client? Here we are faced only with a number of rather briefly expressed ideas about the criteria for the selection of clients. It has been suggested in the literature that clients should be able to relate, be capable of insight, be of good intelligence, and have a capacity for self-criticism. On the other hand, a useful and more considered beginning in the use of more empirical criteria has been made by Harrington.[45] These two approaches need to be combined together with an increased clarification of the different kinds of work psychiatric social workers should attempt.

NOTES

[1] Brown, Clement, 'The Methods of Social Case Workers', in (ed.) Bartlett F., *The Study of Society*, London 1939.

[2] *Social Work*, a quarterly published by The Family Welfare Assoc. is a direct descendant by an almost unbroken line of succession to the first social work journal, the *Charity Organization Reporter* first published in January 1872. In 1885 a monthly *Review* appeared and this was published until

September 1921. After a short interval a *Quarterly* was published which became in April 1939, *Social Work.*

Case Conference, edited and founded by a psychiatric social worker, Mrs. K. McDougall in 1954 is now published 10 times a year and is a periodical for the social worker and administrator.

[3] Ashdown and Brown, *op. cit.,* p. 19.

[4] *Ibid.,* p. 231.

[5] Goldberg E. M., 'Experiences with families of young men with duodenal ulcer and "normal" control families'. *British Journal of Medical Psychology,* Vol. XXVI, Parts 3 and 4, 1953.

[6] Wisdom O., 'Psycho-Analytic Technology', *The British Journal for the Philosophy of Science,* Vol. VII, No. 25, May 1956.

[7] Arsenian J. M., 'Research in Psychiatric Social Work', *Social Service Review,* Vol. XXVI, No. 1, March 1952.

[8] Ashdown and Brown, *op. cit.,* p. 231.

[9] Slater E., and Woodside M., *Patterns of Marriage,* 1951.

Fraser R., (with others including Waldron F. E.) *The Incidences of Neurosis Among Factory Workers,* H.M.S.O. 1947.

[10] Morris P., 'The Psychiatric Social Worker as a Research Interviewer', *British Journal of Psychiatric Social Work,* Vol. V, No. 2, 1959.

[11] See e.g. (1) Bree M. H., *The Dement in the Community,* published by Horton Group Hospital Management Committee.

The author states that this is not a work of scientific research but it constitutes an important study of a topic of considerable contemporary importance; (2) Goldberg E. M., *Family Influences and Psychosomatic Illness,* (1959).

[12] Ashdown M., in the editorial to the first issue of the journal.

[13] Robinson B. H., 'A follow-up study of Ex-patients of the East London Child Guidance Clinic', *British Journal of Psychiatric Social Work,* No. 7, March 1953. Shaw L. A., 'Following up Adoptions', *British Journal of Psychiatric Social Work,* No. 8, November 1953.

[14] Irvine E. E., 'Research into Problem Families', *British Journal of Psychiatric Social Work,* No. 9, May 1954.

[15] Lane M. A., 'The Effect of Leucotomy on Family Life', *British Journal of Psychiatric Social Work,* Vol. III, No. 3, 1956.

[16] Tilley M., 'The Religious Factor in Case-Work', *British Journal of Psychiatric Social Work,* No. 4, 1950.

[17] Armstrong P., 'Aspects of Psychiatric Social Work in a Mental Hospital', *British Journal of Psychiatric Social Work,* No. 1, 1947.

[18] Waldron F. E., 'The Psychiatric Social Worker's Professional Standing', *British Journal of Psychiatric Social Work,* No. 2, August 1948.

[19] Castle M., 'Changes which may effect Methods of Social Case-Work', *British Journal of Psychiatric Social Work,* No. 4, 1950.

[20] Goldberg E. M., 'Some Developments in Professional Collaboration and Research in the U.S.A.', *British Journal of Psychiatric Social Work,* Vol. III, No. 1, 1955.

[21] Beedell C., 'The Psychopathology of Inter-Clinic Conferences', *British Journal of Psychiatric Social Work,* Vol. IV, No. 1, 1957.

[22] Mason E. M., 'The Centenary of Freud: Understanding and Misunder-

standing', *British Journal of Psychiatric Social Work*, Vol. III, No. 4, 1956.

[23] Laquer A. M., 'Interviews with a Mother in the Presence of a Young Child', *British Journal of Psychiatric Social Work*, No. 7, 1953.

[24] Irvine E. E., 'The Function and Use of Relationship between Client and Psychiatric Social Worker', *British Journal of Psychiatric Social Work*, No. 6, June 1952.

[25] Laquer A. M., 'The Caseworker's Task in Meeting the Client's Inner and Outer Needs', *British Journal of Psychiatric Social Work*, No. 10, October 1954.

[26] Goldberg E. M., 'Function and Use of Relationship in Psychiatric Social Work', *British Journal of Psychiatric Social Work*, No. 8, November 1953.

[27] Harrington M., 'Psychiatric Social Work in a Borstal Institution', *British Journal of Psychiatric Social Work*, No. 4, 1950.

[28] Chance E. and Arnold J., 'The Effect of Professional Training, Experience and Preference for a Theoretical System upon Clinical Case Description', *Human Relations*, Vol. 13, No. 3, August 1960.

[29] Ferard M., 'Notes on the Psychiatric Social Treatment of Mental Hospital Patients: Four paranoid Schizophrenics', *British Journal of Psychiatric Social Work*, No. 1, 1947.

[30] Irvine E. E., 'Transference and Reality in the Casework Relationship', *British Journal of Psychiatric Social Work*, Vol. III, No. 4, 1956.

[31] Hutchinson D. M., 'Clinic and Community', *British Journal of Psychiatric Social Work*, No. 2, August 1948.

[32] Lewis K., 'Role of the Psychiatric Social Worker', *British Journal of Psychiatric Social Work*, No. 4, October 1950.

[33] Hay-Shaw C., 'The Short-Contact Interview', *British Journal of Psychiatric Social Work*, No. 4, October 1950.

[34] Rankin T. G., 'Casework in a Community Care Service', *British Journal of Psychiatric Social Work*, No. 6, June 1952.

[35] Tilley M., 'Casework with The Anti-Social Client', *British Journal of Psychiatric Social Work*, No. 11, Spring 1955.

[36] Williams M. and Castle R., 'Notes on Initial Interviews in Child Guidance', *British Journal of Psychiatric Social Work*, No. 1, September 1947.

[37] Ledermann R., 'The Significance of Feeling in the Therapeutic Relationship', *British Journal of Psychiatric Social Work*, No. 9, May 1954. The approach of this article would appear to be Jungian.

[38] *Op. cit.*, pp. 148/9.

[39] Ashdown M., *The Role of the Psychiatric Social Worker*, (1936).

[40] Joseph B., 'A Psychiatric Social Worker in a Maternity and Child Welfare Centre', *British Journal of Psychiatric Social Work*, No. 2, August 1948.

[41] Bree M. H., 'The Function and Use of Relationship between Client and Psychiatric Social Worker', *British Journal of Psychiatric Social Work*, No. 6, June 1952.

[42] Ashdown and Brown, *op. cit.*, p. 153.

[43] Tickle M., 'Indications for successful work with Parents in a Child Guidance Clinic', *British Journal of Psychiatric Social Work*, No. 1, September 1954.

[44] See e.g., Hale M. B. and Hale S. M., *Social Therapy* (1943), p. 73.

[45] Harrington M., 'Some Differing Casework Goals in Child Psychiatry', *British Journal of Psychiatric Social Work*, Vol. IV, No. 1, 1957.

Chapter Eight

THE PROFESSIONAL ASSOCIATION— DEFINITIONS AND PROTECTION OF FUNCTION

INTRODUCTION

I T was around 1917 that social workers first began to claim professional status,[1] and their claims have by now extended over most fields of social work and with increasing intensity. This trend towards some kind of professionalism is one of the obvious characteristics of contemporary social work. What does such a development entail? Social workers are certainly pressing for the rewards of financial and social recognition that accompany professional status in our society; they want to define, protect and further their interests. Yet they are also making claims that involve considerable responsibility. They are claiming recognition for a disciplined and informed skill, based on the selection and training of entrants. They wish to be treated as people governed in important respects by service to their skill, who seek also its improvement for the sake of more effective help to their clients. Social workers try to protect the exercise of their skill, to influence events connected with it, and to improve their conditions of work. To achieve some or all of these objectives they have formed organizations which in varying degrees resemble those of the established professionals. It is within this context that the Association of Psychiatric Social Workers should be considered.

This Association is not the largest of the social work organizations; in 1960 there were almost twice the number of members in the National Association of Probation Officers and 350 more members of the Institute of Almoners. Nor is it the oldest organization; the Hospital Almoners Association was established in 1903 and some form of organization for probation officers has existed since 1912. Yet the Association of Psychiatric Social Workers has undergone fewer structural changes than either of these, and it is the only example of a social work organization based not on the particular post held (like the National Association of Probation Officers), but on full qualification through university training. This means that a significant proportion of members are at any one time not practising as psychiatric social workers and that some of them have never so practised. Some critics have seen this as an anomaly, but it is simply a consequence of the Association's decision to base membership on what we have seen was a broadly based training and not an exclusive preparation for one particular kind of social work. The Association has in this way been able to retain the services of members who have moved on to other forms of social work practice, teaching and research. An analysis of those who have been active in the Association in fact shows that most of them have had some years of clinical experience in psychiatric social work. In the course of its history the Association has gained a reputation both within and outside social work. Younghusband has described it as 'an extremely strong professional body',[2] while Chambers, albeit with some historical licence, has stated that '. . . from the beginning, psychiatric social workers have possessed a strong and well organized professional association'.[3] The Association has, as we shall see, sometimes lacked the strength and the clarity of perception to deal firmly and decisively with the important issues that have confronted it, but its ways of conducting its affairs have changed with the increase in membership, greater experience and enhanced prestige.

The Association of Psychiatric Social Workers began in 1930 with an original membership of 17. It had so few members it was difficult to differentiate the executive committee from the general meeting. It had very few resources, and its life in the early years was often in the balance. In April 1930, the Association possessed a cash balance of 2s. 10d. which by November in the following year had shrunk to 1s. 1d. With few members and resources the programme of activity was restricted and the early general meetings of the Association were simply study groups. The existence of the Association was barely recognized by outside bodies and its influence was non-existent.

The contrast between the early years and the position today is striking. There were, by 1961, 850 members, and contact was maintained with the significant group of those who lived or worked overseas. The structure of the organization had become complex on account of both the increase in membership and expansion of activity in the fields of training, professional development, public relations, publication and conditions of service. There were in 1960, 13 branches of the Association, including one in Scotland, in Ireland and in Wales and two Special Interest Groups of Parents and those interested in Community Care. In the same year the Register of Associates and a disciplinary machinery were established. Financially the Association now handled comparatively large sums of money. In 1960, for example, over £1,300 was paid out in salaries and National Insurance and over £500 in committee travelling expenses. Over £2,600 came in from member's subscriptions.

The history of the Association could be studied in a number of different ways, but the intention of this and the two following chapters will be to trace developments within the Association on a number of key themes—the definition and protection of function, training, influence on social policy and legislation, and conditions of service. It is hoped in this way to show important aspects of the professional activity of the psychiatric social worker, and to avoid the lengthy study of *minutiae* not far removed from gossip or boredom. Some of the topics will have been discussed in previous sections of the book, but they will be viewed now as aspects of the professional life of the Association.

This approach will inevitably convey little of the continuous life of the Association, so before the detailed discussion of themes, some attempt will be made to consider the history, problems and achievements of the Association as a whole.

THE HISTORICAL DEVELOPMENT OF THE ASSOCIATION

The history of the Association cannot be seen as a succession of distinct periods; differences between periods are a matter of emphasis. For example, at the present time, the Association is seeking common ground with other professional social workers, but in 1939 the representation of the Association on the editorial board of the journal *Social Work* was seen as 'indicative of the realization of the common basis of social work and of a desire for closer co-operation amongst those engaged in it.'⁴ It is possible, however, to make certain divisions of emphasis. For the first five or six years of its life, the Association was concerned about its own future existence and that of psychiatric social work. In June 1930, for example, an emergency meeting had to be held to decide how the students qualifying that year should be notified of the existence of the Association; in September 1931, only four of the twelve students had accepted nomination, and it was decided to write to the eight others again. The dangers of introducing a shortened form of training were discussed at length in 1930 and in 1935, and the uncertain position led the Association to adopt a very cautious policy in regard to salaries and conditions of work. Members were also trying to discover what was appropriate behaviour for a professional organization. In 1936, for instance, the tutor of the Mental Health Course asked the Association to provide speakers for University groups with a view to spreading information about psychiatric social workers and their professional activities. The Executive Committee asked if such action could be looked on as propaganda in any sense in which the Association could not co-operate. At a general meeting later in the year it was reported that the Association had been advised (probably by a psychiatrist) that propaganda was unprofessional. These unnecessary niceties contrast with the Association's present concern with publicity and public relations in regard to both mental health and psychiatric social work.

In its earliest years the Association was beginning to work out relationships with the two overshadowing bodies of the London School of Economics and the Child Guidance Council, but it was also concerned with its relationships with other social workers. A simple contrast is sometimes drawn between the present work of the psychiatric social worker with its emphasis on consultation and co-operation with other social workers and that of an earlier period when the psychiatric social worker was isolated from other social workers in her ivory tower. Thus, Younghusband states that 'psychiatric social workers have tended to be separated off from other social workers and to be regarded with a mixture of envy and suspicion as a peculiar people. This more adequate form of training has thus not been able to fertilize the whole field of social work so effectively as would have happened if the course had been more broadly based.'⁵ Such arguments ignore the early ideas about the function of the psychiatric social worker to be found in the records of the Association. From the very beginning members were exercized about themselves in regard to other workers and services.

In June 1931, for example, the General Meeting discussed the report of the sub-committee on co-operation. It was suggested that co-operation was necessary in order to spread principles of mental hygiene and it was decided that cases in a clinic might well be divided into those for which the clinic alone was responsible, those which could be handled in co-operation with other agencies and those which required consultation only. In October 1931, the Executive decided that the report for the British Committee at the Frankfurt International Conference on Social Work should be on the relationship between social work and mental hygiene. Towards the end of the year, when the report was discussed at a General Meeting, it was decided to omit words with controversial associations but the only concession made to the tactics of co-operation was the sacrifice of the term *libido*. In the following years the Association took an active interest in proposals for the formation of some kind of national association of social workers. In 1935 it joined the newly established British Federation of Social Workers, and played a real and continuous part in its deliberations.

The Association was, then, from the first concerned with co-operation with other social workers. Yet this co-operation differed in important respects from present relationships with social workers from other fields. Earlier attempts were based on the view that psychiatric social workers as carriers of the message of mental hygiene had something to give other social workers. The emphasis today is much more on a joint exploration of what is seen as the common nature of social work. It was, moreover, in the earlier period possible to distinguish psychiatric social work, on the one hand, and 'general social work' (that is, the remainder) on the other. Today, 'general social work' is seen as a number of recognized specializations (e.g. child care, probation, etc.).

The first period of the Association's life ends around 1937, when it was decided to explore the possibility of Incorporation as a means of protecting the Association and preserving standards of training. The second period lasted until nearly the end of the War, and the major theme was the identity of psychiatric social work.

This was discussed in terms of training and of specialization and of the relationship between the psychiatric social worker and the medical profession. The Second World War was of the greatest importance to psychiatric social work as Noel Hunnybun was able to conjecture in the report of the Association for the year 1939: 'It may be that the situation caused by the War bears within it the germ of new developments and that the scope and range of psychiatric social work may ultimately be widened by that which at first seemed likely to restrict it.' The developments in the field had their repercussions on the professional organization, and the discussions in the Association 1940/41 are some of the most important in its history.

Towards the end of the War the Association entered its third phase which lasted until about 1953. In this period the Association was concerned with the problems of the psychiatric social worker in what was virtually a new post-war world. New social services were being fashioned, and the Association had to decide on the place psychiatric social workers might occupy in them. Some of the difficulties in this decision are apparent in the comment at an Executive Meeting in 1950 on 'the *opposing* themes of the provision of social services and of professional social work skills', (my italics). The Association began to meet the implications of involvement in new machinery for salary negotiations and the problems raised by the beginning of new courses for psychiatric social workers. This was the period in which the Macintosh Report was published. The evidence of the Association was of a high quality and the Report put before the profession the challenge of consultative work with other social workers. Many in the Association, however, had expected the Report to solve their more pressing professional problem for them. The high and patient expectation which social workers hold of committees of enquiry and government reports is indeed a general feature of the profession. In the last fifteen years social workers have been given ample opportunity to display this quality.

The third period also saw the Association concerned again with the relationship between medicine and psychiatric social work, but now the Association seemed more confident in its refusal of auxiliary status. Within the Association the membership was again exercised by the problems of the identity of psychiatric social work. The discussions in the first year of the 1950's were as important as those in the previous decade, but they had a different emphasis. The discussions in 1940/41 were basically concerned with psychiatric social work as social work in conjunction with psychiatry, while later discussions assumed that it was the exercise of a special kind of human relations skill. Two sides were identified in this second controversy (the 'techniquers' and the 'anti-techniquers') and it was a partial resolution of this struggle around 1953 that led to what may be considered the present period. The ventilation of these important topics was mainly the result of the establishment in 1950 of a working party to form some kind of plan for the general meetings of the Association. This working party, later to become the important Professional Development Sub-Committee, decided that the Association could draw much more on its own members for 'scientific' presentation of the work. The adoption of this principle led to an important series of meetings addressed by psychiatric social workers, and marked a step forward in the Association's progress towards maturity.

In the present period training has once again presented problems and the Association has had to reach a decision on the relationship between training for psychiatric social work and the new movement towards 'generic' training which emphasized an integrated training in which all social workers could participate. The Association was slow to reach a decision, partly because the issues became clear only slowly and partly because of their intrinsic importance. In the general enthusiasm for the new form of training, the Association often appeared as the most important single factor opposing progress. The Association was itself in conflict about the problem and it is possible to see once again an alignment of mental hospital workers against those in child guidance, with the latter more in favour of generic trends. At the same time, in its relations with other professional social work organizations, the Association has taken a leading part in the growing movement towards greater professional unity amongst all social workers. (This spirit is evident in several spheres of activity, including that of salary negotiation.) It is significant in the present period that the Presidents of the Association are not chosen exclusively from the ranks of psychiatry but also from those of sociology and politics.[6]

In the course of its history the Association has achieved success, particularly in the continued education and professional development of its members and the maintenance of standards of training. Yet survival, continuance and growth are themselves an achievement worth recording in view of the organizational problems involved. There have been within the membership a number of important tensions in the Association's history arising from the implicit threat to unity contained in the issues of London versus the provinces, 'therapy' versus social work, child guidance versus mental hospital, community care versus other fields and, of course, men versus women. There were, for example, in 1947, signs that male psychiatric social workers were unsure of their position in the work—one wrote to the Executive asking if male psychiatric social workers were simply stop gaps; another tried, but failed, to elicit an opinion on their clinical role.[7] How has the Association kept its unity? It has been composed not simply of people with different interests, but of social workers and for various different reasons social workers present a problem to any association that would organize them, especially for 'political' action.

Firstly, social workers are trained to accept the other person's viewpoint sympathetically and this would seem to be the exact opposite of the attitude required, for instance, in salary negotiation. Their training in the past emphasized, moreover, the one-to-one relationship rather than the group situation, and political action must often have seemed akin to the manipulation they were taught to avoid in work with clients. Psychiatric social workers in particular have been trained to believe that growth and change are slow and to work at another's pace. These attitudes are, of course, appropriate in clinical work, but their generalization to problems of organization and 'politics' have tended to produce a professional outlook which is often cautious, slow and sometimes lacking in clarity. Thus, there is a danger in clinical work of curtailing diagnostic thinking due to despair of thoroughly understanding complex problems presenting so many elements of uncertainty. A quick diagnosis may be made and held, or no clear diagnosis formulated at all. The history of the Association will show examples of both dangers transferred to policy considerations. Finally, psychiatric social workers are a minority group working for the acceptance of their role in the community. The missionary outlook of their work has often entailed some diffidence in making claims for themselves on the community.

167

The Association has taken a number of steps to maintain unity amongst its members. The continued emphasis on standards of training, and the work of the Standing Advisory Committee on Training for Psychiatric Social Work, have gone some way towards ensuring that the training, which is the main link between members, has certain constant elements. The Association has also attempted to adapt its organization to meet the real problems of communication that have arisen as the membership increased in size and spread over the British Isles.

In 1942 the need for two vice-chairmen was raised, and it was decided that one of these should be from outside London. One general meeting of the Association each year has been held out of London since 1942 and as members spread over the country branches have been formed. The first 'branch' was recognized in 1940 when the Scottish group of psychiatric social workers formed a sub-committee of the Association, and in 1941 a North of England branch was formed.[8] Towards the end of the war some serious discussions were held about the apathy of the membership, especially in regard to policy discussions and it was decided to co-opt on to the policy sub-committee each year a representative from those newly qualifying. The Association has had success in recruiting new members to its ranks and in retaining the services of those who have worked on its various committees, but attracting new members to serve on the committees has always been a problem. This is a complex matter. The Association has tended to treat new members with caution and the newly qualified were until fairly recently likely to be working on committees with those who had been their teachers only a short while before. This made for difficulties for both sides. The Association, like other bodies, has had both a formal admissions procedure and an informal recognition that the member is in fact 'one of us'. This informal procedure is, of course, difficult to detect, but it would seem that acceptance within the Association is conditional on the member obtaining experience in the fields of psychiatric social work. One of the questions psychiatric social workers most frequently ask about their colleagues is, how much clinical work have they done?

In 1949, the Association considered proposals for the decentralization of some of its business. The central problem was defined as one of transition from being 'a family group' to becoming a professional group concerned with other than face-to-face activities amongst members. It was not until 1958, however, that regional representatives were appointed to the Executive. The issue was discussed in 1951 and 1952, but it was decided that it would be too expensive and increase the Executive to an unmanageable size. Meanwhile, in 1951, a liaison officer had been appointed to convene an annual meeting of branch secretaries, to communicate with them and, if possible, visit at regular intervals. The reports of the liaison officer showed that the problem of unity was not simply a question of communication from the central office, but also of passing information from the branches to other branches and to London. The loyalty of other members depended less on overcoming a feeling of geographical isolation and more on the capture of their interest. Here the Association has formed special interest groups and two such groups now exist for psychiatric social workers who are Parents and for those interested in problems of Community Care.

This is a very brief account of some aspects of the history of the Association as a whole, its organizational problems and some of the measures taken to solve them. We shall now consider the development of the main themes outlined at the beginning of this chapter, starting with the definition and protection of function.

Definition

One of the main issues for the Association in the attempts to reach a definition of psychiatric social work has been the working out of the relationship of workers to medical colleagues and their place in the growing complexity of the National Health Service. The problem of the relationship between psychiatric social worker and doctor first appeared in 1936, though in October 1935 Dr. Kimber had given a talk to the General Meeting on Psychiatric Social Work in the Mental Hospital in which he stated a preference for the term 'psychiatric assistant'. The issue raised in 1936, however, was that of the registration of psychiatric social workers as medical auxiliaries. This presented the Association with a problem. Traditionally, social work has relied heavily on analogies with medicine,[9] and medicine was the discipline to which psychiatric social work looked for support. At the same time the psychiatric social worker saw herself, in important respects, as independent. At an executive meeting in March, 1936, members could see no advantage in applying for inclusion on the register of medical auxiliaries and a disadvantage in the rule that an auxiliary should work only under the control and direction of a medical practitioner. However, the subject was postponed until the next meeting. In May a member was asked to discuss the problem with a certain psychiatrist, but in June it was decided to bring up the question again in a year's time, following reception of a letter from the Hospital Almoners saying that they would take no action to be registered as medical auxiliaries. Postponement was partly due to the complexity of detail (in March 1936 it was reported that the regulations for auxiliaries fill a book), but also to difficulty in reaching a decision in spite of the apparently clear views of the March meeting.

The question of auxiliaries does not reappear in the Executive Minutes until February 1938, though it is clear that the Policy Sub-Committee had been considering the question for some time. At this meeting it was reported that 'the position would need very thorough exploration before an opinion could be expressed. The expected report of the Feversham Committee would also have to be taken into account. The Committee was not in a position to report to the general meeting at this stage'. Once again there was postponement. The leaders of the Association found the issue overwhelming and failed to give an adequate lead to its members on a vital question, which concerned the nature of psychiatric and, by implication, other kinds of social work. No more was heard of this question until October 6th, in the same year, when a psychiatrist known to the Association, suggested that the secretary should approach the British Medical Association requesting inclusion as a Medical Auxiliary Service in any scheme of medical organization created as a result of the emergency and stating a desire to be placed at the disposal of the British Medical Association. No decision on this request is recorded, but in January 1939 when the British Medical Association pressed for a decision the Association replied that they had decided not to apply for registration.

This question of registration as auxiliaries of another profession was not raised again until 1952, but the relationship between medicine and psychiatric social work became an important issue quite early in the war. As we have seen, the war encouraged psychiatric social workers to enter new fields of work, to assist in evacuation and after-care schemes and to become generally much more active outside the clinical setting. It was not every psychiatric social worker who felt the need to respond to this challenge, and there developed in fact a split within the Association between those who wished to extend the work and those who were anxious to preserve the more classical idea of practice within a clinical setting. The new kinds of service raised the question of relationships with psychiatrists. In February 1941, the Chairman of the Association reported on her prompt action to dispel the idea of a new medical member of the Mental Health Emergency Committee that psychiatric social workers preferred to work independently, and not under the guidance of a psychiatrist. In June regret was expressed by the Association that the Child Guidance Auxiliary Service (psychologist and psychiatric social worker) should have been established before the Association had been consulted, since the psychiatric leadership of the clinical term was highly valued. In March, 1942, the position of members working independently of psychiatrists was discussed at a general meeting. It was emphasized that in fact psychiatric social workers were often working in areas where there were no psychiatrists, that they were *social* workers and their work was environmental. (Unfortunately, the term 'environment' produces ambiguity rather than clarification.) A resolution that 'No psychiatric social worker appointed as such should hold any post for casework unless she is professionally related to a psychiatrist or clinic (with a psychiatrist or medical practitioner) who will accept and advise as regards cases she wants to refer' was passed to the Executive for closer consideration. This was seen, correctly, as an important question of policy, and a sub-committee was appointed to investigate the function of the psychiatric social worker.

The sub-committee reported in June 1942 the results of a questionnaire circulated to members, thirty-six of whom replied, (i.e. approximately 20 per cent of all those trained as psychiatric social workers). The replies were unanimous that psychiatric social workers should aim at working under medical direction, especially since they were trained to work in a team. They expressed the view that members would get into disrepute with the medical profession if they exceeded their function, but they also argued that psychiatrists should shoulder their own burdens in this matter of treatment. It was suggested that some psychiatric social workers could undertake unsupervized psychotherapy because of special experience which might include a personal analysis. It was this suggestion and the content of the psychiatric social worker's 'treatment' that were taken up in the discussion at the General Meeting. One member stated that it was very strange that they should still be wondering what they were doing. She tried to clarify the question by asking what were psychiatric social workers doing now that was different from the social work they did before training. This was an important question, and the issue of treatment and of the identity of psychiatric social work was taken up again at a conference in July 1942.

This conference was called to consider a memorandum by Dr. Gordon of the Child Guidance Council on problems of the role of the psychiatric social worker. The memorandum suggested that 'the need to adapt to war conditions and to new claims on their services have necessitated adjustment to a type of work not envisaged in their original training.' Two general questions were posed: should workers specialize in child guidance or adult work, and how much responsibility could the worker take who was not attached to a clinical team? Amongst other questions raised in the memorandum were: the function of the psychiatric social worker in relation to hostels for difficult children and foster home placement, an increase in the number of training courses, and the possibility of training the three members of the clinic team together. The General Meeting discussed the memorandum and reached a number of decisions. It was considered impossible to separate the two sides of the training (child guidance and mental hospital) and that, while there was undoubted scope for psychiatric social workers in administrative and liaison work in the mental health services, the aim should always be to link up with a clinic or psychiatrist. There was general agreement that 'child psychiatry should not be undertaken by psychiatric social workers without further training', but that 'a therapeutic relationship is entered into in a psychiatric social worker's contact with the parents of children attending a Child Guidance Clinic, and with some patients. Psychiatric social work *is* treatment, and has a special technique'. This question of treatment was to engage the attention of the Association a great deal in 1951 and 1952 and we shall have to return to it later.

Definitions and Protection of Function

So far we have considered one attempt on the part of the Association to define some aspects of the relationship between doctors and psychiatric social workers. Psychiatric social workers did not wish to be considered medical auxiliaries, but they relied on certain members of the medical profession for a great deal of advice on critical matters that faced the professional organization from time to time; many of them worked under psychiatric direction and some were learning to develop their own work with clients with the theoretical and practical help of psychiatrists. There were, moreover, difficulties in asserting that psychiatric social workers were first and foremost social workers. There was no identifiable general group of social workers and very little systematic thinking about the role of the social worker. Moreover, it was natural to ask if psychiatric social workers were social workers before they trained, what were they after such training? Surely, they were not still simply social workers? This question about identity led the Association, as we have seen, to discuss the role of the psychiatric social worker as some kind of 'therapist'. What was in fact happening was that the Association was following two different definitions of psychiatric social work. In discussing relationships with doctors, the implied definition of psychiatric social work was social work undertaken in collaboration with psychiatry. In discussing the issue of 'therapy' or 'treatment' members were searching for a definition in terms of a special kind of work different from 'general' social work.

The issues were, of course, complex and it was not only the psychiatric social worker who was confused in her role expectations. Doctors themselves were also not in substantial agreement. As we shall see, Dr. Hadfield in 1942 pointed out that many psychiatric social workers were already doing therapy and his proposed new training course would regularize their position in the eyes of the medical profession. In January 1943, Dr. Winnicott read a paper to a General Meeting which argued against the idea of teamwork, and in the same year Aubrey Lewis in his Presidential Address called for more emphasis on the psychiatric social worker as the expert in knowledge of social conditions and social stress. Another kind of role was implied in Dr. Burns' comments in the same year at the Sixth Biennial Interclinic Conference. Referring to the different kinds of child guidance clinic he said that some were 'quite complete, some with essential parts missing, some of the non-parlour type, without a psychologist, and others of the non-bathroom type, without a social worker'. In view of such vague and differing expectations on the part of psychiatrists it was perhaps understandable that the definition of psychiatric social work as social work in conjunction with psychiatry presented difficulties as a starting point for study and discussion.

The Association was faced with a new problem of definition when it became clear that some kind of National Health Service would be created. What was to be the place of the psychiatric social worker in such a Service? This was a subject that found the Association unprepared and hesitant. At a meeting of the Health Workers' Council in 1943, it became clear that there was insufficient evidence about the position of the Association in relation to any of the schemes for a reorganized Health Service. At a meeting of the Executive of the Association in October, it was pointed out that in the past associations which did not know where they stood had been forced to make quick policy decisions and as a result had not been able to make an effective contribution. It was agreed that further study of the issue was important and this was linked with a proposal to hold a general meeting on 'What is Mental Health?' The proposal of such a subject, replete with possibilities of abstract argument and semantic confusion, looks more like an escape from a decision rather than a means of reaching one. In May 1944 a general meeting was held on the White Paper on the National Health Service, in the hope that agreement might be reached in the Association, but this seemed to produce little result. (Indeed in 1947 when the Executive discuss the apathy of the membership the difficulty of obtaining general opinions on this Government White Paper is cited as an example.) In January 1946, the Health Workers' Council requested a memorandum from the Association on the place of the psychiatric social worker in the National Health Service. In February it was decided to send a copy of the resolutions passed at the General Meeting in May 1944, and 'to emphasize our desire to maintain high professional standards of work.' The resolutions were all of a very general character: the psychiatric social worker must be part of a team which included a psychiatrist; she had a function outside the specialist service in a liaison and advisory capacity; she had a function in the community to encourage the proper understanding of mental health; there was room for mutual

education amongst health workers, e.g. psychiatric social workers
and health visitors had much to learn from one another.

An example of the specific questions that the new Health
Service could raise for psychiatric social workers was presented in
the following year: would psychiatric social workers be willing to
serve as Duly Authorized Officers when the National Health
Service Act transferred the duties of the Relieving Officers in
connection with Lunacy and Mental Defect to the D.A.O. in the
Local Health Authority?
It was agreed that a general meeting should discuss the question.
In April, however, the Chairman decided that this was pre-
mature, and she contacted the Board of Control (with whom
the scheme originated) to see how matters stood. It was felt
generally that the Branches should discuss the question before a
General Meeting was held. In June 1947, the policy Sub-
Committee discussed the issue and decided to circulate all
members in adult work for their views. In July the Secretary
reported that some replies had been received and they indicated
that the matter was causing a good deal of feeling. Some of the
points in question were raised in an article in the 1949 issue of the
Journal: 'Some of our profession feel that the Duly Authorized
Officer's duties are as remote from psychiatric social work as are
the duties of the constable on his beat. Those of us who feel our
special skill applies more to the field of prevention, education, and
community care than in intensive work with selected patients and
therapy divorced from environment, yet rightly doubt whether
the Psychiatric Social Work training is not a definite handicap in
the material task of getting a patient out of his home and into
hospital . . . The answer to these problems surely lies in team
work . . .'[10] This division of opinion was reflected in the Executive,
and it was decided to devote the September general meeting to a
discussion of the issue. As a result of this meeting two memoranda
were drawn up. The first gave a general description of the work
of the psychiatric social worker which was suitable for wide
circulation, while the second was intended for the Board of Control, and gave suggestions as to the most effective way in which
psychiatric social workers might work in the new Health Service.
The nucleus of a new group of mental health activities was seen
in local authority work with the possibility of some preventive
action; joint-user arrangements between hospitals and local

authorities would have to be made because of the shortage of psychiatric social workers; the new role of consultant to untrained workers was envisaged for psychiatric social workers. The second memorandum was discussed with representatives of the Board of Control, who suggested that it might be more useful if it were worked out in co-operation with the Mental Health Workers' Association, giving a view of the whole field. At the Executive Meeting at which the meeting with the Board of Control was discussed (May 1st, 1948) the Chairman stated that a new point had arisen, namely the place of the psychiatric social worker in a co-ordinated service and her relation to other workers in the mental health field. This issue, which has a familiar sound, was referred to the Policy Sub-Committee. Meanwhile no agreed policy on the D.A.O. question had been worked out. Some opinion had been formulated, but the point at issue had now changed to the larger question of social work in the mental health services.

This was not the first time that the Association had been called on to define the function of the psychiatric social worker in relation not to medicine but to other kinds of social work. In his Presidential Address in 1943, Aubrey Lewis had warned the Association of the difficulties that might ensue with the hospital almoners once the latter were able to free themselves from administrative routine. In March 1944 a joint meeting was held, and some attempt was made to distinguish two spheres of work. The Almoners suggested as a distinguishing criterion the degree of maladjustment; if the general physician could deal with the patient, then the social work could be carried out by the almoner. The psychiatric social workers suggested as criteria the existence of physical illness, or of mainly psychological causes of illness. The first kind of case should go to the almoner, the second to the psychiatric social worker. Both groups agreed that a common basic training was required and both urged a more scientific approach to social work. (This latter seems to have been a way of saying that social workers should be more clear about their objectives.) The criteria agreed do not stand close scrutiny, and illustrate some of the difficulties in defining the function of psychiatric social workers. What, however, was required of the Association in 1948 was a consideration of the relationship between psychiatric social workers and untrained social workers within the total mental health service.

The Association decided to meet representatives of the Mental Health Workers to discuss the memorandum on 'The place of the Psychiatric Social Worker in the National Health Service'. There had been earlier contact with these workers, who had, in July 1937, raised with psychiatric social workers the issue of a single recognized training for work in mental health. The two executives had met in October 1937 and agreement had been reached that a psychiatric social worker should be employed when a full psychiatric service was required. The meeting in 1948 was perhaps less concerned with the ideal demarcation of jobs. It was agreed that it was important to let local authorities know that the Association was aware of the shortage of trained workers: it was also thought that something less rigid than a statement on the need for trained workers should be included in the statement. The Executive agreed to meet further with Mental Health Workers and draw up a joint statement. In September the Executive agreed to the draft in principle—no one should be appointed to any post involving responsible social work in mental health who cannot produce evidence of adequate practical experience in some form of social casework. This represents a change towards realism.

The importance of a consideration of the place of the psychiatric social worker in the mental health services was emphasized when the Macintosh Committee was appointed in July 1948 'to consider and make recommendations upon questions arising in regard to the supply and demand, training and qualifications of social workers in the Mental Health Service'. The two points of particular importance in this connection were the place of the psychiatric social worker in the local authority, and her ability to undertake social work on behalf of mental defectives. These were considered largely from the point of view of training and will, therefore, be discussed later. Following the issue of the Report of the Macintosh Committee, the Association took the initiative in calling a meeting of representatives of the D.A.O's and the Association of Mental Health Workers, and from this meeting grew the Joint Standing Committee of Workers in the Mental Health Field.

Gradually, it seems, some policy was beginning to form in the Association on the place of the psychiatric social worker in the new mental health service or, if this is too optimistic a view, the Association was beginning to lose some of the defensiveness which previously led it to interpret such questions as the shortage of workers in mental health as a veiled attack on psychiatric social work training. The challenge of the mental health service seen as a whole was beginning to be faced. A comparison between Association policy in 1935 and in 1951 illustrates this important change.

In July 1934 Miss Fox, of the Central Association for Mental Welfare, suggested the formation of a committee to consider the shortage of psychiatric social workers. The September meeting of the Association reported considerable discussion on the relationship between psychiatric social worker and the untrained workers appointed to psychiatric social work posts. Members should always do what they could to assist such workers, but should also point out to them and their senior officers that such help was a very inadequate substitute for training which should be taken wherever possible. The Association would always write if requested to this effect to Medical Superintendents and other officers. When, in January 1936, the chairman of the Association was invited to sit on the Committee, the Association formulated resolutions for the Committee which were entirely concerned with the Mental Health Course:

(i) No curtailment in the course was consistent with efficiency.
(ii) A good grounding in social work was an essential qualification for the Course.
(iii) The Course was a sufficient qualification for work with mental defectives.

In 1951, on the other hand, when considering the Macintosh Report, the majority of members felt that psychiatric social workers should begin to equip themselves for leadership in the tasks of supervision and consultation of the untrained and partially trained mental welfare officers, whilst some are concerned at the insufficient attention paid to Child Guidance Clinics. The fact that the mental health service could not be staffed by trained psychiatric social workers was beginning to be faced. The difference between these two attitudes is not surprising in view of the precarious position of psychiatric social workers in the earlier period. The new attitude was partly the result of a growing self-confidence, and partly of a growing sense of identity with social work.

This second factor was clearly visible in the reaction of the

Association to the renewed discussion in 1952 of the question of registration as medical auxiliaries. There was still doubt and confusion on this question, but some of the views expressed and the final decision reached show a kind of reasoning different from that of the earlier period. In January the Ministry of Health informed the Association that the recommendation on registration made in the majority reports of the Cope Committees would now be taken as a basis for discussion with appropriate professional bodies, adding that the Macintosh Report indicated that psychiatric social workers should be brought into any scheme at the outset. An original answer to the Ministry was not sent because in the Chairman's view insufficient time had been given to a consideration of the question. In the meantime some of the Association's medical friends had been consulted. One had no views; another thought that the Association could not fight the issue, but could fight to be included on its own terms; another considered that the Association should discuss the constitution of the proposed Council of Auxiliaries, so that social work might have a wider representation. This rather pessimistic advice reflects perhaps the ambivalence of the medical profession towards another professional group concerned at least in part with 'therapy'. It was not, however, taken and a reply was delayed until the Association had consulted colleagues, the university departments concerned and so on. Representatives chosen to go to the Ministry were to discuss: the possible effects of such registration on training; the danger of the relegation of skilled social caseworkers to an auxiliary status in the field of medicine; further divisions rather than the unification of social workers in the field of mental health. The University Departments concerned with training psychiatric social workers stressed that their courses were based on the university disciplines of sociology and psychology and that psychiatric social workers were members of a profession in their own right. In a meeting with the Board of Control in March, it was made clear by the representatives of the Association that psychiatric social workers belonged to the social services.

This way of regarding psychiatric social workers was partly a result of the increase in the number and importance of the social services following post-war legislation. They had developed to the point at which they constituted a possible reference point for psychiatric social workers, who have looked now to psychiatry, now to social work for a firmer sense of identity and purpose. Placing themselves in the context of the social services, they faced, however, certain important problems which only slowly became apparent. Relationships with clients would always be of central importance, irrespective of the profession's point of reference, but as a 'social servant' communication with colleagues (in social work or not) and an understanding of administrative structures would be almost as important. The function of the agency would also become crucial, though psychiatric social workers have not found this an easy or tractable concept.

Before these implications could be more than tentatively grasped, there was considerable work to be done within the Association in defining the content of psychiatric social work. We have already seen that the idea of such work as 'treatment' had been in the minds of psychiatric social workers almost from the earliest days of training. Sometimes as we have seen in reviewing the writings of psychiatric social workers, the idea caused considerable controversy. Perhaps the most important controversy arose in the course of the influential meetings in June and December, 1951, on the function and use of the relationship in psychiatric social work. Some aspects of this have already been considered. It is important in the present context to note that there was a considerable divergence within the profession on a number of connected issues. There was disagreement over the description of the work in terms of 'technique': some saw a technique as something 'dead', others as the opposite. One group emphasized the importance of the reality situation, the other stressed the unconscious aspects of the relationship. For one group spontaneous interaction was of the essence of the work. As Bree remarked in the discussion in December, 1951: '. . . over and above all this I recognize that the most potent and least predictable factor in any relationship is the influence of one personality on another'.[11] For the other group conscious understanding and use of the relationship was the aim. There was, moreover, a tendency to identify these two groups in terms of child guidance and mental hospital experience. As a result of the discovery and partial formulation of these differences, a series of meetings was arranged by the newly formed Professional Development Committee on the Inner and Outer Needs of Clients, and this was followed in 1954 with a series on the ways in which the setting of the service affected the work. These meetings helped the further expression of feeling and thought on this subject, and were instrumental in achieving some kind of reconciliation between the two viewpoints. Speakers in the first series, from child guidance and mental hospitals, denied the validity of any split between inner and outer needs, while those in the second series went some way towards an affirmative answer to the original cautious question: 'Are there *legitimate* varieties of approach?' (my italics).

Discussions on this and kindred subjects have helped the members of the Association towards a more clear view of their function, or perhaps to be less concerned about certain differences between members on this score. There has certainly been in the last few years a noticeable easing of tension between the different fields of psychiatric social work, and between psychiatric social workers and their colleagues in other services and disciplines. As Irvine wrote in the latest publication of the Association, '. . . we seem to be less preoccupied with the demarcation of boundaries, and more interested in the extension of the teamwork concept. This involves on the one hand colleagues within the psychiatric services who were not fully included before (mental nurses, for instance) and on the other hand the building up of therapeutic teams which transcend the barriers of the hospital and include those working in the community, such as medical officers and health visitors.'[12] Yet considerable attention still needs to be given to the definition of function. In 1955 the Professional Development Committee was asked to discuss the view of the Scottish Branch that the Association only seemed interested in individual cases and not in wider issues in the mental health field. In particular there seemed no priority in regard to the 'spheres where psychiatric social work skills were thought to be most important at the present stage of development, as it was clear that psychiatric social workers could not possibly man all types of job.' The Association has come a long way on the question of the definition of psychiatric social work, but there is still no policy in regard to priorities and no factual information on which to base such a policy. Should psychiatric social workers concentrate on long-term work with the comparatively small number of cases which would show basic change in attitude or spread their work more widely or concentrate on helping other workers to carry a larger proportion of mentally ill cases? Or should their time be divided in some way between these demands?

The Association has become aware of the need to move away from a defensive policy as it becomes more conscious of the demands made by entry into the complicated bureaucratic structure of the social services. Yet we still know little of what psychiatric social workers in fact do in their jobs. Attempts to begin an investigation along these lines have met with little success. In October 1945, for example, a member raised the question of the caseload that might be allocated to a single worker. The question was discussed and considered important in view of the category of posts with special responsibility in the salary scale. It was referred to the Policy Sub-Committee. In June 1946, however, it was reported that the questionnaire sent out had been so variously interpreted that a new form had been designed and had been submitted to an expert. In January 1947 it was reported that 31 replies had been received on the questionnaire in regard to hospital caseloads. The Policy Sub-Committee was to judge if they were representative. Nothing further was heard and when in May 1949 a member of the Macintosh Committee asked for some figures on caseloads '. . . it was decided to request the General Purposes Sub-Committee to pick out a few clinics and ask them to let us have approximate figures of the number of patients dealt with per annum'. It seems that a more promising venture was started in 1958, when a study group was convened to study present developments in Mental Hospital and Community Care, including the expectations of medical staff and their requirements of psychiatric social work. The report of this group in 1960, however, satisfied no one because of its general character, and the earlier suggestions of a similar study of child guidance clinics was unfortunately not taken up.

PROTECTION OF MEMBERS, TITLE AND FUNCTION

There has been a gradual, if uneven, development from discussion within the Association of the importance of conditions for good psychiatric social work to the creation of a register of psychiatric social workers, the use of certain letters to denote membership of the Association, and the establishment of disciplinary machinery.

The early meetings of the Association had functions of mutual support and discussion, but as numbers and confidence grew the Association began to form relationships with other social workers and to take, somewhat later, steps to protect its members. In 1934 the Executive considered asking the Child Guidance Council to publish a pamphlet on the standards and qualifications of psychiatric social workers, but decided that it was impossible to make such a request. In the same year discussions with the Women Public Health Officers' Association and the Institute of Almoners was started on common professional problems. The protection of members was suggested as a possible subject, but the Executive decided that the Association has not reached the stage at which it could envisage such a function.

From this time the protection of the title and function of the psychiatric social worker seems to take three main forms: protest over individual cases of misuse of the title, clarification with other workers, and the attempt to secure some form of legal, or administrative protection.

A good example of protest over individual cases can be found in March 1946, when the Executive discussed an instance of an untrained worker calling herself a psychiatric social worker. The worker concerned had been trained on the After-Care Scheme of the Provisional National Council on Mental Health. The Executive decided to write to the Council pointing out that the danger they had foreseen had materialized. The Hospital concerned was to be informed of 'what the title "psychiatric social worker" had come to represent', a copy of this letter was to be sent to the worker and the chairman of the local Branch was asked to see her. This kind of action sometimes led to the social worker ceasing to use the title, but often it had little effect. Sometimes the superintendent would reply by requesting that the worker be recognized by the Association. This proved impossible, of course, because of the training basis of membership. Yet to respond to medical superintendents with this information alone sometimes produced an impression of 'closed shop' tactics. In fact the Association attempted to become more helpful on this question. In May 1948, for example, no immediate action was taken over a social worker misusing the title in order to enable the Policy Sub-Committee to consider some aspects of training (i.e. the use of bloc placements as opposed to fieldwork concurrent with

183

academic work) so that some constructive proposals might be made in connection with the shortage of psychiatric social workers.

The social workers most concerned in any 'demarcation' dispute were, of course, the medico-social workers or almoners. On three separate occasions this question has been discussed with them. In May 1944 the Association asked the Almoners for views on their members working in the mental health field. The Association by October had clarified its own policy and it was decided that the psychiatric social worker should belong to the social welfare department of a hospital if one existed, but that if the department was purely an almoner's department she should maintain her independence. This, as might be imagined, did not really solve the problem of working relationships between psychiatric social workers and almoners, and in July 1946 an informal meeting was arranged to discuss psychiatric social workers in almoner's departments. This produced no agreed formula, but gave each side the opportunity to state a case. Some almoners criticized a tendency amongst psychiatric social workers to reject responsibility for certain practical aspects of the work, such as financing and arranging convalescence. Psychiatric social workers replied that in general they accepted responsibility for any social work which had a direct bearing on the case from 'the psychiatric aspect'. This emphasis on the psychiatric approach or aspect constituted one important phase, as we have seen, in the attempt to distinguish psychiatric social work from other kinds of social work.

The third of these discussions occurred in 1959 when the Institute of Almoners asked for the Association's views on requests they had been receiving from Mental Hospitals for almoners. By January 1960 it is reported that as a result of discussions the Institute would not, as a policy, encourage almoners to work in mental hospitals as psychiatric social workers, but would accept advertisements for posts of medico-social workers in such hospitals. It is perhaps appropriate at this point to continue the account of relationships between the almoners and psychiatric social workers to the present day. After the publication of the Younghusband Report, a Joint Standing Committee was established with the Institute of Almoners and the Association of General and Family Caseworkers. This explored the implication of the Report for social work in the local authority and issued a useful memorandum on the subject. Partly as a result of this successful outcome and partly because of the long, if discontinuous, connections between the Institute and the Association, the Institute at the end of 1961 approached the Association with a view to joint consideration of a closer professional grouping between the two professions. This matter is now being jointly explored by the two bodies.

More general aspects of the protection of title are apparent in attempts by the Association to secure administrative and legal protection. The necessity for looking at ways of general protection probably first became apparent after the publication of the Feversham Committee. In July 1940, the Association considered the important fact that the report did not use the term 'psychiatric social worker', but referred instead generally to 'mental health worker'. This seemed likely to hinder the Association in its attempt to maintain professional standards. In October of the same year, some members expressed the view that the term 'psychiatric social worker' was not clearly understood in England. The matter was discussed but, as we saw in Chapter One, none of the alternatives seemed preferable. The Association took no general action until 1948/9, when a number of attempts were made to obtain some administrative protection. In September 1948 a scheme for appointing untrained workers under the supervision of psychiatric social workers was proposed by the Ministry of Health, and the Association decided that it would agree to take part in the arrangements on condition that the title of 'psychiatric social worker' was used only by qualified people. In the following year, the Board of Control was approached and informed that the use of the title by unqualified workers was increasing. The letter suggested that the Association was not only concerned with its status, but also with the fact that psychiatrists were finding it difficult to know if a 'psychiatric social worker' was trained or not. In September verified concrete examples of misuse of title were sent to the Ministry of Health and it was stated that the Ministry of Education had for a long time kept the title exclusively for the trained person. No definite undertaking was forthcoming from the Ministry of Health and the Association began to consider legal protection.

In 1950 the Association began to collect information on various methods of securing legal protection of the title. A Charter was considered; it seemed this would give some honour but little protection. An injunction could be taken out against a person wrongfully using the title, but this would require an obvious case and very good evidence. Depositions from well-known people would also be needed to prove the validity of the title and the value of the work. The cost would apparently be about £150. The Executive decided to approach certain doctors informally before taking any action. In February 1951, however, the question of proceeding by way of injunction was postponed until the Macintosh Report or for six months. Little seems to have been done until 1958 when legal advice on the use of letters after the worker's name was taken. This question was taken up in the following year by the Standing Advisory Committee, who suggested the use of letters and the keeping of a register. In 1960 a Register of Associates of the Association of Psychiatric Social Workers was created, and for the first time members were given a way of indicating both their function and training. This register will not prevent unqualified workers from calling themselves psychiatric social workers but if the letters (A.A.P.S.W.) are widely used by qualified psychiatric social workers it will provide an easy way of distinguishing the trained from the untrained.

NOTES

[1] See, e.g., 'The Organization of Social Workers', *Charity Organisation Review*, No. 256, New Series, April 1918, which refers to a conference held in 1917 at the London School of Economics. As a result of this a Provisional Committee was established, representing 'both voluntary and professional social workers'. This Committee considered that social workers should form themselves into groups in accordance with the work they did and 'these groups should discuss and decide their own particular problems, and make what regulations, demands, and suggestions in regard to training, salaries, and general conditions of employment as they think fit.'

[2] Younghusband E., *Social Work in Great Britain* (1951), p. 39.

[3] Chambers R., 'Professionalism in Social Work', Appendix II in Wootton B., *Social Science and Social Pathology*, 1959.

[4] *Annual Report of Association of Psychiatric Social Workers*, 1939.

[5] Younghusband E., 'Forward to 1903', *Social Work*, Vol. 10, No. 3, July 1953.

[6] Between 1937 and 1955, eight of the nine Presidents of the Association were drawn from the field of psychiatry, and the exception (Miss Darwen)

had been associated with the administration of the mental health services. Since 1955 and in a much shorter space of time Presidents have included Professor R. Titmuss and Mr. Kenneth Robinson, M.P.

[7] This is a useful subject for research. A recent study of therapists reported a tendency for women therapists to be preoccupied with the assumption that their patients were typically passive, characterized in particular by positive dependency.

See Chance E., 'Mutual Expectations of Patients and Therapists in Individual Treatment', *Human Relations*, Vol. X, No. 2.

[8] For some brief historical reflections on the branch see Brown M. A., 'Psychiatric Social Work in the North of England', *British Journal of Psychiatric Social Work*, No. 10, October 1954.

[9] The vocabulary of social work is, of course, full of medical terms (e.g. diagnosis, treatment, etc.) and from the late nineteenth century the social worker has often seen herself as some kind of social physician. C. S. Loch, for example, writes in his diary, May 28th, 1877 of the friendly visitor who makes herself into a 'good physician'. Quoted in Woodroofe, K., *From Charity to Social Work* (1962), p. 136.

[10] Le Mesurier, A., 'The Duly Authorised Officer', *British Journal of Psychiatric Social Work*, No. 3, November 1949.

[11] Bree M. H., 'The Function and Use of Relationship between Client and Psychiatric Social Worker', *British Journal of Psychiatric Social Work*, No. 6, June 1952.

[12] *Ventures in Professional Co-operation*, Foreword.

Chapter Nine

THE PROFESSIONAL ASSOCIATION—
TRAINING

TRAINING for social work, after a period of relative neglect
from 1910 until towards the end of the Second World War, has
become a topic of general importance to social workers and some
interest for those outside the profession. It has been a continuing
and critical concern of the Association of Psychiatric Social
Workers since its foundation. The Association has always based
membership on a training qualification and is in this unlike other
professional social work associations, with the exception of the
Institute of Almoners. Unlike all the other Associations it has
attempted to maintain the quality of training both in regard to the
selection of entrants to the profession and also to the standards of
the university courses they followed. Indeed it is largely in terms
of a training policy that the Association is judged by critics and
friends alike. How has the Association defined its training problems and what has it done about them? An answer to this question
has obvious importance for a study of psychiatric social work, but
its significance is much wider. Social workers and others are still
asking what should be the content, methods and objectives of training, whilst those outside social work still wish to know what dis-
tinguishes the trained from the untrained, in theory and in practice.

The training activities of the Association can be divided into
four main groups, the protection of training for psychiatric social
work, the improvement and extension of such training, and
measures to establish and maintain standards.

PROTECTION

The Association has been limited in what it could do to protect training for psychiatric social work. The selection of students, the content of the courses and the decision about final qualification are all primarily university matters. It has, however, achieved a measure of protection largely by formulating and attempting to maintain common standards of training. This is, however, mainly a post-war development. Prior to this, the Association discussed and acted upon rumours and possibilities of a shortened form of training and attempted to maintain a training that would distinguish its students from the more traditional mental health social worker, on the one hand, and, on the other, the alluring psychotherapist. During the first decade of the Association's history a shortened form of training for social workers in the field of mental health several times seemed a possibility. In 1930, for example, a considerable amount of time was spent considering rumours of a proposed short course in mental hygiene. Information was requested, and the Association discussed the nature of the course, its likely effect on standards of training; it also questioned the idea that the demand for workers was in excess of supply. It was, however, decided to express no definite view on the subject. The danger of a shortened course was again discussed in 1935 in connection with a Child Guidance Council committee on the shortage of psychiatric social workers, and we have already seen the resolutions adopted by the Association.

This illustrates some of the early uncertainty about the future of the Mental Health Course and of psychiatric social work, and the Association considered at one stage taking up a strong position in regard to training. In October 1936, the Executive suggested that the Association should itself become a certificate-granting body, and in November a report was received from a sub-committee on the methods of the Speech Therapists, R.M.P.A. and the Women Housing Property Managers in granting certificates. The importance of co-operation with the B.M.A. was stressed in the Association's discussions. It appeared clear that the Incorporation of the Association was a necessary first step and the Association was finally incorporated in 1945. It has, however, never considered since 1936 the possibility of granting certificates itself.

The identity of training for psychiatric social work was largely worked out in the 1930's and 1940's in regard to the fields of psychotherapy and mental health social work. The question of identity which arose later, with the 'generic' movement in social work training (with the stress on the common core of social work in whatever kind of agency it was practised), posed a different problem and will be considered later.

The question of the identity of training in regard to other mental health workers was raised in the 30's and early 40's largely in relation to work with mental defectives. This work was seen over this period largely as a matter of providing supervision and the field of service had little enthusiasm of its own and a low estimation from those outside. The Association wanted, therefore, to distinguish psychiatric social work from this kind of work, while also arguing the sufficiency of psychiatric social work training for the general field of mental health. In 1931, for example, when a psychiatrist wrote to the Association expressing concern that more time on the Course was not given to mental deficiency work a defensive reply was sent pointing out that considerable time was given.

In January 1941, the policy sub-committee reported on the Feversham Report, regretting that no clear distinction had been made between the functions of social workers in relation to mental defectives and psychiatric patients. The committee stated that full psychiatric training was unnecessary for mental deficiency work. The general issue of the relationship between such workers and psychiatric social workers was raised again in discussions of evidence to the Macintosh Committee in November 1948. In February 1949, a meeting was held with representatives of the Mental Health Workers. One of these argued that mental deficiency should be given an equal status on the course with Child Guidance and Adult Work, but in the discussion the supervisors on the courses argued strongly against such a proposal. It was agreed that more mental deficiency training was needed for the senior worker and that, in view of the implications of the new Health Service, mental health courses should be extended to give more practical training in mental deficiency. This discussion in fact produced no results, but recent changes in the organization of the mental health services and in the status of work with mental deficients have changed this particular problem in training. Work with mental deficiency has now been given both status and interest through research projects,[1] and by the creation of a unified mental health service.

Training

The second problem of identity concerned the distinction between psychotherapy and psychiatric social work. This has already been discussed in terms of techniques, and we shall here refer only to training. The most important discussion of this took place in 1942. In July Dr. Hadfield wrote a letter proposing that a course be established to help psychiatric social workers and psychologists to train in therapy. This, as might be expected, was welcomed by some members of the Association, and the matter was referred to the Training Sub-Committee (established in 1941). A group was appointed to meet Dr. Hadfield, and their report was considered by the Executive in September 1942. 'The special function of the psychiatric social worker had been emphasized, and it had been pointed out that association with the proposed scheme might prejudice the development of their own technique . . . Dr. Hadfield drew attention to the shortage of therapists, and said as psychiatric social workers were already doing therapy in many instances this training would regularize their position in a way which would be acceptable to the medical profession.' In the course of discussion one of the senior members of the profession suggested that it might become necessary to define the function of the psychiatric social worker more clearly and she felt the Association should give careful consideration to this point. Dr. Hadfield's suggestions were not considered appropriate for psychiatric social workers, but further clarification of function was not pursued.

IMPROVEMENT

In its early years the Association, whilst defensive to outsiders about the training courses, was not uncritical and it has maintained a critical attitude ever since. In particular, members have shown concern at what they consider to be the short amount of time spent on the training courses, and have from time to time proposed an advanced course of some kind or another. The issue of a post-graduate or an advanced diploma course was first raised in 1941 when its consideration was deferred and finally postponed until after the War. In 1950 a Training Research Committee was appointed, but within two years its uncertain life was over. Interestingly enough it was not until the issue of the generic courses was debated that proposals for an advanced course were considered in any detail. There was a fair degree of unanimity that an advanced course should be made available, but few clear ideas as to how it might be established.

As psychiatric social workers have become more established their awareness of some of the limitations of training has grown as their work has extended to the direct helping of many disturbed and mentally ill people. Two factors in particular have encouraged them to turn to the idea of further training. Heightened awareness created by the training already available has enabled them to face any inadequacies in their own casework and higher standards of work have also made workers more ambitious to achieve something more than a superficial contact with their clients. Many cases in this field are highly complex and require considerable skill in diagnosis and treatment. To illustrate this statement three brief extracts from the records of psychiatric social workers have been selected:

(a) *Mental Hospital*
Client (aged 34) referred to the psychiatric social worker on discharge from hospital; she could not attend the out-patient clinic because of distance. She had been admitted after her third suicide attempt.

At the first interview client was depressed and aggressive. She said she did not know how she survived day by day. She demanded of the worker, 'You've got to make me feel better.' The worker suggested that she was looking for someone who would change things in a flash. This quietened the client who said she could only live for her father, since she was sorry for him because of her mother's nagging. Yet she hated him and could not bear him to show her any affection.

At the second interview the client arrived 55 minutes late for her hour's appointment. Worker explained that she had another appointment in five minutes and the client retorted that she might not come at all next time. She seemed relieved, however, when the worker said her appointment for the following week would be kept for her.

At the third meeting client seemed restless. She complained of feeling empty and asked about the psychiatrist at the hospital, saying she loved him. The client suggested she was wasting the worker's time since she could not say all she wanted to say. Worker suggested that perhaps the client felt she would suggest that it was not worth their while meeting. Client glowered at the worker but said nothing. The worker said that possibly the client felt that when she became fond of people, sooner or later they disappeared from her life. Client was silent for about ten minutes and got up to go. Worker reaffirmed the next appointment and as the client went she asked in an aggressive manner, 'I wonder how you knew', presumably in connection with the worker's comment about her feelings.

(b) *Child Guidance*
A boy, aged 10, was referred to the Clinic for persistent truancy; his father was undergoing analysis. The clinic psychiatrist decided to take the boy on for regular treatment, while the mother saw the psychiatric social worker.

First interview (after a social history had been obtained). Mother wondered why she was being seen; it was not as if she was the truant. Worker sympathized with her feeling, but before she could say any more mother had launched into an angry tirade against the school. The school was to blame—it was too strict and was always making her son do things he did not like. Worker suggested that the Clinic must seem like school to mother and mother replied 'I knew you'd say that. I must be more clever than I think'. The worker asked how mother knew and mother said it was the sort of thing her husband had told her his analyst said. Worker suggested they might talk about some of the differences between a social worker and an analyst.

Fourth interview. Mother told worker about a recent dream. Worker listened, but when she made no response, mother added a rather defiant 'Well?' The worker suggested that mother was wanting her dreams analysed like her husband's and was perhaps feeling she was getting an inferior sort of help. Mother got up and walked up and down the room reciting 'What are little boys made of . . .'

(c) *Community Care*
David first came to the notice of the Mental Health Service in 1956. His widowed mother had been sent by the Youth Employment Officer after she had called seeking help for him. She ex-

plained that he was 18 and had not worked for a year and had refused to go out of the house for a long time.

The psychiatric social worker visited the home. David complained of various aches and pains and wondered whether he had a weak heart or kidney trouble. He said he could not go out because he was afraid to face people. He thought of himself as a complete failure, but readily accepted that he might in fact be ill and agreed to see a psychiatrist after the worker had discussed this with him.

This mother was seen again in order to obtain a personal and social history. David left school soon after the death of his father and worked for a few months. He was made redundant after five months but found another job where he worked for two months. He then had influenza and from that point lost confidence in himself refusing to leave the house or even answer the front door. Mother kept him supplied with cigarettes and sweets from her own small earnings but felt she could not go on.

David was taken to the psychiatrist by psychiatric social worker. The consultant felt this might be the beginning of an insidious schizophrenic process or a chronic anxiety. He advised admission to hospital. David refused to enter hospital and the worker spent some time helping him to clarify his feelings about this. He felt going into hospital would mean facing people again—after some time he was eventually persuaded to enter.

In hospital David made rapid progress, but refused all contact or visits from his mother. Eventually he was discharged from hospital and given parole to find employment—he appeared extremely confident. He was offered a job and started work the following day. Three days later when the psychiatric social worker visited, David had been in bed all day 'talking to myself to pass the time'. He said he could not face people again and could not go back to work. He said he wished he was dead. Worker discussed these feelings with him and agreed to return to work with him to explain his difficulties to the manager. David agreed to resume work. He worked for four days and again retired to his home where he sat with the curtains drawn and the oven full on. He remained like this for a week and the worker contacted the hospital who agreed to his re-admission. Two days later worker called to get David to agree to enter hospital. He would not consider it at all but put forward various excuses from

'They do not know how I feel' to 'I don't want to get better.' Eventually after discussing his objections in great detail David agreed to enter hospital. The next day mother telephoned to say he had changed his mind and would not go.

These brief extracts will, it is hoped, show why the psychiatric social worker is concerned about further training (and indeed maintaining the standards of training already achieved). In the past it was never assumed that psychiatric social workers would be fully trained as the result of a year's course, but it was considered that training would be continued within the agency by means of support and guidance from the psychiatrist. However, such help has been available in very few cases and at the same time we have begun to appreciate that the help of a psychiatric social worker is often the only help available or accessible to many disturbed clients. To suggest transferring every such case to senior workers is unrealistic in view of the staffing situation.

Consequently, in July 1956 the Training Committee of the Association considered the establishment of an advanced course and suggested that the essential first step before an approach was made to a university was the demonstration that an appropriate body of knowledge existed. A group of members and social workers from other settings was convened, but its deliberations came to nothing. This was largely due to a fear amongst some of the members that too much theoretical study would somehow destroy a student's 'feeling response' and that too much theoretical speculation would take members of the group themselves away from the emotional realities of casework. In view of the importance of advanced training, this was an unnecessary and unfortunate conclusion.

Part of an advanced course would be concerned with training supervisors. The improvement of supervision and the gradual extension of facilities for good supervision has been the subject of some concern to the Association in the last decade.

This concern has been prompted by a critical awareness of the limitations of the existing provisions for student training within social work agencies both within the psychiatric field and in other fields of social work. The majority of training courses for social workers insist on practical experience within social work agencies as an essential ingredient of training but it has become increasingly obvious that the mere contact of a student with clients is not a sufficiently enlightening experience nor is mere observation of established social workers carrying out their functions necessarily rewarding. What the student requires is more direct teaching within the agency so that skill in handling cases is not merely demonstrated by example but encouraged by the prudential guidance of a student handling his own caseload. Obviously such supervision needs to be highly skilled, first and foremost as a safeguard to the clients involved and secondly because the supervisor must be someone with an informed intelligence able both to explain the validity of her judgments to the student and understand the difficulties of the student in appreciating and absorbing the implications of applied casework knowledge. The student is taught the general principles of his profession in the training centre, but he has to learn to organize his theoretical knowledge in conjunction with his own personality, for the benefit of his clients in the casework setting. It is the supervisor's job to help the student by a perceptive intrusion into his working experiences which will guide and improve his particular potential for casework.

There is another aspect of supervision also that must not be ignored. There are few caseworkers who would claim that as a result of their one year's professional training they felt confident or adequate enough to deal with every type of client or situation. Indeed, training is envisaged as the commencement of a period of learning that will extend over most of a professional life. Consequently, the majority of the profession would endorse any attempts to introduce or improve the quality of staff supervision.

The question of a register of supervisors was raised in 1957, and a questionnaire was sent out to members of the Association enquiring about their experience in this respect. This was completed by about 23 per cent of the Association (161 members out of 690). Of this 161, 33 had had no experience of supervising or being supervised since their own training; 12 were currently being supervised, while 116 had experience of supervising one or more of the four kinds of social worker listed. The Register was discussed throughout 1959, but no decision seems to have been reached; the project could not overcome the basic difficulty of deciding what body might keep the register and maintain standards. However, the Association began to organize and run courses on supervision (and on consultation), to help those already supervising and those who had so far no such experience. The Association has here begun to make an important contribution to training.

EXTENSION

It has sometimes been suggested that the Association has not attempted to extend training to other groups in the mental health field. In the Annual Report for 1959, for example, it was considered necessary to remark on the opinion 'expressed among some employing bodies, psychiatrists and medical officers of health, that the Association has deliberately restricted entry in order to force up salaries.' Has the Association in fact shown concern for the training problems of the mental health field generally?

In the first decade of its existence the Association was largely on the defensive. Its reaction, for example, to the Feversham Report was largely in terms of measures to secure the protection of the title psychiatric social worker. Such an attitude is understandable in view of the small number of psychiatric social workers and their uncertain standing in the social services. At various times in the 30's members of the Association could not find employment.[2] Yet the Association assumed that the social workers required in the psychiatric services would all ultimately be trained as psychiatric social workers. This idea was still operative in the early 1950's though it is the last decade that has seen the Association begin to adopt a more realistic policy, which attempts to make a contribution to the problems of the now greatly expanded mental health services. There are two interesting examples of attempts to do this—the first following the important Macintosh Report, the second concerned with a scheme of in-service training within the mental hospital service for unqualified social workers.

The Report of the Macintosh Committee was published in April 1951. This recommended amongst other things that the term psychiatric social worker should be restricted to persons holding a university mental health qualification, and that psychiatric social workers should be regarded as specialists in their own sphere. It explicitly recognized the position of the psychiatric social worker, in marked contrast to the earlier Feversham Report. It was, however, similarly concerned with the wider field of the mental health service and it is in this area that the Association took initiative. In June 1951, the Salaries and Conditions of Work Sub-Committee recommended that the Association should call an informal conference of the bodies mentioned in the Report in connection with the trainee scheme (par. 132). This was agreed, and the Provisional Committee (Macintosh Report) came into existence. This was a virtual continuation of events of the previous two or three years when the Association of Psychiatric Social Workers and the Association of Mental Welfare Officers drew closer together after the beginning of the National Health Service in 1948. In 1950 a Joint Standing Committee had been formed consisting of the Duly Authorized Officers, the Association of Mental Welfare Officers, the National Association of the Local Government Health and Welfare Officers and the Association.

The Provisional Committee (Macintosh Report) met until the end of 1953. Much of its work was concerned with attempting to secure the implementation of the Macintosh Report, particularly in relation to the training of mental welfare officers.

In January 1952, the Committee agreed to send a short summary of points to the Ministers of Health and Education. Their statement would be based on the following proposals for basic training for Mental Welfare Officers:—

1. There should be only two recognized trainings for professional social work in the mental health field:—full-time University training for Psychiatric Social Workers, and in-service training for mental welfare officers;
2. There should be a recognized training for Mental Welfare Officers with a national body awarding a qualification—this should be primarily in-service training;
3. Selection of recruits of the right personality was essential;
4. A basic training in social science suited to in-service training should be aimed at for all trainees after a preliminary five years.
5. There should be a committee comparable to the present informal meeting as recommended in the Macintosh Report to advise upon:
   (a) co-ordination of recruitment and training of social workers in the mental health field;
   (b) standards of training in the field;
   (c) selection;

Training

(d) how best professional duties of such social workers may be undertaken to meet varying social work needs in mental health.

By 1953, however, it was clear that the Ministry has postponed consideration of the Macintosh Report until the results of the enquiry into the Training of Health Visitors had become known. The Association was, moreover, beginning to realize some of the difficulties in joining a specialized federation of mental health workers in view of the new tendency towards a generic approach to social work. Once again the psychiatric social worker seemed to be pulled in two directions—the psychiatric and the social. Consequently, by November 1953 the Provisional Committee was dissolved, the Association feeling it could not continue responsibility for the struggle which the Associations of Duly Authorized Officers and Mental Health Workers would have to carry on with the Ministry of Health. There was, however, an implicit promise of continued support, and in 1956 a Standing Committee with Mental Welfare Officers was established.

Relationship between psychiatric social workers and mental welfare officers since 1948 in fact show that the latter have persistently tried to secure some form of general recognized training for themselves, and that the former have made strong efforts to support them. Psychiatric social workers have not in this area of interest appeared to be clinging defensively to an ivory tower. This attitude of concern for the service as a whole is seen also in recent discussions on the social worker in the mental health field.[4]

In 1957 the Association set up a Sub-Committee in Birmingham to discuss the problem of the employment of unqualified workers and to suggest how the Association might participate in some system of in-service training. This committee drew up a scheme of In-Service Training in the Birmingham area for social workers in the Mental Health Services. The Association approved the scheme in June 1958, and suggested that the sub-committee should continue to investigate the problem of the unqualified worker in the mental health field and proceed with the proposed pilot scheme. This, however, was brought to a stand-still when the Regional Hospital Board decided that they could not participate in the scheme until the Younghusband Working Party had reported. An approach to members of parliament was suggested,

199

but the issue was not pressed on the advice of an interested M.P. In March 1960 the scheme was taken over by local bodies, and the sub-committee was wound up.

These two examples—the Provisional Committee (Macintosh Report) and the Birmingham pilot scheme—show that the Association has not been indifferent to the needs of the mental health service. They also show that the comparative failure of attempts to make a significant contribution was due to factors outside rather than inside the Association.

The most successful intervention of the Association in the field of training was the inauguration of the trainee scheme, which was intended to increase the numbers of students on the mental health course and to provide an opportunity for them to obtain experience in social work before taking the Course. The aim was to encourage recruits to psychiatric social work by providing that trainees could be placed for a period of not more than two years in certain selected hospitals with a view to proceeding, if suitable, at the end of their period as trainees to one of the courses of University training. The scheme began in 1950, when the Trainee Sub-Committee first met in July to receive applications from prospective trainees and from mental hospitals offering places. By November 1952, 60 applications had been received from prospective trainees, and 42 had been accepted. The successful candidates were between 22 and 30 years of age. By this date 11 hospitals were taking trainees, having an establishment for 15. Of the trainees placed in mental hospitals, 12 had been accepted for training on University courses. By March 1956, 97 applications had been received, and 65 accepted, but of those accepted only 47 had been found places in mental hospitals. A total of 35 had been accepted on University courses (72 per cent) and of these five were in training, 28 had qualified and two had failed. The scheme, as we shall see, created several difficulties for the Association, and its maintenance and improvement over the years has involved the trainee sub-committee in a considerable amount of work. Yet the figures indicate that the scheme has been successful in attracting workers to university training in psychiatric social work, and also perhaps to work in the provinces and in mental hospitals. Of the 28 who had qualified by 1956, 24 were employed, 15 in adult work and 9 in child guidance, 15 in the provinces and 9 in London.

Training

The difficulties encountered in running the scheme have consisted in the Ministry's failure to give official approval and the gradual discovery of certain implications and side-effects of the plan.

Initially the Association hoped that the Ministry would support the Trainee Scheme, so that it could be promoted by the Regional Hospital Boards rather than the Hospital Management Committees, who might be less enthusiastic to the trainee coming on their establishment. However, in January 1952 the Minister postponed meeting a deputation on the recognition of the Scheme, until the position in regard to medical auxiliaries was clarified. By 1953 a policy of economy was in force, and in June the Minister informed the Association that he could not recognize the scheme. He was prepared, however, to write to Regional Hospital Boards, encouraging the use of trainees where hospitals had an establishment for more than one psychiatric social worker and vacancies were unfilled. The Minister was informed by the Association that they should be consulted when a hospital intended to employ a trainee. As a result of this correspondence an interview was arranged with the Ministry. Official recognition was still withheld, though the Association was encouraged to continue. The representatives gave the Minister particulars of the trainee scheme and a list of hospitals considered suitable by the Association.

One of the major complications over non-recognition concerned salaries. Originally the Association wished to keep out of the salary question in regard to trainees, beyond stating that their salary should be lower than that of the psychiatric social worker. Gradually, the responsibilities incurred by the Association in sponsoring the scheme were grasped, and the salary of trainees was discussed. In December 1952, for example, it was suggested that trainees would receive higher salaries if they were graded as assistant social workers. Yet the committee was reluctant to suggest this to supervisors; at that time the Association still envisaged a service fully staffed by professionally trained psychiatric social workers. There seemed to be, however, no reason why trainees should be in a different category from 'unqualified' psychiatric social workers. In a general discussion of the scheme in April 1956 the Association's representative on the Whitley Council faced the Executive with the dilemma of this policy. The position then was that the status of the psychiatric social worker was being threatened by increases in the salary of unqualified workers. Yet the Association, through its Trainee Scheme was sponsoring unqualified workers. However, the dilemma was not resolved and the Trainee Scheme continues up to the present as a way of helping the Health Service and the Universities with some of their recruitment problems.

The Scheme continues, but it has undergone several changes. Some attempt has been made to extend it to the other two fields of psychiatric social work, child guidance and the local health authority service. Of the 47 trainees placed by March 1956, only two had been alloted to local authorities. The placement of trainees, in child guidance clinics proved even more difficult. In 1952 the Branches were asked to consider the possibility of employing trainees in Child Guidance Clinics, but the response was not encouraging, even though the matter had been raised in a forceful manner during the general discussion on the Macintosh Report. A member of the Association, who was also a member of the Macintosh Committe, commented on the disappointment of some members at the insufficient mention of Child Guidance in the Report. This, she argued, was largely due to the failure of the Association to mention the possibility of trainees in child guidance in its evidence. In fact, workers with only a social science qualification were being used in the clinics, so perhaps there was a need to revise ideas about trainees. By 1957 two Child Guidance placements had been offered, but, as the Annual Report noted, neither attracted a trainee that year.

The most obvious change in the Scheme since its beginning has been in the attention given to the supervision of trainees. In September 1952, the Trainee Sub-Committee considered the selection of supervisors, and recommended to the Executive that a supervisor of trainees should have had two years experience as a psychiatric social worker, of which one should have been in the hospital she was at present serving, unless it had a well-established social work department. The Sub-Committee stated that the only available evidence of the suitability of hospitals for trainees was the opinion of the psychiatric social workers on the spot; no other method of approving hospitals could be found. The inauguration in 1952 of meetings of supervisors of trainees proved an important development, and further useful changes came about

Training

as a result of a meeting in 1954 of ex-trainees who had qualified as psychiatric social workers. In 1955 it was decided that trainees should be visited by a member of the Sub-Committee during their placement and be encouraged to ask for advice. In the following year, as a result of a questionnaire sent to ex-trainees, it was decided to assign to each trainee an experienced psychiatric social worker in the area to act as counsellor, and to be available to the supervisor also if she wished. This was an attempt to combat a feeling of isolation on the part of both trainee and supervisor which had been revealed by answers to the questionnaire. This feeling can partly be explained by geographical factors, but it is also true that the trainee scheme, in spite of considerable success, has attracted little status within the Association.

STANDARDS OF TRAINING

The Association never seems to have taken any initiative in the establishment of new courses of training for psychiatric social work, and its policy has been extremely cautious. However, it came to appreciate during the War the importance of maintaining standards in the likely event of new centres of training being started. It was suggested that a common examining body be established, but the Association decided eventually to pursue a policy of recognizing new courses as they arose.

Such a policy was, of course, likely to encounter difficulties. Training for the profession was carried on in University departments, and issues like that of 'recognition' of such training by a professional body (small and lacking the status of older professional organizations) were bound sooner or later to cause problems. The first difficulty encountered was concerned with the problems of prior consultation. In March 1944 a file of correspondence was received by the Association concerning the proposed course for training psychiatric social workers at Edinburgh University. This was the first official intimation received and, because it involved the first 'break-away' in training, it created some disturbance among the Executive. It was difficult to appreciate the problems of protocol within a university met by any individual department wishing to install a new course of training. However, the Executive, relying, as it often did in the 30's and early 40's, on the advice of those of its members already associated with the training course, took pains to ensure that good relations were maintained between Edinburgh University and the Association. In June the training Sub-Committee, having seen the syllabus of the proposed Scottish Course, recommended that interest be expressed and the importance of training stressed, since membership of the Association was on a training basis and it was hoped to extend it to workers trained in Scotland. The difficulty of providing adequate facilities for field work training in Scotland was mentioned. The Course began in spite of difficulties (the tutor of the course was also supervisor for the work of students with adult patients) but the Association decided to take no further action until February 1946, when the Course was recognized.

More action was taken by the Association at the beginning of the course at Manchester, though the first idea members had of this course was through seeing an advertisement for a tutor. The University was approached, and a memorandum (drawn up by the tutor on the L.S.E. Course and agreed by Edinburgh) on basic requirements was sent. One of the points at issue concerned the desire of Manchester to place psychiatric social worker students in such fields as blind welfare. The Association declared that it was not opposed to new developments, but emphasized that salary negotiations were conducted on the understanding that members of the Association had certain qualities amongst which sound clinical training should be included. The Course was in fact organized on very much the same lines as the existing trainings and was recognized by the Association in September 1947.

The nature of the 'recognition' is not easy to define. The Association is inevitably concerned with training because of the basis of its membership and yet training is given on University courses run by bodies independent of the professional association. The implications of this tension have only gradually been appreciated. In June 1947, the general question of recognition of new courses was discussed. It was agreed that a minimum standard should be laid down, and the memorandum drawn up between L.S.E. and Edinburgh should be used for this purpose with certain amendments. A memorandum on these points was agreed in July. The most important points in this were:

'Training for psychiatric social work should be regarded as a specialized branch of training for social work . . . Preference should be given to those who have reached the age of twenty-four and have already been employed as social workers.'

'A reasonable minimum period of time for casework training in each of the two main branches of work has been found to be 60 days spread over three or four months . . . Theoretical teaching should include the subjects of general and developmental psychology; psychiatry, related both to children and adults (including mental deficiency); physiology; relevant law and social administration, and its historical background; principles and methods of psychiatric social work; social aspects of the mental health services.'

It was not until 1954 that the general nature of 'recognition' was discussed and in May of that year the Training Committee was asked to reconsider its terms of reference. In July the Committee proposed that a Standing Committee on standards of training should be appointed. This was to be a more formal and independent body than a sub-committee, and to have the limited but important functions of considering standards of training, and advising the Association on the recognition of the qualification of candidates from new courses and on the maintenance of standards on existing courses. In August the terms of reference of the new body were considered. At the same meeting comments on a proposed new course of training for psychiatric social workers illustrate the importance of the maintenance of standards. The proposed course made no reference to obligatory casework experience before admission; the examination could be taken with the student having had no experience in adult work; and there were difficulties in providing adequate fieldwork facilities.

The creation of the Standing Advisory Committee on Training for Psychiatric Social Work has certainly placed the recognition of courses on a formal basis, and the visitation of courses by members of this Committee have often been the occasion of helpful discussion between the Profession and the University department. However, there was still doubt after the Committee had begun its work about what exactly was being recognized. For example, the General Purposes Committee in April 1955 discussed a letter enquiring if the . . . course is recognized. 'It was suggested that in the reply to this letter it should be explained that the A.P.S.W. does not recognize training courses but that students who have finished an established course are recognized as members of the A.P.S.W. The . . . course is therefore still under consideration and it was suggested that meanwhile students from . . . should attend the three recognized courses'. This difficulty is further illustrated by the Executive Minutes of April 30th, 1955. The question here raised is of the possibility 'of accepting' a course temporarily, subject to subsequent review. 'This decision had been reached as there were not very clear grounds on which the Association could turn down the course—it was largely a question of the quality of supervision. The Standing Advisory Committee now proposed to study this question and draw up a document, which would have to be approved by the general membership, giving guidance on the selection of supervisors.'

The attempt by the Association to define and maintain standards of training raises two important questions; how effective has the Association been and what significance has the attempt in the evolving relationship between the University and the Professional Organization?

Undoubtedly, the fact that existing courses for psychiatric social workers teach a common fieldwork and academic syllabus (as we saw in Chapter Two) is due, to a considerable extent, to the activities of the Association. The maintenance of a minimum standard, particularly in regard to supervised fieldwork, has been much more difficult. The Association has been most successful when it has offered, and the University has been able to accept, an advisory service. This has been particularly so in the case of those university departments who have been able to consult the Association at an early stage in their own consideration of the possibility of training psychiatric social workers.

The issue of the recognition of courses established and run by the Universities is complex: the Universities are anxious to preserve their independence of judgment in regard to the students selected, the subjects taught and the teachers appointed. Yet it is sometimes forgotten that the traditional functions of a University have been intimately connected with training for the professions and there seems no reason for distinguishing between the well-established professions and the new professions emerging in our new society. Not only is it difficult to make, let alone maintain, this distinction on logical grounds, there are good reasons for arguing that training for such emerging professions as social work should become an accepted and full part of the University's task, rather than a not entirely respectable sideline. Such training should be given in a University both because of the growing influence of the newly developing professions on the ways in which our culture is maintained, transmitted and transformed and also because these professions are becoming increasingly dependent on the theoretical knowledge and research which the Universities should be concerned to promote. If it is admitted that training for social work is a legitimate part of a University's task, then some kind of partnership with the professional organizations seems indicated. In training for the new professions, Universities will often not have the specialized knowledge and developed judgment necessary for this unfamiliar task, nor any clear ideas about adequacy of standards in such new subjects as supervised fieldwork. It is likely that the relationship between the University and the new professions will find expression in formal machinery, and it is this which sometimes seems an affront to university autonomy. Yet the professions are often seeking through formal procedures the kinds of safeguard in relation to the definition and maintenance of standards which are already in force in training for the older professions through informal and less obvious means.

It is within this broader context that the work of the Association should be seen. The issues involved have not been faced either in the Universities or amongst social workers generally. The Institute of Almoners has attempted to express a judgment on the suitability of particular social science courses as a basis for almoners' training, and found considerable difficulty in actually making recognition depend on certain objective standards, and in withdrawing 'recognition' once it had been given. It has, however, not attempted this kind of formal appraisal in regard to professional training, nor does it review its own training in the way the Standing Committee of the Association 'recognizes' and reviews all training for psychiatric social work. In this sphere the Association has at least attempted to shoulder its professional responsibilities. Opinions on its success or failure may differ, but it has at least seen the importance of the question and tried to do something to answer it.

If the Association is to achieve co-operation and respect in regard to this function, however, at least one important change is desirable. Means must be found whereby the work of the Standing Advisory Committee can be made more open to public scrutiny, so that it can be seen to be based on reasonable criteria used in a responsible manner. Obviously, much of the detail must and should remain confidential, but the work of the Committee will be respected if its basis and the intention of its operation are clear. This can be achieved—to the extent required—in two ways: by the clarification of the criteria used in deciding on the suitability of courses and by inviting observers from outside the profession to attend meetings of the committee, (for example, from the Royal Medical Psychological Association and possibly the Ministries of Health and Education).

A new and important feature of standard-setting emerged when the Association began to consider training other than that for psychiatric social work towards the end of the 1940's. The Association started by examining the social science diploma as a basic training in social work. Before this the Association had been almost exclusively concerned with training for psychiatric social work as such and with the real and imaginary attacks upon it. Two factors are responsible for this interest in the social science diploma. Firstly, in 1947 the British Federation of Social Work proposed the formation of an Institute of Social Work. Secondly, the Association was beginning to give realistic consideration to the shortage of qualified social workers in the mental health field. This was leading members to the view that more stress should be laid on the need for a basic training in general social work. The proposal in 1948 that a trainee scheme be inaugurated lead the Association to consider the content of the diploma courses with a view to broadening and expanding them as a basic training for general social workers and thus increasing the equipment and capacity of future candidates for Mental Health Courses. Three issues were involved in this approach to the problem, the nature of the social science courses, the necessity for basic training for social work, and the extent to which such training might prove something more than an introduction to, or preparation for, psychiatric social work.

The Association certainly acted on the view that the social science courses were badly designed as training courses. This was understandable at the time, and it is certainly arguable that at the present time Universities may be abandoning the two year social science diploma too hastily, without considering the possibility of its reorganization. The Association spent a considerable amount of time and energy in discussions of the two year diploma. In October 1948, for example, the Training Committee of the Association and the Institute of Almoners considered an 'ideal' syllabus for psychology in the Social Science Course. The following suggestions were made:—

(a) Course should include psychology of human relationships, starting with family relationships and widening out into social and industrial relationships;

(b) Lecturers should be people who were in touch with clinical material of their own;

(c) There was general criticism of the present social science courses, and a feeling that they should be radically changed to meet the needs of the new services. At a joint meeting with the Mental Health Workers in February 1949, it was agreed that as a long term policy all Mental Health workers should have a basic social science training, which assured that there would be more adequate casework training and more emphasis on the psychological aspects of human relationships and behaviour.

However, the most important issues in training that faced the Association were those connected with the movement for an improved professional education for social work, which began soon after the war and out of which grew the new 'generic' courses. As the movement developed three distinct ideas can be identified, but it was difficult at the time to appreciate which of the three was being discussed on any one occasion. The first concerned the improvement of the social science diploma as a basic qualification for most forms of social work. This had been a perennial concern of the British Federation of Social Workers. The second involved the inauguration of a year's course of training in social casework and the third that such a course would replace existing University professional training for social work. In the early 1950's the Association considered the first and second ideas, but it did not become apparent until 1953 that the discussion in general social work circles had moved on to the third.

The reactions of the Association to these changing ideas are of interest. First and foremost, stress was laid on the importance of preserving standards. In December 1950, the Training Committee was asked to discuss proposals for a basic training in casework submitted by the Association of Family Caseworkers in conjunction with other professional bodies. In 1951, the Training Committee reported that such proposals sought to build on a structure that was non-existent, and their alternative proposal suggested a social work training centre and special courses for training supervisors. This question of training supervisors was and is vital, but it seems as if the real importance of the proposals for a year's professional training had not been grasped. In the following year one of the founder members of the Association suggested that a small group from some of the main bodies with specialist training should meet to discuss the possibility of compiling a syllabus for the year's training. By the end of the year, however, only two members of the A.P.S.W. had accepted nomination, and the Training Committee was asked to discuss a possible syllabus with the help of these two members. In January 1953, their report was discussed. Much of it was taken up in discussion of the organization of an Institute, and the syllabus was seen to consist mainly in dynamic psychology and the principles of casework. In discussion it was agreed that the Association's wish to have the opportunity of establishing an adequate theory of casework should be expressed.

In March 1953, some of the confusion was revealed at a meeting of the proposed Standing Conference on Casework, composed of representatives from the social work organizations. The chairman of the meeting was under the mistaken impression that an agreed report would be sent to the Joint Universities Council, whilst others attending saw the meeting as a way of securing agreement amongst those present. There was an implicit assumption that a training in basic casework was to be an alternative to specialist training, and that to think of a lengthening of social work training was a hopeless aspiration. Only the psychiatric social workers and the moral welfare workers were opposed to agreeing beforehand to accept the proposals for a year's professional training common to all branches of social work. The representatives of the Association tried without success to begin discussion of the kinds of agency used and the quality of supervision necessary. It is clear that the Association was again seeking to maintain standards of training, but was failing to appreciate the new force at work in the formulation of training policies.

Training

The Association's views on Generic Training received more clarification when a memorandum on such training submitted by the Proposed Standing Conference on Casework was considered (September 1953). Stress was laid on the importance of a long period of supervised experience in one agency under the same supervisor, and because such facilities were rare it was conjectured that the number of students was likely to be small. Successful students on such a course would, it was thought, be at an advantage in applying for psychiatric social work courses, as the requirement of intervening experience could be waived. The question of possible modifications in length and type of existing specialist training could only be considered after such courses had been running for some time. The Executive made it quite clear that the present psychiatric social work training was too short, and 'therefore rather than give up this specialized training, they considered that the course in generic casework would be a means of raising the standard of training for psychiatric social work.' For the next few years the Association was concerned with formulating a policy towards the new generic courses. This was the most important single issue ever faced by the Association, since it concerned the identity of psychiatric social work, the continued existence of specialist training in this field and, therefore, the traditionally maintained basis of membership of the Association. Even so, it was not until 1955 that the Association began in earnest to discuss the problems involved.

The issues were difficult to grasp, and the Association attempted to look at possible differences between psychiatric social work and other forms of social work in terms of clientèle, of training requirements and of the actual facts of training. In July 1955, for example, the Professional Development Sub-Committee discussed the question of priorities in psychiatric social work with particular reference to the mental hospitals, non-clinical posts and a consultative service to other social workers. As a result of this discussion it was considered essential to make a clear differentiation between those cases that required specifically psychiatric casework and those emotionally disturbed people who could be helped by other caseworkers. It was thought that psychopathic clients could be more easily carried by non-psychiatric social workers, but the reverse was true in the case of psychotics. In these deliberations the committee were working on a number of different assumptions. They were viewing psychiatric social work as a special kind of casework (psychiatric casework) rather than as social work carried out in a particular kind of agency which had psychopathic and psychotic patients for whom help should be given through the means of, and towards the objectives specific to, that agency. It could, of course, be argued that the shortage of psychiatric social workers prevented help being given to all who required it, and that non-psychiatric social workers (i.e. social workers in a non-psychiatric setting) should be encouraged to carry those cases for which they were most suited. In such a situation some kind of *ad hoc* division between kinds of case has obvious attractiveness, but provides no help in a discussion of the basis of different training programmes. The distinction made by the committee, however, rested also on other assumptions, one important and valid, the other persuasive and dubious. The important assumption was that the psychiatric social worker could more easily carry psychotic patients. This was an assumption connected directly with training and function, since all psychiatric social workers had supervised fieldwork in a mental hospital as part of this training, and those who went into hospital work have been, as we have seen, increasingly concerned in face-to-face work with patients. This means that they have met, explored and tried to understand the fantasies of madness in patients and also in themselves. The second assumption in the committee's distinction was that work with psychopathic clients was less likely to produce change in the client or movement in the case, and was, therefore, less suitable for the psychiatric social worker. In some senses this appears a persuasive notion, along the general lines of using skilled help where it makes most impact, but, on the other hand, it obviously requires the maximum skill and the most subtle understanding to attain even small successes in the most difficult cases.

At a meeting in October the distinctive features of psychiatric social work were considered, and these were seen as work in a team and work amongst clients who had psychopathological conditions. Such a description could, of course, be applied to other branches of social work, depending on the definition of psychopathology. Consequently, when the committee came to discuss the distinctive features of psychiatric social work in relation to generic training, it is not surprising to discover a sharp difference of opinion. Some maintained that psychiatric social workers required more skill than social workers in other settings because of the complexities of teamwork in the psychiatric setting, the essential importance of psychiatric knowledge and the kinds of treatment carried out with clients. Others argued that the same knowledge of human development was required in all branches of social work since the clients of the probation officer, child care worker and so on were likely to be as disturbed as the psychiatric social worker's and that just as medico-social work was casework in the setting of hospital or local authority health department, so psychiatric social work was casework in a psychiatric setting.

Meanwhile, the Training Committee was no more successful in reaching agreement. This committee in 1955 compared psychiatric social work training and generic training. It was thought that the former gave more weight to previous experience in social work and placed heavy emphasis on psychiatry and psychopathology, whilst the Generic casework course emphasized the teaching of casework in clearly defined stages. Some members were in favour of a 'wait and see' policy, whilst others supported a swift move away from specialist training. This made it practically impossible to answer the question: do other social workers require the same skills and knowledge as the psychiatric social worker? The committee concluded: 'In the end this controversial question must be left on one side, no doubt to be considered many times in the future.'

In January 1956, the Training Committee compared statistics from the three psychiatric social work courses in connection with age of students and their previous experience. Having left aside the question of the skills and knowledge required in other kinds of social work, the Committee were approaching the issue along more empirical lines: were students on the psychiatric social work courses so very different from those who might be accepted on generic courses? The figures showed that since 1954, 20 per cent of the students at Edinburgh and Manchester were under 25, and 16 per cent at London; at Manchester 20-25 per cent of students were without previous experience in social work, 27 per cent at Edinburgh and, in the last two years, 7 per cent in London. We must remember, however, that the percentages refer to very small actual numbers of students.

The Professional Association

As a result of the deliberations of this and other committees, an Extraordinary Executive Meeting on 28th January 1956 considered two policies in regard to generic training. As a short-term policy it was proposed that any generic course with one psychiatric placement might claim special consideration, and in that case the course should be evaluated by the Standing Advisory Committee, paying special attention to adequate teaching in psychiatry; generic courses extended by six months in a complementary psychiatric placement could be acceptable as a membership qualification. It was decided to watch and study these generic courses in regard to age and previous experience, and to ensure that psychiatric social work tutors and supervisors on each course should be consulted on selection. For a long-term policy two suggestions of the training committee were discussed (i) The Association should work towards a two year training for psychiatric social work—students might transfer to second year of this from a generic year. (ii) an advanced University course for experienced caseworkers, from all settings, to give special qualifications to teachers, supervisors, administrative and research workers and other leaders in the field of social work. The Training Sub-Committee asked to consider further how the Association could work towards (ii) and the Professional Development Committee was asked to arrange two general meetings on the whole issue.

Finally, in November 1957 the Association's Working Party on Generic Courses reported to the Executive and their resolution was later passed by a general meeting, that for an experimental period of five years a generic course (with one psychiatric placement), followed by an additional complementary psychiatric placement of four months, would qualify students for membership of the Association, subject to certain safeguards. These safeguards were that the generic course should be in accordance with the standards laid down in the Association's Memorandum on Training, that selection of students should be on the basis of suitability according to the Memorandum, that theoretical work should be as detailed in the Memorandum, that supervision in psychiatric placements should be carried out by psychiatric social workers. This is, in fact, the present basis of policy in regard to generic courses and a number of such courses have applied for recognition, the first being Southampton in February 1958.

Training

This issue has been followed in some detail because of its importance for the Association and the Association's reputation. Psychiatric social workers have earned the reputation of standing against the mainstream of development towards a common training for all branches of social work. Is this reputation deserved and if so what was and is really at stake?

Historically, the slowness of the Association to grasp the challenge of generic training, should cause no surprise. There is, as we have seen, good reason to look on the Mental Health Course as the first generic course. Students come from many different fields and, at the end of the course, go to work in many fields other than psychiatric social work. The whole basis of such training was that probation officers, almoners etc. came on the courses and either returned to probation, almoning etc. or became psychiatric social workers. It is, therefore, understandable that psychiatric social workers should see improved training in probation, almoning etc. as an improvement in the preliminaries of training on psychiatric social work courses. Training for psychiatric social work had, moreover, been a part of social work training in this country for a number of years, and the Association was certainly justified in hesitating to jettison this tradition and experience in favour of fashionable but untried projects. The question at issue for psychiatric social workers was not whether generic training would raise standards of probation work, child care, and so on, but whether it would maintain even existing standards for mental health work. For probation officers and almoners participation in a full year's professional training at a university represented a new kind of recognition but for psychiatric social work the 'generic' movement had of course no such appeal.

Yet, given these historical reasons for the Association's attitude, has the special position of psychiatric social work any present justification? Superficially, it sounds simple and logical to refer to all specializations as casework in particular settings. As probation work is casework in a court setting, so psychiatric social work is seen as casework in a psychiatric setting. Yet how far is this separation of casework from its setting possible save in a superficial analysis? It seems that in our initial enthusiasm for 'generic' training we tried to generalize about casework practice before we had sufficiently grasped and appreciated the impact of setting.

215

What are the features of psychiatric social work that might justify specialized training?

It does not seem fruitful to compare psychiatric social work with other kinds of social work in terms of difficulty. How does one, for example, compare the difficulty of helping a discharged patient keep a job with that of removing a child from his foster-home? Nor is it helpful to confuse 'psychiatric' with 'psycho-therapeutic', and maintain that psychiatric social work is some kind of therapy. It may on occasions be a form of therapy, but so is much social work in probation, almoning and so on. In fact, the 'therapy' of psychiatric social work has developed largely in response to one of the main institutional aspects of the work, day-to-day work with psychiatrists. It is the institutional aspects of the work which provide the most fruitful way of examining the specialization of psychiatric social work. The main features of the settings of psychiatric social work would seem to follow from the fact that the worker has been trained to work with psychiatrists in agencies carrying out community sponsored treatment of the maladjusted and mentally ill. In this work familiarity with the changing world of psychiatry is essential and has in fact proved the most important growing point for the clinical work of the psychiatric social worker. Thus, the psychiatric social worker has a place in specialized agencies, recognized by the community for specific objectives (treatment) in relation to a defined class of people. The agencies are of sufficient complexity to allow and encourage the social worker to made a distinctive contribution to the management of internal affairs, as well as the execution of policies in regard to patients.

This, then, is the field of psychiatric social work and these are its special aspects, which must be the concern of any training course which proposes to train psychiatric social workers.

NOTES

[1] See, for example, Tizard J. and Grad J., *The Mentally Handicapped and their Families*, 1961.

[2] As the Macintosh Report stated in connection with the development of psychiatric social work before and at the outbreak of the Second World War, 'Each step of the way had to be demonstrated by service. Anxiety over the future employment of each student in a group which before the war varied

in size from 11 to 25 had hardly passed when the very existence of the training was threatened, owing to conditions created by the war,' p. 11.

[3] See, for example, the comprehensive Statement on the Professional social worker in the local health and welfare services prepared by the Standing Joint Committee of the Association of General and Family Caseworkers, the A.P.S.W. and the Institute of Almoners, September 1961.

[4] The British Federation of Social Workers was founded in 1935. It was a small body aiming to represent the views of social workers in general. It was important for its aims rather than its achievements.

Chapter Ten

THE PROFESSIONAL ASSOCIATION—
PUBLIC INFLUENCE AND
PROFESSIONAL WELFARE

IN this chapter two contrasting aspects of the history of the Association will be discussed; the attempts to influence legislation and policy and the work of attending to the welfare of members. The Association began as a 'promotional' group,[1] concerned not with salaries and negotiation, but with advancing the cause of mental hygiene. It soon became interested in salaries, but the force of conviction placed behind negotiations was often weak. It took the Association many years before it could admit freely to being a 'sectional' group concerned with the economic interest and vocation of its members. Early discussions of methods of spreading knowledge of psychiatric social work were, for example, seen by many members as 'propaganda', and the dangers of such 'unprofessional' behaviour were stressed. Now the Association pursues salary negotiations with some vigour and a very high proportion of its members are members of N.A.L.G.O. Some of the older members consider that the younger sections of the Association are concerned only with the 'trade union' aspects of the life of the Association. It is to be hoped that these two aspects of the Association, the vocational and the sectional, can be combined, but any attempt to give them equal emphasis must be based on a realization of the ways in which policy and legislation are in fact influenced, and of the pressures brought about by the attempt to play the roles of 'reformer' and 'therapist'.

The roles of 'reformer' and 'therapist' in social work have recently been given some attention by Wootton and others.[2] Social workers themselves have made critical reference to the fact that they no longer participate in reform movements or 'carry the banners'. It is true that psychiatric social workers have given the better part of their time and attention to the establishment and operation of child guidance clinics, and hospital departments. These are not the sort of task to elicit large desires for radical social reform, and in fact such work emphasizes compromise, adaptation and a wait-and-see attitude. Yet the topic of the child has always roused the psychiatric social worker, and some members of the profession showed a continuing interest in the law relating to children which culminated in the nomination of one psychiatric social worker (Miss Clement Brown) to membership of the Curtis Committee in 1946. In this context reference should be made to Reifen, a psychiatric social worker trained in this country, who helped to shape the juvenile court system in Israel and to introduce changes in the law relating to children involved in sexual assaults.

A very few psychiatric social workers have been able to use their social work skill and knowledge in research which leads to proposals for reform. The work of Pauline Morris on the after-care of prisoners is perhaps a good example of this. In general, however, something in the nature of a split can be observed in the attitude of the psychiatric social worker towards 'reform' and 'therapy'. Reform, it is assumed is one thing and therapy another and usually these are the separate activities of two different people. Take, for example, the viewpoint of a psychiatric social worker writing of her work in a Borstal institute: 'I myself have come to feel, however, that a worker "inside" must start with an acceptance of the position as it now is: an acceptance of the present stage of social opinion and, above all, of the work of the people operating the system—having, in short, a caseworker's approach rather than a reformer's. Let us have reformers in plenty in administrative quarters but let us also have psychiatric social workers as colleagues of non-psychiatric personnel, willing to work with them at the point where they now stand.'³

Yet this kind of splitting has probably been a problem in social work since its beginning in the second half of the nineteenth century.⁴ We have seen that arguments about the value of knowledge derived from the social sciences are sometimes supported by reference to some supposed time when such knowledge was in fact fruitfully used. Arguments about the 'reform' function of social work sometimes receive similar support. What has received inadequate attention are the sources from which the social worker might derive a factual basis for proposals of reform, and the ways in which such knowledge could best be used in the support of the reform programme. To use a metaphor frequently employed in discussions of this issue, it is little good 'carrying a banner' if one is unsure what to inscribe thereon, and has moreover an uncertain idea of one's route.

A study of the attempts by the Association to influence legislation and policy shows some of the important problems involved in 'reform' activity.

The first topic which exercised the Association was the Children and Young Person's Bill in 1932. A letter containing recommendations on necessary standards for approval of places as remand homes and on the facilities that should be available for the examination of children on remand was sent to the Home Secretary, and simply acknowledged. The Executive then decided to collect data urgently in May from hospitals and clinics concerning children who had been charged with an offence and had been referred for study by the courts. The newspapers were to be watched so that an appropriate member of the Lords could be approached. By October the data had been sent but no reply had been received. In November, a member devised a questionnaire on the use of clinics by the courts and in January 1933 she reported that there were no insurmountable obstacles to the clinic examination of children brought before the courts. The possibility was explored of publishing her report in the Magistrate's Journal with the express intention of helping to change the attitude of the magistrates, but nothing further was heard of this. In June 1934, the General Meeting passed a resolution on the need for a central authority to deal with the placement of children removed from their homes. The Executive were to consider how to forward the resolution to the appropriate authority, but no action was taken.

The first subject in which the Association shows interest did not produce very satisfactory results. Attempts to influence legislation showed the Association not unexpectedly lacking in the sophistication of public affairs. It was, moreover, hampered by the smallness of membership and the delays consequent on monthly meetings. On the other hand, the Association had grasped an important issue in the operation of the social services and seen the necessity of collecting data and influencing, for example, the attitudes of magistrates. In this particular episode, however, resources were not equal to intention.

It was natural for the committee to feel some diffidence when, in October 1934, (only three years after the formation of the Association) the question of giving evidence to the Departmental Committee on Probation was raised. Members of the Executive wondered if the Committee would accept evidence from the Association and if the Association had in fact anything to say on the subject. By December the doubts were still unresolved and a sub-committee was appointed to consider the question. In January (1935) the sub-committee reported that the Association had information and opinion which it could usefully send to the Committee; in particular, views on the after-care of children discharged from Home Office schools, remand and observations homes, the training of adult Probation Officers, and the co-ordination of work for delinquents. The sub-committee was asked to circulate a questionnaire to the various clinics. In May a draft report from this committee was very fully discussed, and an amended draft was to be sent to the Clinic Social Workers, 'to be passed by the directors of their clinics'. Further amendments are made in July and August, especially on training. The Executive evidently felt the need for caution, and decided that training should be dealt with 'on very general lines', though they suggested the need for 'general social work training with practical work under a probation officer who has qualified in the Mental Health Course.' In March the document for the Committee was considered, but there was some uneasiness as psychiatric social workers had been reminded that they were not actually concerned with the courts. Evidence was, however, eventually submitted.

This episode is more successful than the first venture and raises a number of interesting questions. It took the Association approximately ten months to decide to produce a report and actually to compile it. When a reasonable draft was ready it had to be *passed* by the clinic directors. This illustrates the hindrances to the exercise of independent influences on legislation and policy, the deference of the psychiatric social worker to the clinic director at that point in time. Occupational subordination created a similar kind of dependence in professional activity. Moreover, the psychiatric social worker was conscious of being part of the child guidance movement. This had the effect of emphasizing the '*missionary*' outlook of psychiatric social workers so that they felt 'compelled' to give opinions on many areas of activity, even though their competence was not always obvious. On the other hand, the Association clearly saw the importance of training in other branches of social work and the part that could be played by those trained on the Mental Health Course.

Very near to the interests of the psychiatric social worker, of course, was the Feversham Committee on the voluntary mental health services. Two groups of psychiatric social workers were formed to prepare answers to the questionnaire sent from the Committee (October, 1936). In November, however, the Child Guidance group reported that the Association as such played no part, and it would be better to comment on reports of individual clinics. So far, however, individual clinics seem to have done very little. The Hospital Group presented a draft report for circularization. This was considered at the next meeting, but the child guidance group still had difficulty in getting individual reports from clinics, and eventually reported without them. In February 1937 six copies of the Association's report were sent to the Feversham Committee. The difficulty of collecting evidence for this committee was due, of course, not to the Association, but to the slowness of the individual clinics in presenting reports.

The Feversham Committee recommended the amalgamation of the four main voluntary societies connected with mental health and the creation of what amounted to an all-purpose mental health social worker. 'The training and qualification of the mental health social worker', commented the Committee, 'are very important... we recommend the appointment of fully-trained mental health social workers for all purposes, and not only for the service of a single branch . . . The course of training for mental health social workers should be sufficiently comprehensive to cover experience in all branches of community care, including the supervision of early cases of mental and functional nervous disorders, the after-care of mental hospital patients, the statutory and voluntary supervision of mental defectives, and the follow-up of children presenting problems in behaviour.'[5] There should be a single minimum standard of training and a national qualification corresponding to the training of psychiatric social workers. In this the Committee were not so much making detailed recommendations (such as were made in later years by the Younghusband Report), but expressing a hope for a future all-purpose mental health social worker. This was an important and progressive proposal, though the position of the psychiatric social worker was left rather ambiguous. How did the Association react to the Feversham Report?

The views of the Association were not finally formulated until early in 1941, but the conditions of the war years have to be remembered. In January 1941 the policy sub-committee reported agreement with the Feversham Committee's recommendation in regard to standardization of mental health social work, but regretted that the term 'mental health social worker' had been used instead of psychiatric social worker. It also regretted that no clear distinction had been made between the supervision of mental defectives and that of psychiatric patients and stated that full psychiatric training (i.e. psychiatric social work training) was unnecessary for work with the former. This cautious and critical response to an idea which foreshadowed some aspects of present mental health policy was partly a reaction to immediate stress and partly the result of an established policy. The immediate stress was due to the fact that training for psychiatric social work was very much in doubt because of the war. The policy was that of enhancing the status and maintaining the separate identity of psychiatric social work by emphasizing its difference from the supervision of mental defectives. Early in the life of the Association, members had had to decide if they would join with a larger group of social workers mainly concerned with defectives, but, as the first annual report of the Association delicately said, it was 'wiser not to risk a confusion'.[6] Basically, the Association was accepting the low valuation placed on social work with defectives at that time, though psychiatric social workers have since shown that when such work is more highly valued they can follow the pioneering of others. It was certainly understandable, and perhaps necessary, that psychiatric social workers should devote themselves to the development of a particular and characteristic way of working, but progress in this obscured the needs of some for whom it was *apparently* inappropriate.

The next important issue on questions of social policy concerned the proposals to establish a National Health Service. This has already been referred to, but is mentioned again because of its importance in the discussion of the Association's attempt to influence policy. To pass a general resolution in favour of the Beveridge Report was comparatively easy, but it proved very difficult to establish where psychiatric social workers stood in relation to the new Health Service. The question arose through the attendance as observers of members of the Association at the Health Workers' Council. This Council was formed largely on the initiative of the Socialist Medical Association, and its political flavour unsettled many psychiatric social workers. It was not until May 1944 that the Executive decided that it could see no reason to advise the General Meeting against affiliation. But this hesitation was part of a considerable incapacity to think with clarity and firmness about the possible place of the psychiatric social worker in the new health service. In March 1945, the Socialist Medical Association suggested that the Association of Psychiatric Social Workers should assist in the campaign to secure the new Health Service. It was decided by the A.P.S.W. that an approach to M.P.s was an individual matter, but the Association might write to the Ministry of Health, expressing views on questions of staffing and the general organization of Child Guidance clinics, with particular reference to the shortage of psychiatric social workers. However, it was found at the next meeting that there was insufficient agreement on which to base a letter to the Minister. The main resolutions passed by the General Meeting had, in fact, been concerned with child guidance—the psychiatrist should be in charge, the family should be the basis of treatment, and the clinic should be part of a comprehensive health centre. It was considered that only a general letter should be sent to the Minister in support of the White Paper. Further delay was inevitable when in January 1946 the Ministry asked for a memorandum on the place of the psychiatric social worker in the National Health Service and the Executive decided that it was not clear what kind of information was sought. In February it was decided to send a copy of the resolutions passed at the general meeting in May 1944 when the White Paper was discussed and to emphasize the importance of high professional standards of work.

This series of incidents illustrates one important aspect of the professional association as a pressure group. The membership of the Association is composed of members of all political parties and it is obviously difficult to obtain a general consensus on such a political issue as the proposed Health Service, and to press such an opinion in a political manner. Yet such difficulties seem to have paralysed any attempt to work out a professional policy on this important issue.

Most issues, however, have not this scale of importance. They could, perhaps, be divided into problems to which an administrative solution is possible and problems under consideration by the Government for legislative change.

As regards the former, we can see that from time to time a considerable range of anomalies are brought to the attention of the Association from a number of different sources. In April 1942, a small group of members were to contact psychiatric social workers employed on selection work at the Admiralty because of a suggestion from one member that commissions were being given to people with the wrong kind of personality, but this suggestion was dropped. In May 1942, the Association was asked to collect evidence for the Committee of the British Federation of Social Work on Rehabilitation: by July some critical comments had been collected and sent. In January 1943, a member wrote that the South West Branch had become very concerned about conditions in Day Nurseries. Discussions of this question showed a wide divergence of opinion. It was decided that no action should be taken at present, but members of the Executive were to watch conditions in their localities, and were reminded of the existence of the Advisory Service of the Provisional National Council for Mental Health. In December 1956 a member pointed out that if part of the cost of maintenance was recovered from patients in mental institutions who went out to work, the patient was often left in a worse financial position than before he went out to work. She wondered if others were finding that this regulation worked unsatisfactorily, and she was referred to another member for information. As the chairman remarked, this letter showed how frequently members did not know how to set about making contact with one another. In September 1957 the President drew the Chairman's attention to the proposed new regulations affecting child dependants' allowances under sickness benefit. The proposal was to stop such allowances after three months unless need was proved. The Association sent a letter of protest to the Minister.

The Professional Association

These random examples show the different sources from which anomalies and minor abuses are referred to the Association. They show also the different disposals that are effected. Some issues prove abortive, on others the Association does not have strong or detailed opinion. Some minor abuses appear to be purely local, others are bewildering and are lost sight of, and others result in a letter to the Ministry. How reasonable is this treatment?

It is at once obvious that the Association could not answer all the calls made for an expression of opinion, or attempt to remedy every minor abuse. Yet the operation of our social services is often clumsy and sometimes malignant and a way must be found of pooling information about such effects and of attempting to see that effective action is taken to remove them. The present attention paid to such questions by individuals and by the Association is clearly too haphazard.

The second kind of issue in which the Association has been consulted and on which an attempt has been made to influence legislation is the problem brought before an official committee or commission of enquiry. Since the Feversham Committee the Association has given evidence to a large number of enquiries: to the Curtis Committee on the Homeless Child in 1945, The Underwood Committee on the Maladjusted Child, the Ingleby Committee on Children and Young Persons and the Younghusband Working Party.

In considering the evidence given to these committees two general developments appear. Firstly, evidence offered seems in the earlier instances to rest on rather narrow professional concerns, or on a too direct transference from the situation of psychiatric social work to other situations. Secondly, the Association has become more aware of its functions in producing evidence for enquiries, more sophisticated in the presentation of such evidence and conscious of the need to follow up the report itself once it has been published.

Illustrations of the way in which evidence has reflected too directly the situation of the psychiatric social worker can be given from the evidence to the Committee on Adoption in 1953, and to the enquiry on the Training of Health Visitors. In March 1953, a member suggested that the Association might give evidence to the Royal Commission on Adoption. The Association decided to ask the National Association for Mental Health whether they could use any evidence the Association might collect. Meanwhile, however, the Home Office approached the A.P.S.W., and an *ad hoc* committee was established. In April there was some discussion as to whether the Association was in a position to give evidence at all. It was considered that any evidence would have to consist of individual case material, with indications of the complexity of the whole problem and the necessity for specially trained people. In June, when the evidence was considered in draft, some members pointed out that it was entirely from the point of view of the child. This was precisely the criticism made by the Working Party on the Training of Health Visitors when the Association presented evidence to them in June 1954.

The Annual Report for 1958 clearly recognized the importance of the function of collecting evidence for committees of enquiry: 'The collection of evidence for government committees and working parties has become a major part of the Association's activities in recent years. The time and energy which this involves proves very rewarding, not only because we often find the Association's opinions valued but also because it requires us to think more clearly. We have now had sufficient experience of the problems of collecting and co-ordinating evidence to draw up a memorandum for the guidance of future chairmen of *ad hoc* committees.' There has also been an improvement in the manner of collecting data. In 1955 a member who had given oral evidence to the Royal Commission on Mental Illness warned members of the great importance of clear thought and of the necessity to produce facts to substantiate opinions. This warning seems to have been heeded by the time evidence was collected for the Young-husband Working Party.

It is not enough, however, to give evidence, and the Association has grasped the usefulness of following-up both its evidence and the Report once it has been published. For example, the Association formed an *ad hoc* committee with other interested organizations to discuss the Underwood Report. In December 1957, the General Purposes Committee considered the circular from the Ministry issued as a result of the Underwood Report, and suggested that particular stress should be laid on the preventive aspects of child guidance and on the importance of consulting the parents before their child was referred to a child guidance clinic. In 1955, the Association gave evidence to the

Royal Commission on Mental Illness. As soon as the Report appeared, several members of the sub-committee which had drafted the evidence met and their findings, together with comments from a General Meeting on the subject were sent to the Ministry. The Association devoted the Autumn issue of the Journal (1958) to the papers presented at the General Meeting. Extra copies were printed, and a descriptive leaflet was produced to 'bring the Journal to the notice of administrators at policy-making level. In this way we are continuing the work started by the *ad hoc* committee which originally gave evidence to the Commission'. The enthusiasm kindled by reflection on the Report can be seen also in the response of the Public Relations Sub-Committee. This was formed in 1957, so that the work of the Association and its members should be brought to the attention of the public. In the Annual Report for 1958 this sub-committee stated: 'letters are useful to correct mistakes and misrepresentations, but letters are not enough at a time when we have a valuable contribution to make to informed public opinion. The Report of the Royal Commission has given us an historic opportunity, and we therefore support wholeheartedly the call to action by the Editor of the Journal and urge, with her, that psychiatric social workers should write articles for the daily and weekly press on the discharged mental patient in the community. It could be argued that it is our duty to do so; it is also in our best interest." Such calls to write, however, produced very little response and the Sub-Committee reported in 1960 that several other projects concerning publicising the work of the psychiatric social worker had not materialized.

Meanwhile the Association had shown a sophisticated reaction to the Younghusband Working Party. Evidence for the enquiry was carefully collected and clearly presented, and the Association called a Press Conference on the day the Report was published. Soon afterwards, a memorandum was sent to the Ministry of Health generally welcoming the proposals, and the Association joined with the Association of General and Family Caseworkers and the Institute of Almoners in forming a Standing Joint Committee to consider the implications of the Report for the three professions. More recently, members of the Association responded quickly to a call for information on the working of the Mental Health Act, and their replies were used as the basis for the opening of a debate in the Lords by the Earl of Feversham (4th July, 1962).

Reviewing the history of the Association's attempts to influence legislation and policy, certain general trends are apparent. The mental hygiene ideology, which was the original basis of the Association's attention to these wider issues, gave way to a greater concern with the identity and interests of the profession. At the same time the Association has become more versed in the ways of such methods of investigation as the Committee of Enquiry, and more aware of the importance of both having and declaring a clear policy. The problems of the 'gap' in a social service, of administrative anomaly and other side effects of the day to day working of the services remained, however, to be faced. On the whole, it has been the social research workers, rather than social workers who have called attention to the conditions in mental hospitals, the inadequacy of child guidance clinics and other failures in the world of welfare. The Association of Psychiatric Social Workers has become a more efficient and more conscious group, at times a pressure group amongst other such groups. Many in the population have, however, no group to represent their interests. Many such people are clients of the social worker. A way of ensuring that this interest is not neglected would be through action taken by the professional social work associations. The interests of the client, which might become those of the Association are those that fall outside the scope both of individual casework and of proposed or prepared changes of policy. Such interests have, as we have seen, come before the Association, but they have not been dealt with in a systematic way.[7] If this were to become a recognized part of the work of the Association, certain changes in organization would be necessary so that the protection of those who have no pressure group of their own would become a specialized function of one committee or group. It is certainly appropriate that the Association should consider this aspect of its work if 'It is . . . the function of a professional body to keep constantly before its members its own ideal of a professional worker. In doing this it should be our endeavour to avoid at all costs the worst aspects of professionalism which we are all quick to condemn in others. If we succeed in this, then the question of training, function and status will fall into place behind the overall purpose of providing a high standard of service to those who need our help.'[8] This is an important viewpoint, since the very use of the term 'profession' may encourage psychiatric social workers in the comfortable assumption what what is good for the worker is automatically good for the client.

This section has been concerned with tracing policy, but some brief reference should be made to the influence of individual psychiatric social workers. It would clearly be invidious to refer to such workers by name, but at the level of central government and elsewhere individual workers have not been without influence. This is perhaps particularly so in training matters concerning both psychiatric and other kinds of social work. The early development and continued expansion of training in the new field of child care, for example, owes much to psychiatric social workers in the central government department and in the universities. Individual members of the profession served on the Curtis Committee (the care of the deprived child), on the Macintosh Committee (social workers in the mental health services), on the Underwood Committee (maladjusted children) and on the Younghusband Working Party (social workers in the health and welfare services.

PROFESSIONAL WELFARE

A professional association is concerned with increasing the skill and furthering the interests of its members, and the welfare of any one group is consequently a wide topic. One aspect only has been selected for consideration in this section, that of salary negotiation.

Salary negotiation
The history of this activity of the Association of Psychiatric Social Workers falls into three periods. The first, from 1930 until 1944, was marked by the Association's hesitant entry into discussions of salary, and the gradual solution of some of the problems of dependency on the Child Guidance Council and on psychiatrists. In the second period, 1945 to 1955, the Association used machinery for negotiation established in the form of the Joint Negotiation Committee consisting of representatives of the employers of various professional staff (voluntary hospitals, local authorities etc.) and the professional staffs committee representing psychiatric social workers, almoners, public pharmacists, physio-

therapists and radiographers. In this period the Association obtained for the first time a career structure for psychiatric social workers, but the problems of negotiation in such a complex organization as the Health Service had been apparent for some time. In 1955, the third period began and the services of the National Local Government Officer's Association were obtained in negotiation and arbitration, and over 90 per cent of members of the Association of Psychiatric Social Workers joined. These three periods will now be discussed with the intention of emphasizing the main problems facing the Association in this branch of its activities, rather than providing a detailed narrative of events.

One of the objects of the 1929 constitution of the Association was 'To raise and maintain professional standards, and to encourage the employment of fully trained workers at adequate salaries.' The Association first took action in this field through the circularization of posts. This was originally a service provided through the Child Guidance Council, and in July 1931 the question of the minimum salary to be circularized was referred to a general meeting. In January 1932 the general meeting decided that only posts offering a minimum of £250 per annum should be circularized. In the same year two members wrote to the Association about the holidays under the L.C.C. Only two weeks summer holiday have been allowed because they were classified as clerical workers. The Association decided to ask the Child Guidance Council to take the matter up with the L.C.C. and the National Committee on Mental Hygiene. In October the L.C.C. replied that there was only one such officer on their permanent staff and that workers loaned by the Child Guidance Council had their holidays arranged by this body. The L.C.C. stated that they had decided to postpone consideration of the Association's views until it was certain that the temporary worker was to be made permanent. A reply from the Association was considered but by December it was felt to be inappropriate. This delay underlines the difficulties in the Association's situation. A small group of workers was caught in a dilemma; how could they safeguard the rights of existing workers without jeopardizing the future of psychiatric social work in the eyes of employing bodies?

This basic issue was more fully explored in 1934. In February an appointment was advertised in Warwick with a maximum of

£5 above the minimum scale sanctioned by the Association. One of the founder members suggested that the Warwick scale might become a precedent for other local authorities, and outlined the drop in salaries since the first child guidance appointments. At the following general meeting members wondered whether in the event of protests an untrained worker would be appointed. It was decided to attempt to arrange a meeting with the Warwick authorities and with the Child Guidance Council. The former did not materialize as the appointment was not proceeded with, but the Child Guidance Council was asked not to circularize posts below the Association's minimum. In May, the Association at the suggestion of a sub-committee on Conditions of Work appointed in January, held a special meeting on salaries. Two scales were suggested, one a minimum and one as an ideal aim. The first ran from £275 × £12 10s. – £350, the second from £300 × £5 – £420. Scales were to be uniform for London and the provinces. The Child Guidance Council was to be informed of this scale, and the hope was expressed that the next provisional loan service posts would conform, though the Association would for the present circulate posts at a minimum of £260.

Towards the end of the year, however, the Association seems to become hesitant. In September a special meeting of the Executive was called to hear the full correspondence with the L.C.C. and one of the founder members reported that she had heard much criticism of the Association's action, and underlined the dangers of a new short course of training being introduced. It is in line with this feeling that in November the Executive decided that a letter should be sent to the Child Guidance Council offering help to their sub-committee on social work salaries but in a way that 'makes it easy to refuse without embarrassment.' This followed an October meeting with representatives of the Council, at which some of the Council expressed a fear of the Association adopting strike tactics. These members of the Council were opposed to the formulation of any scale because local authorities had not yet accepted the necessity for a psychiatric service. They considered that some sacrifice on the part of individuals might be necessary. This is the kind of appeal which social workers used to find hard to resist.

In February 1935 the Child Guidance Council recommended to the Association that no rigid scale be adopted, but that two classes of psychiatric social worker should be recognized. These were assistants with a salary £225-£275, and seniors at £275-£400. The minimum salary had been calculated by taking £190 as an average salary for a social worker and adding two increments for the mental health certificate. In discussion at the Executive it was pointed out that £225 was lower even than the L.C.C. salary, and that the notion of assistant was ambiguous. The Association has, on questions of salary, always argued that the beginning worker was fully responsible for her own work. However, the Secretary stated that it was important to avoid further correspondence with the Child Guidance Council and a letter from a senior member requested that discussion of salaries be dropped. It was decided to write to the Council, but not to express an opinion. One has some sympathy with the Secretary who reported in March that she found it impossible to write without some expression of opinion slipping through. It was decided that, since controversy was to be avoided, the report from the Council on salaries should merely be acknowledged and a crystallization of the position thus avoided. It is interesting to note that in June L.C.C. posts below the A.P.S.W. scale were being circulated, and in October a 'diplomatic' letter to the L.C.C. was considered. In February 1936, the Association decided to take no action on behalf of psychiatric social workers employed by the L.C.C., leaving them free to take whatever action they thought desirable themselves. In 1937, there seems to have been some hardening in attitude towards the L.C.C., and in April the Executive decided that no L.C.C. posts were to be circularized, but at the following meeting the fear of antagonizing the L.C.C. was again raised. A psychiatrist known to the Association was to be consulted, and a General Meeting was called. A founder member expressed the fear that the L.C.C. might start a short training of their own. This fear proved illusory, but the Association continued to have difficulty in formulating and adhering to a consistent policy. In 1938 the Association decided not to circularize posts at less than £275 and to make no exceptions, but in 1941 the Appointments Secretary explained to the General Meeting that the L.C.C. posts which were below scale had been circulated because of their greater security and their higher maximum. Sometimes the Association successfully made representations to authorities, who then raised their scales, but in the absence of any general machinery, this was a matter for the individual hospital or clinic.

In June 1937, the Association circularized to members a Memorandum on the Salaries of Qualified Social Workers. This showed the salary offered at that time to those in full time salaried employment for which the Mental Health Course was regarded as an essential qualification; those employed by Public Bodies earned an average of £260 in the salary range £235-310, while those employed by voluntary Agencies earned an average of £291, in the range of £225-400. Those starting work with voluntary Agencies enjoyed a higher salary than their colleagues in public bodies, but after five years their salary tended to become slightly less. Moreover, very few of the private employees had any guarantee of permanent employment or were entitled to pensions. This contrasted with the conditions of employment in the statutory sector. Salary figures, however, mean very little unless they are used as the basis for comparisons.

In 1937 the majority of successful students could expect a higher salary after training. A small number had been faced with a loss of between 5 per cent and 25 per cent, but the majority had gained between 3 per cent and 57 per cent. The average salary after the Mental Health Course was 19 per cent higher than the average salary before. A more important comparison is that with other kinds of social work and 'kindred' occupations. The following are some of the comparisons made in the Memorandum: District Organizers, L.C.C. Children's Care Committees, £300-400; Health Visitors £250-300 or £200-300 or £280-450 according to different scales in different parts of the country; almoners £225-275; teachers (graduates) in secondary schools, London £264 × £12 to £420 and Provinces £216 × £12 to £380. This shows that in some instances the starting salary and the maximum are lower for psychiatric social workers, though entry to such work was tied usually to a minimum age and a minimum pre-professional qualification.

One of the most difficult tasks the Association has faced in the field of salary is that of the establishment of grades,[9] so that the profession could have a career structure. This was first considered in 1938 in two general meetings, September and December. The first proposal was for the creation of a second scale, £275-£450 for posts with administrative responsibility, but this proved difficult to define and in December such posts were defined as requiring either administrative responsibility or considerable experience. This question was taken up again in October 1944, when there was a General Meeting on Salaries. There was considerable discussion on the minimum of £275—would this attract social workers to take the Course, how did it compare with the salaries of other social workers or with the new scale for almoners? The minimum was very heavily defeated, and a new figure of £300 was carried. Increments were to be by £20 to a maximum of £500 for ordinary posts (which, it was pointed out, was below the maximum for psychologists) and of £750 for special posts. The principle of two grades was questioned, but carried. The posts requiring experience and special qualification were to have a scale of £400 × £20 to £750, but this was not settled finally. The commencing salary was to be fixed in accordance with experience not as a psychiatric social worker, but as a social worker. The question of the higher salary was discussed again in the November General Meeting and in January 1945 the higher salary was carried, though it was pointed out that it is high compared to hospital matrons. However, argued the majority, the profession had to compete for recruits and had to maintain its status.

The first period in the history of the Association's attempts at salary negotiation ended in 1944. By that date interest in salary negotiations as a proper activity of the Association had become more apparent. If the profession had to recruit in competition with other professional groups, then the salary of a psychiatric social worker would have to be made more attractive. Also there were legitimate status ambitions amongst psychiatric social workers. Yet what was the appropriate professional reference group? The profession clearly should possess a career structure, but how could this ensure a suitable reward for those in 'special' posts and what previous experience was to be considered relevant? If experience in social work before training was to be seen as relevant, was the Association not defining psychiatric social work as some kind of continuation of social work? These and other questions were posed more sharply in the second and third periods.

In 1945, the Association became a constituent member of the Professional Staffs Committee, consisting of representatives from the Institute of Hospital Almoners, the Guild of Public Pharmacists, the Chartered Society of Physiotherapy and the Society of

Radiographers. This body established permanent machinery for salary negotiations with the Joint Committee on Salaries and Wages representing the L.C.C., the British Hospitals Association, the County Councils Association, the Mental Hospitals Association and the Municipal Corporations Association. In October the Executive received the employers' offer of £320 × £20 to £460 plus £75 for extra responsibilities. A general meeting was called to consider this in December. At this meeting it was urged that the Association should not agree to any scale that would be lower than the Almoners. Members asked about the scale for teachers and suggested that their scale should be fixed in accordance with that of teachers or psychologists. The meeting decided against the offer, and pressed for a maximum of £500. The commencing salary was to be fixed in accordance with the worker's experience in psychiatric social work, but the employers were to be asked to recognize previous experience in almoning and teaching. The definition of posts of special responsibility created real difficulty. It was considered that this referred to teaching and administration, but what of the clinical worker? Was her position not thus undermined? Members asked if the tradition should be abandoned whereby in departments where several psychiatric social workers are working together none was considered senior to the others. The result of the demand for an increased salary was an agreement that from April 1946 the scale for psychiatric social workers would run from £320 to £480 with £75 for special responsibilities.

In 1948, when the Health Service came into operation, a Whitley Council was formed to deal with salaries for psychiatric social workers and other professional staff, including almoners, physiotherapists, occupational therapists, orthoptists, dieticians, etc.

In September 1948, the Executive suggested re-opening negotiations on the basis of £450 × £25 to £740, with a responsibility allowance of £100. There should be a minimum of a month's holiday, subsistence allowance and the consideration of experience other than in psychiatric social work when the starting salary is fixed. This was passed at the November General Meeting. The negotiations on this scale began, but in April 1949, the issue of 'special responsibility' had to be decided. It was thought that 'posts requiring a senior worker or posts in a department or clinic where there are not less than two other social workers' should also include a clause stipulating that the psychiatric social workers concerned should have had not less than two years continuous clinical experience as psychiatric social workers. However, the scales submitted were turned down by the management side. There was delay in the negotiations and in November 1949 it was decided to write to the Staff side pointing out that psychiatric social workers were starting at a lower salary than untrained workers, and asking that an approach be made to employers to discuss at any rate an increase of £20-25 above the £390 for untrained workers. The anomaly was, however, merely brought to the notice of the Staff side as the Staffs' side were anxious to press on with general negotiations.

It is indeed in this period that the problems of the untrained worker became most evident to the Association. Psychiatric social workers were now in a unified National Health Service, and involved in negotiations for national scales. For the Association there were two problems, the definition of the untrained worker, and the maintenance of salary incentives for training as a psychiatric social worker. Initially, the Association wished to make a distinction between the qualified and the unqualified psychiatric social worker. In 1949, for instance, the Association asked the regional psychiatrists to approach hospital management committees and local health authorities with a view to their distinguishing the trained worker as a 'qualified psychiatric social worker.' Gradually, however, it was realized that this kind of distinction implicitly admitted that the unqualified also was doing psychiatric social work, and this encouraged the claim made by some of the Management Representatives on the Whitley Council that salaries should be negotiated on the basis of the rate for the job. However, by 1953 agreement was reached that the untrained worker should be called a social worker in a psychiatric department.

The problem of the differential between the untrained and the trained can best be illustrated from an advertisement which appeared in 1950, which attracted considerable attention within the Association. This advertisement stated that 'preference will be given to a duly qualified psychiatric social worker or candidates with a Diploma or Certificate in Social Science, and if so qualified the salary will be £370 × £20 to £530 per annum, commencing according to experience. For unqualified persons the salary would be £480 × £15 to £525 per annum.' This illustrates two difficulties, firstly the fact that psychiatric social workers and candidates with a Diploma in Social Science are treated as equally trained, and secondly the way in which such training was in fact being penalized. The Association on this particular issue gained the public support of several psychiatrists, and action on the immediate problem was followed by an attempt to formulate a general policy, though the representative of the Association on the Whitley Council had to remind the Executive of the importance of this.

In 1952, the Association circulated a questionnaire to members on the position of unqualified social workers in their areas, and replies indicated that the 'training' of such workers (i.e. any non-psychiatric social work courses) was very varied, that the titles used to describe them officially were also varied, and that their salaries ranged from £300-575 (this maximum being £15 above the maximum for psychiatric social workers). By this time the introduction of the trainee scheme had complicated the Association's position, and it was decided that the unqualified should start below the trainee, but be able to rise to a higher maximum salary. The Professional Staffs Committee suggested that the unqualified should start three 'increments' below the psychiatric social worker, but the Executive of the Association countered with a suggestion of five 'increments' below, since psychiatric social workers had both experience in social work and a certificate. In 1953, a compromise was reached with the Professional Staffs Committee that those unqualified who were appointed before July 1948 should be paid the rate for the job, but that those appointed afterwards should be paid two 'increments' less than the psychiatric social worker. The eventual agreement on the Whitley Council gave the unqualified appointed before April 1946 a scale very near that of the psychiatric social worker.

Meanwhile the Association had been continuing its work of establishing grades within a career structure and seeking a basis of comparison with other professional groups. In 1950 a three stage scale was discussed—a basic stage; senior workers with two workers under them, single-handed posts and new pioneer jobs; a third stage where the establishment was for over three, research posts, supervisors of students or of other social workers. The following year a four-stage scale was submitted—(1) general grade, (2) single handed posts, teaching posts, senior workers, experienced workers who would develop a new post, additional qualifications (3) senior posts in a department with 3 p.s.w's or with supervision of psychiatric social worker students (4) senior teacher or senior post in a department with over three psychiatric social workers, trainees or social workers. In negotiation, the staff side proposed that the basic grade should be connected with a definite age, but the Association opposed this, wanting the rate for the job and maintaining that their scales were comparable to those of the almoners and not those of the Duly Authorized Officers. Towards the end of the year (1952), however, the Association felt it should be placed for negotiation purposes in the group containing psychologists, and the representative was asked to discover the sessional rates of psychologists and doctors so that they might be related to those of the psychiatric social workers.

In September 1953 it was considered desirable to reconsider the grades so that they could be brought in line with the psychologists who were able to have in the same clinic an overall senior, several seniors and some psychologists on the basic grade.

The scales negotiated in 1952 were not very favourably regarded by the membership, and the small increase in 1955 emphasized their dissatisfaction. Encouraged largely by an unofficial group of male psychiatric social workers, the Association once more considered the question of affiliation to a Trade Union, so that it might obtain the services of a skilled negotiator. This issue had been raised in 1948, when a member suggested that affiliation should be investigated with the Association of Scientific Workers, since the salaries of psychiatric social workers should be considered in relation to psychologists. This was held over until the interim report of the Macintosh Committee. After an investigation of the legal position, a referendum was held, but though the majority voted in favour of affiliation, the total number of replies was below the agreed figure of 70 per cent. The matter was dropped until 1956, when a group of male psychiatric social workers asked for a meeting with the chairman and the Whitley representative. They later submitted a memorandum pressing for a cost of living increase, and stressing the need to publicize psychiatric social work more actively. The Whitley representative

239

stated that negotiating was a very special skill, which could in her view only be carried out successfully by experienced Trade Union representatives. She reported that N.A.L.G.O. had a scheme of co-operation with professional organizations to which many of those represented on various Whitley Councils belonged. In return for 60 per cent affiliation of working members, the professional organization could have a seat on a joint consulative committee run by N.A.L.G.O. and arrangements could be made to help with negotiations.

The issue of a connection between a professional organization and a Trade Union is a matter of general interest; to many members of the Association it appeared at first an unprofessional idea. Some were in favour of a connection, but, still looking for parity with the psychologists, wanted this to be with the Association of Scientific Workers. What perhaps reassured many members was the extent to which the representative of N.A.L.G.O. most concerned with salary negotiation took the time to become acquainted with the work of the psychiatric social worker in child guidance clinics, hospitals and local authority. In 1955 membership of N.A.L.G.O. was recommended by the Association and over 90 per cent of the members joined.

That body then undertook the main task of negotiations and arbitrations for psychiatric social workers, and an agreement was reached giving a revised grading structure and a new salary scale for psychiatric social workers in hospital and local authority services, which was operative from 1st May 1955. This agreement provided, not merely a substantial increase in salaries, but also an assurance of a main career grade for psychiatric social workers working without professional supervision who could not hope or did not wish to become heads of departments. There is no doubt that this agreement was assisted by the recommendations of the Macintosh Committee, which drew attention to the low salaries paid to psychiatric social workers.

Further negotiations took place within the Whitley Council with the result that there were further increases on the 1955 agreement in 1957, 1958 and 1959.

In 1961 the Association of Psychiatric Social Workers and N.A.L.G.O. considered the recommendations of the Younghusband Committee, which again drew attention to the low level of salaries for psychiatric social workers as compared with those of unqualified social workers and social welfare workers in Local Government and other public services, and a claim was made on the basis of these comparisons by the Staff Side of the Whitley Council. The claim was rejected by the Minister of Health who at that time was acting upon a Cabinet decision that increases in pay should be regulated by the pay pause policy of the Government and that increases in pay for psychiatric social workers should not therefore be more than $2\frac{1}{2}$ per cent. This policy was opposed by the Staff Side, and the issue was eventually taken to the Industrial Court on the 18th May, 1962. The Ministry of Health spokesman of the Management Side urged the Court to make an award consistent with Government policy. In the event the Court made an award operative from 1st April, 1962, which increased the pay of the psychiatric social workers by 13 to 14 per cent.

In 1962, how does the salary of the psychiatric social worker compare with that of his or her colleagues in the social services or in kindred occupations? Taking 1951 as the year of comparison, the starting salary of the qualified psychiatric social worker at the age of 27 has risen from £420 to exactly double by 1962. Comparing this with the fields of teaching, probation and clinical psychology, only the probation officers have received a higher percentage increase, though their starting salary (at age of 22) is much lower (it was £305 in 1951 and £625 in 1962). The male graduate teacher had a higher starting salary than the psychiatric social worker in 1951 (£471), but a lower one in 1961, though he would begin his teaching career at an earlier age than 27. The gap between the salary of the psychiatric social worker and that of the clinical psychologist has been considerably reduced during the period. The salary of a clinical psychologist at the age of 27 in 1951 was £580 and £860 in 1962 (an increase of 48 per cent). A similar reduction is observable between the senior grades of the two professions. The maximum of a senior psychiatric social worker in 1951 was £725 and in 1962, £1,310; for a senior clinical psychologist the figures were respectively £1,170 and £1,500.

The main problems facing the Association in this field have been fairly simple, though their solution has taken time and involved considerable difficulties. They have been concerned with obtaining a career structure that satisfied those in clinical practice and recognized the special claims of those with teaching responsibilities or in posts carrying special responsibility. Secondly, the work of the psychiatric social worker had to be set in some context so that both the career structure and the claims for higher salary could be supported in terms of parity with some other field of work. Thus, the question of salary negotiation raises once more the question of the identity of psychiatric social work, since one of the basic questions in this field has been what other professional group are psychiatric social workers like. In salary negotiation comparison has been made with other qualified social workers (e.g. almoners), with psychologists and teachers, but the emphasis at present is on abandoning the policy of linking the salaries of psychiatric social workers with those of psychologists and exploring a common scale for all qualified social workers. Thirdly, the Association has been concerned with the salaries of the untrained social worker in the mental health field. Initially the psychiatric social workers expected that the health service would one day be staffed by trained psychiatric social workers, and therefore the problem was largely one of maintaining incentives for training. Now they feel much less threatened by the untrained, and the present attitude is perhaps well represented by the Executive's reaction when the North Eastern branch in 1957 pointed out that a rise in salary for psychiatric social workers was usually followed by a rise in local authority scales, thus re-creating the invidious position of the former in relation to the latter. The Executive suggested that members should not begrudge mental welfare officers their new salary in view of their heavy responsibilities.

NOTES

[1] The terms 'promotional' and 'sectional' are taken from a recent classification of pressure groups. See McKenzie R. T., 'Pressure Groups and the British Political Process', *Political Quarterly*, Vol. 29, 1958.

[2] See e.g. papers on Reform and Therapy by Donnison, D. V., Brown M. A., Bantock G. H., in ed. Halmos P., *Moral Issues in the Training of Teachers and Social Workers*, Sociological Review Monograph No. 3.

[3] Harrington M., 'Psychiatric Social Work in a Borstal Institution', *British Journal of Psychiatric Social Work*, No. 4, October 1950.

[4] See e.g. editorial in *Charity Organisation Reporter*, Vol. X, No. 406, December 1881: 'The kind-hearted almsgiver experiences a shock that can

never be forgotten when . . . he discovers it is his duty to leave a great part of those miseries alone . . . The almsgiver . . . watching the great multitude, the unskilled masses of the cities, as they strive, with a dumb despairing patience, against the seemingly inevitable miseries of their lot. With the struggle itself he cannot interfere; he can only wait for some stray case that, by reason of some exceptional circumstance, is swept within the reach of his succouring arm; or he can go apart from the actual strife, and study the causes that produce it, with a view to their gradual abatement and removal.'

[5] Ministry of Health, Departmental Committee on the Voluntary Mental Health Services, 1939 (Feversham Report), p. 206.

[6] *Annual Report*, 1937.

[7] One kind of systematic attention to problems arising in the course of work can be seen in the investigation in 1951 by the psychiatric social workers of the North West Metropolitan Region into difficulties in placing severely disturbed children. This was submitted to the Advisory Committee on Psychiatry and the workers were asked to make another enquiry.

[8] *Annual Report of the Association of Psychiatric Social Workers*, 1959.

[9] The grades operative at various times and the salaries awarded can be seen from Table I.

Table I: Salaries of Psychiatric Social Workers, 1948–62: Authorization and Date

Grade	Joint Negotiating Committee 1948 — England	Joint Negotiating Committee 1948 — Scotland	P.T.A. Circular 7 1.4.51	P.T.A. Circular 17 1.5.52	P.T.A. Circular 33 1.5.55	P.T.A. Circular 49 1.2.57	P.T.A. Circular 67 1.11.58	P.T.A. Circular 81 1.11.59	P.T.A. Circular 95 29.8.62
Basic	£ 370 × 20 — 530	£ 380 × 20 — 540	£ Increase of 50	*470 × 15 — 560	*495 × 15 — 510 × 20 — 550 × 25 — 750	*585 × 25 — 810	*610 × 25 — 785 × 30 — 845	*740 × 25 — 790 × 30 — 1,000	840 × 30 — 930 × 35 — 1,140
Posts of Special Responsibility	As above plus up to £75 per annum	As above plus up to £75 per annum	at all points of previous scale	No Scales					
Senior I—Single handed or in charge of 1	No Scales			500 × 20 — 640		No Scales			
Senior II—In charge of 2	No Scales			560 × 20 — 660		No Scales			
Senior III—In charge of 3 and over	No Scales			625 × 20 — 725	†645 × 25 — 820 × 30 — 850	†700 × 25 — 775 × 30 — 925	†730 × 25 — 780 × 30 — 960	†880 × 30 — 1,000 × 35 — 1,070 × 40 — 1,150	†1,000 × 35 — 1,210 × 50 — 1,310
Teacher Supervisor	No Scales			560 × 20 — 680	590 × 25 — 790	640 × 25 — 740 × 30 — 860	665 × 25 — 715 × 30 — 895	845 × 30 — 995 × 35 — 1,005	960 × 35 — 1,205
Senior Teacher	No Scales			625 × 20 — 725	645 × 25 — 820 × 30 — 850	700 × 25 — 775 × 30 — 925	730 × 25 — 780 × 40 — 960	880 × 30 — 1,000 × 35 — 1,070 × 40 — 1,150	1,000 × 35 — 1,210 × 50 — 1,310

* At age 27. Minimum abated for younger entrants for each year or part of year below the minimum. † Senior in charge of 4 p.s.w.'s.

Chapter Eleven

CONCLUSIONS

THE history of the profession is not easy to summarize, but it is basically concerned with the interplay between changing definitions of psychiatric social work and wider social forces. The definitions in question are sometimes those assumed or propounded by the workers themselves; at one time or another they have seen their work as a special kind of therapy (therapeutic social work), as social work carried out in conjunction with psychiatry, or as social work which carries a particular responsibility for stimulating 'teamwork' on the problems of the mentally ill. Definitions have also been attempted by those outside the profession, and these have reacted upon those made by psychiatric social workers. The medical profession, for example, at one time wished to define such workers as medical auxiliaries, and the Board of Control emphasized in its Reports in the 1930's the extent to which they could save the doctor's time by doing what perhaps he could have done himself in happier circumstances. The various views of psychiatric social work have interacted with each other, and with some of the important changes in the thirty or so years of the profession's existence. Of particular importance to the development of psychiatric social work, as we have seen, have been the social experiments during the Second World War and the extension of the social services, especially for mental and physical health, in the years after.

Psychiatric social work, beginning as a new venture in both psychiatry and social work, has enjoyed the advantages and suffered the limitations of its dual situation. To psychiatry it could offer the encouragement to explore the significance of social relationships and conditions in the aetiology and treatment of mental illness; to social work in general it offered ideas of mental health and 'the psychiatric point of view'. Yet it has often appeared a peripheral activity, necessary for the perfection rather than the existence of the institutions it served. Psychiatric social workers in mental hospitals, like hospital almoners, have never been essential to the life of the institutions for which and in which they worked. In this respect they differ substantially from other, larger, groups of social workers. Children's Departments and Probation Offices cannot fulfil their statutorily imposed functions without child care and probation officers. The psychiatric social worker seems more essential, at first sight, in the child guidance clinic, but the service itself is apparently not as indispensable in many parts of the country as, for example, the mental hospital. The child guidance clinic can be defined, moreover, in several different ways; some kind of help for the maladjusted child can be (and often is) provided in a service staffed by untrained social workers or by none at all. (Such services are a reflection of the shortage of psychiatric social workers and sometimes of the views of local authorities and clinic directors.) In the field of community care, there were before the Mental Health Act (1959) comparatively few psychiatric social workers, and it is clear that the new local government mental health services will have to be staffed by those trained on the recently established courses in Colleges of Advanced Technology (Younghusband Courses).

The special position of the psychiatric social worker in relation to the psychiatric services has had a number of important implications. The training policies of the Association, for instance, have never had to face the challenge of the necessity of staffing a nation-wide statutory service. Psychiatric social workers have been concerned for most of their history with 'treatment' rather than the provision of a concrete service or the fulfilment of a statutory requirement. An approach to the problems of society by means of 'treatment' may have blunted a zeal for reform, but it has also exposed the psychiatric social worker to the demands and needs of many sections of the population for help with mental health problems. Sensitivity to this need and an awareness of the skill necessary in meeting it have been one of the basic forces in the development of the work and professional policy of this group of social workers. It has been at the root of their concern for standards, their realization of the necessity for supervision and consultation and the changes in their role in clinics, hospitals and community care towards more face-to-face contacts with patients. This, of course, constitutes no denial of the fact that professional ambition has sometimes made their attitude to social workers in the mental health services (or indeed in other fields also) hesitant and defensive. Psychiatric social workers have not identified themselves so closely with the mental health services that they have always given as much help as they could to the mental welfare officers. Their first task was, of course, the definition and establishment of their own function, but their realization of the problems of the mental health services as a whole could perhaps have been quicker. Their present sustained flexibility to such problems is partly due to the facts that the new local authority services must be staffed, whether by trained personnel or not, and that such officers cannot be regarded in any sense as auxiliaries in a wider institution. In this branch of psychiatric social work the Association has been faced with a situation that resembles in some ways that confronting the professional associations of child care officers and of probation officers—how far can standards of training be strictly maintained when a service has to be staffed in some way or other?

The history of psychiatric social work in this country can be seen as variations on a number of connected themes. Psychiatric social workers have been faced throughout their history with problems of identity. Most of them came from the field of social work, though for a significant minority training in psychiatric social work was an entry into social work. If, then, they had been social workers before, what were they after training? A new kind of therapist or a special sort of social worker? And how could this therapy or social work be distinguished from that of others? Certainly, they valued highly their special nature (as they saw it at the time) and were concerned with the improvement and protection of the training which had conferred it upon them. They were conscious, too, of their special place in social work, and their conception of themselves as leaders in this field was certainly one of the factors that limited the number of those who became trained psychotherapists. In many ways psychiatric social workers have been the most fortunate of all groups of social worker, having been professionally trained from the start, and having had a long association with psychiatry and with the world of mental illness, in which the operation of fantasy is most readily visible.

Conclusions

Yet these factors had also their negative aspects. Psychiatrists were often threatened by the therapeutic activities of these case-workers, and made insecure by their demands for help and leadership. For the psychiatric social worker a dependent relationship with what soon became a high status profession (psychiatric medicine) had its disadvantages.

The psychiatric social worker is created by the successful completion of a year's training course,[1] irrespective of the work subsequently undertaken. The training is given in the field of psychiatric service for mental illness and maladjustment. The demanding nature of such work is widely recognized, and it is expected that personnel should be carefully selected and taught certain subjects that form the basis of the curricula in all the training courses. Psychiatric social workers themselves have always emphasized the importance of personal selection for training, though they have given insufficient attention to delineating the personality characteristics of the psychiatric social worker and to ascertaining the means by which they might be assessed. Psychiatric social workers have always argued that training should be lengthened and improved rather than curtailed. Such a view may seem unrealistic, and indeed it is if we attend to issues of immediate practicability. It serves, however, an important critical function at the present time, when we need to be reminded of the considerable limitations in professional social work training at the universities in view of the present emphasis on other (non-university) kinds of training which seem to be built on the assumption of educational and professional leadership from those trained in the universities.

If psychiatric social workers are to work in conjunction with psychiatry, to attempt to help mentally ill patients, singly or in groups, to work with patient's relatives and to help other social workers deal with mental illness or maladjustment, no lowering of present training standards seems justified. It is perhaps more arguable that selection procedures have set standards that are too high or too stereotyped. It has in fact always been possible for universities to accept students without formal university qualifications and up to 1962 eight per cent have been admitted as exceptional cases. Recently, the universities have accepted the recommendation of the Association of Psychiatric Social Workers that for an experimental period of five years there should be a relaxation in the academic requirements in the case of experienced mental welfare officers. Some of those previously admitted for training without formal academic qualifications have made an important contribution to the profession, but a general relaxation of such qualifications does not seem possible in view of the content of training. What is required in the field of selection is an analysis of the role and function of the psychiatric social worker, and also a consideration of what Emmet has described as 'vocation' or 'creativeness within certain kinds of role'.[2] Role and function need to be clearly specified, but we should also consider that too close a matching of the applicant to the work he is to do afterwards may encourage the acceptance for training only of those who come within a fairly narrow personality range. The profession might in this way be deprived of the fruits of an essential 'interplay of purpose, function and vocational creativeness.'[3]

Training could be improved if we had more systematic knowledge about the clients who come to the psychiatric social worker for help. This is more complicated than it sounds. Each agency selects from the total number of referrals the kinds of client considered likely to respond to the service offered and some agencies (e.g. local health authorities) allow their workers considerable choice of client within an agreed general policy. The workers encourage those who refer clients to them to concentrate on particular kinds of referral. The position is further complicated by the fact that clients also select themselves, withdrawing from or continuing with contacts that they find respectively helpful or uncongenial. Thus, the group of clients actually served by any agency is a product of the interaction of worker, agency and the general population. Knowledge of the different kinds of clientèle, however, could come from research and the training courses should recognize their responsibilities in furthering this, directly by undertaking enquiries and indirectly by encouraging students to become aware of this necessary dimension of their experience. Research is necessary, both to improve existing service to clients and also to make some intelligent provision for new kinds of clientèle in the future. The need for research should be faced by individual psychiatric social workers, training courses and the Association. To fail to increase our knowledge or to fail in putting new knowledge to use is to retreat on the position that science and therapy are somehow incompatible. To rely exclusively on research of the kind required being undertaken by outside bodies is to entertain unhelpful fantasies.

Recent criticism of social work has been based on the impression that methods which might well be appropriate to work in a psychiatric setting, were being extended to other forms of social work. As we have seen, a significant proportion of those who qualify in psychiatric social work (particularly at the London School of Economics) enter or return to a wide range of social work occupation. What aspects of training are most valuable to those working in other fields, and which features of training may have proved inappropriate for these settings? Courses in psychiatric social work constituted the first training in this country to stress the value of the worker's knowledge of self. The function of such knowledge has sometimes been misunderstood (it has sometimes appeared that it was sufficient to point to some personal satisfaction that a worker might obtain from a particular action to rule it out of court), but its value is unquestionable. This is so whether casework is seen as a learning or a treatment situation for the client or as a situation in which concrete services are requested and given. In all these situations self-knowledge on the part of the helper, in so far as it relates to the work in hand, is an essential ingredient of help that is not restricted in range or effectiveness to any special setting.

Equally important for casework in any setting is knowledge of the interaction between client and worker. Some aspects of this will be considered later, but on the training courses this element, seen primarily in terms of 'relationship', has been given valuable stress. It has been taught to some extent through theoretical concepts, particularly those of psychoanalysis, but especially through supervised practice in the two periods of fieldwork. This supervision has consisted of a largely educational experience in which the student learns about his work with clients through discussion with the supervisor on the basis of an evolving relationship.

A consideration of supervision and, indeed, of professional education for social work reveal both the theoretical and practical contribution of psychiatric social workers to the development of a method of education and also to teaching in many fields other than psychiatric social work. The literature on supervision published in this country has been contributed exclusively by psychiatric social workers,[4] and as a method of education it has proved indispensible in training for all kinds of social work. It is, moreover, one of the truly original contributions of social work to professional education in general.

In training for psychiatric social work, the student social worker who was not going to practice as such, had the opportunity of working in varying degrees of co-operation with psychiatry. This was sometimes described as training for teamwork, though whenever this term is used in social work it is stressed by social workers rather than other professions represented in the 'team'. It had, however, some disadvantages, particularly in the child guidance field. It is these that made for difficulties in the adaptation of the training to other kinds of social work. Social work in child guidance obviously contained important ingredients for all social work (the emotional interaction between client and worker, the ways in which the mother could be helped to describe and see her problems, etc.), but the 'ideology' of child guidance proved less helpful. This ideology split off material relief from help given on personal problems; it stressed the avoidance of authority and the slow progress along the road to self-discovery. Much of this is now passing, but whenever the child-guidance situation is taken as a model for social work it should be appreciated that the main patient has the status of a minor, that he has yet to meet the full force of social expectation over a range of behaviour, and that he is given considerable time in which to change and develop. These features of the child-guidance clinic are essential to its nature, but they may nonetheless present problems for those who would adapt work appropriate for child guidance to other settings.

Psychiatric social workers have often been considered, and have considered themselves to be leaders in the field of social work. Their journal began as a form of internal communication amongst psychiatric social workers, but increasingly psychiatric social workers have written for a wider social work public. What kind of leadership has their writing provided in the task of theorizing about social work?

We have seen that very little fruitful work has been done on the rather abstract questions of the status of social casework, or on questions concerning what kind of thing casework is. Reference is increasingly made to a body of casework knowledge, but the writings of psychiatric social workers provide little clear evidence either of the range of such knowledge (what aspects are psychological, what sociological, in the technical sense of the term) or of its content. It may be that different ways of describing content (for example, different ways of describing the way in which the past influences the present) make no difference to the worker's activity, but if social workers claim knowledge clear formulation is necessary before such claims can be tested.

On the other hand, it was largely through psychiatric social work that psychoanalysis was admitted into social work. This, of course, constitutes no commendation in the eyes of some but this is to ignore the reasons for the appeal of this group of theories. We have seen that psychiatric social workers are often by the nature of their work placed in extremely unstructured situations. This was perhaps even more the case in the first decade of psychiatric social work when its pioneering nature was most evident. In such situations it was natural to look for a body of theory which could give a structure, and at that time and to a large extent since, psychoanalysis has been the only theory sufficiently developed to supply it. It had, moreover, the advantage of giving the psychiatric social worker prestige and clearly marked her off from other social workers and identified, at least to some extent, what she was doing.

It had, however, disadvantages. It tended to establish a model of casework based directly on the psychoanalytic situation with length of contact, passivity on the part of the worker, and uncovering of past relationships given great emphasis. It tended to divert attention from the consideration and use of the concept of agency function, and encourage avoidance of roles with the element of authority within them. In striving to be as like analysts as possible, some of the early psychiatric social workers were imitating rather than adapting. Psychiatric social workers were in an exciting and potentially important position in society. They had contact with psychoanalytic ideas, and with men and women in various social roles, living according to differing standards, sometimes considering themselves sick and in need of therapy, and sometimes not. Analysis was impossible for each and every one of them, even if it was desirable, but help based on psychoanalytic understanding of themselves and their situation was possible. In this way psychoanalysis would be extended as a

Conclusions

helpful theoretical basis of understanding to a range of situations. Psychiatric social workers have begun to take part in this extension, realizing that for many of the problems of the vast majority of mentally ill people there is no other professionally trained help available.

It was during the War that psychiatric social workers began to appreciate the dangers of 'going for a walk with a relationship' (to adapt a phrase of Paul Klee). There had always been psychiatric social workers who talked of the worker in roles other than that of 'intensive treatment', but they did not develop either the methods or the *rationale* of such an approach. In the early 1950's psychiatric social workers began to question whether there was one correct approach to helping people and to consider the effects of different settings on the practice of psychiatric social work. From then onwards the influence of setting on other forms of social work has been studied. The present position seems to be one in which the need for a variety of approach is more generally recognized, but little has been published about the kinds of people for whom different approaches are appropriate. It would now be agreed that advice was necessary in some cases, that reassurance was sometimes appropriate, but while we have 'therapy' and the relationship on the one hand, with its developed and evolving *rationale*, we have, on the other hand a wandering empiricism with no *rationale* at all.

In some respects this is part of a split in psychiatric social work thinking between dealing with the real material problem and helping through a relationship. The most extreme phase of this has passed, but the separation of material help, advice and reassurance over concrete problems, etc. from help with 'real' emotional problems was a feature of psychiatric social work thought and practice in the 1930's and 1940's, and today workers are still struggling with ideas of treating the 'deep-down' cause and not the superficial symptom. This is part of a split which is one of the traditional dangers of social work; the split between cause and symptom, matter and mind, ordinary living and 're-lationship', material help and help with real problems. (This kind of splitting is also apparent in the critics of social work. It is, for example, at the basis of much of Wootton's recent criticism.) This is important because psychiatric social workers were not simply engaging in technical discussions, they were trying to influence people's perception of their world. To this extent this attitude can be appropriately criticized from a wider framework. 'The attempt to separate material needs, and the ways in which they are to be met, from human purpose and the development of being and relationship, is the suburban separation of 'work' and 'life' which has been the most common response of all to the difficulties of industrialism.'[5]

The integration of these two facets in a truly helping relationship has not yet been accomplished. Psychiatric social workers have made an important beginning in the consideration of the place of the worker's personality in such a relationship, but so much of the discussion has emphasised the worker as interpreter or listener rather than as actor. In so far as action has been envisaged it has been largely in wide and vague terms. It is difficult to see what terms like insight, problem-solving, support and so on mean without a clear idea of the actual operations involved. Once, however, one begins to analyse and describe such operations the need for a frame of reference is apparent. The idea of role-relationship, role-taking and role-making suggest themselves, and it has been suggested that in many cases the worker plays out a parent-child relationship.[6] This, however, like ideas of transference emphasizes the infantile or child-like aspects of such situations rather than those elements in the personality of the client that are struggling to maintain and possibly develop a precarious adulthood. What, however, is of greater importance is the emphasis any idea of role relationship places on the interaction between client and worker. This in its turn highlights the personality of the worker as one who is able to play a range of roles rather than use a number of isolated techniques.

The range of roles to which I refer are not easily identifiable 'blocks' of behaviour, for example, the role of mother, inspector, neighbour and so on, but a more tentative exploration of the ideas that a person holds about his self-role and the role of others towards him. To suggest that a worker should play a maternal role with the emotionally immature client, for instance, neglects the complexity of the conceptions the client holds of himself and of others. Role always implies reciprocity; there can be no mother-role without someone in a child-role. So in the case of the immature client we have someone who may see himself in the role of a child and may wish others to respond to this idea, but this is not his only conception of himself; others have treated him perhaps as very much not-a-child and this will have had an impact on his image of himself. The social worker can, then, be seen not as playing one leading part, but as someone who can respond to the range of roles imputed to him by the client by confirming, denying or questioning the conception the client seems to hold of his own reality, his value and the reality of the world.

The challenge of this problem has not been met in psychiatric social work. There has been considerable confusion about the status of techniques—sometimes these are spoken of as the policy in regard to a case, sometimes as specific means to limited ends. Yet the technical equipment (in the latter sense) of a psychiatric social worker, is extremely difficult to describe, as we have seen. It is much more feasible to think in terms of a person trained in understanding social and psychological situations, who can respond to these according to his judgment and according to the function of the social agency he represents.

So far we have considered some of the important aspects of training for psychiatric social work and of the literature of the profession. Yet characteristically the psychiatric social worker is not a student, teacher or writer, whatever her contribution to teaching and writing. What of the work of the psychiatric social worker in child guidance clinics, mental hospitals, and in local authorities? Undoubtedly, the psychiatric social worker has contributed to the development of child guidance, to important changes in the mental hospital, and to the more recent development of community care. To work in conjunction with psychiatry does not entail accepting automatically the prescriptions for action of every psychiatrist; in fact it offers to many psychiatrists an opportunity to learn from the work of people who may have more training or more experience in helping people to talk about, define and try to solve their problems. Psychiatric social workers have originated work of major importance in the social services. We have seen this in the development, still in its initial stages, of work in maternity and child welfare services, in community care and in the more recent theorizing and action in regard to consultation with other workers. These can be seen as realistic and original attempts to deploy their scarce resources in the most helpful way. Such an attitude has not, of course, always been uppermost and some psychiatric social workers may have merely followed fashion in therapy and other matters, content to rely on outside authorities. This is perhaps a general tendency in social workers and Polansky has suggested that the reason for this is their predominant character as orally-dependent personalities.[7] It is difficult to see how such a statement could be validated: it appears more reasonable to look for the roots of the attitudes of psychiatric social workers less in personality and more in their situation in relation to the medical profession. One perceptive social work commentator warned against such dangers at the beginning of psychiatric social work in England, when he spoke of the new 'science which converts all our reforming zeal into the ancillary of specialized medical treatment.'[8] In fairness to psychiatric social work it should perhaps be added that 'reforming zeal' was hardly a feature of social work in the 1920's; it perhaps seemed most precious when it was most in danger of being lost as an idea.

The idea of 'treatment' in psychiatric social work has perhaps not been as heuristic as might at first have been imagined. To talk of 'treatment' implies that you can, to some extent, categorize the 'illness' and select treatment procedures to 'cure' or alleviate it, and also that there is a way of judging if these have been successful. There has been in fact little progress along these lines, and in the present stage of the mental health services it is worth considering how much time and energy can be devoted to this essential enterprize. In the first two decades of psychiatric social work practitioners assumed that the mental health services should eventually be entirely staffed by trained psychiatric social workers, but technically the advance was in the direction of work most suited to one particular group, the intelligent neurotics. Work was, of course, undertaken with other groups, but this has, on the whole, not been extensively described, and its *rationale* is only just developing.[9] The position now seems to be that psychiatric social workers are claiming, with justification, to work with a wide range of personality and problem. Some service, it is argued, can be given to most people, even though particularized help with specific problems relies for its success largely on the ability to understand the significance of these problems in the wider context of the individual's relationships to other people. To achieve a small success in a very difficult case calls for the highest skill. Yet in the mental health services it is clear—as the demands from psychiatric social workers for some order of priority in their work testify—that the psychiatric social worker cannot now offer some service to most people in need. Now, when the workers could be exploiting their new security in the services and their new flexibility of approach, so that we can begin to see which groups of people seem to benefit from which particular combination of responses in the worker, they are already being asked to develop the skill and the *rationale* of ways of helping other social workers do these very things.

Finally, psychiatric social workers have developed a strong professional association to further their work and protect their interests. How successful has this been, and how far can the professional association be trusted as an intermediary between the psychiatric social worker and society? Any historical appraisal must begin from a realistic view of the situation facing the Association. It began as a very small group and is still small, compared, for example, to the professional groups of probation officers and child care officers. Yet size has been only a part of the story. The group of psychiatric social workers have been associated with psychiatry and with psychoanalysis, and with a somewhat missionary concern for mental hygiene. This has resulted in some suspicion from those outside such activities; and the apparently intangible nature of psychiatric social work made it difficult to remove this suspicion. Within this field of activity, however, the psychiatric social worker was seen, at times, as an intruder or as a potential hand-maid for other professions, and these professions were sometimes realistically threatened by the psychiatric social worker's concern with therapy. These were considerable difficulties for any professional group to face.

The Association's success in maintaining its existence and in evolving a professional identity has been seen in previous chapters, and of all social work groups the A.P.S.W. has been most successful in the continued education of its members. In training it has perhaps been hesitant in regard to new training courses and its attitude to generic training has formed only very slowly. This issue roused the old questions about the identity of psychiatric social work, and perhaps threatened to revive the old tensions between child guidance and mental hospital. It also raised a question about the continued leadership of the psychiatric social worker in the field of social work. It was for these reasons a difficult decision. For many the question seemed to pose the problem of the essence of psychiatric social work, but it seems to me that the search for a final definition is a barren one. The work of the psychiatric social worker has developed through a number of phases in response to changing pressures (internal and external) and changing needs. This does not, however, mean that the history of the profession would not have been more fruitful and, at times, less frustrating if at particular periods of its growth the Association, the training courses, and indeed workers themselves had undertaken some kind of reassessment, had examined their objectives, long-term and immediate, and expressed them clearly. The question is not what is the essence or nature of psychiatric social work, but what are our objectives on training courses, and in professional life and practice. A concern for a clear identity could then flourish alongside a desire for new features or a reorganization of the old. This kind of self-consciousness would itself have proved a safeguard for standards and helped the profession to be more confident and less cautious about the issue of generic training.

This book, concerned with the history of psychiatric social work, has been written at an important juncture of the profession's life. We have seen the recent approach from the Almoners for an exploration of a closer professional grouping and the A.P.S.W. has been active in promoting wider discussions of the possibility of a single professional organization for social work. A review of the history of the organization should not, of course, be expected to solve the problem. As in its solution of clinical problems, psychiatric social work is more than applied psychoanalysis or applied sociology, so in the solution of professional problems 'applied history' has its limitations. Yet history sheds some light on the problem. It shows clearly the tensions within the Association about the identity of psychiatric social work, and also the ways in which it has been drawn into the main stream of events in social work. It shows also that membership of the Association and the term 'psychiatric social worker' covers a heterogeneous group of people. Perhaps most clearly it shows the disadvantages of delaying decisions on important issues, and the disappointment that seems to follow with some inevitability from the expectation that others (be they psychiatrists or members of a committee of enquiry) will solve one's problems for one. At the present time the Association could perhaps give priority to three distinct projects. Firstly the clarification of the current objectives of psychiatric social work by means of discussion and research. Secondly, as a leading organization in social work, it should press rapidly for a general professional organization of all social work in which it could take its place as a special section, and to which it could entrust such functions as education, publication and influence on general social policy. Thirdly, it should continue to explore the specific nature and function of a social work professional organization—with particular reference to the suggestions in Chapter Ten.

Within the first of these tasks two subjects in particular call for close attention: the new mental health programme and problems of training. The policy of community care requires continual evaluation. Psychiatric social workers are aware of some of the main problems and dangers: the problems arising from the fact that some people now find it difficult to obtain care in mental hospitals; the danger of hastily conceived schemes of in-service training which will produce only a kind of clerical assistant home visitor who will exactly carry out 'treatment' medically prescribed; the importance of co-operation between the main kinds of worker involved (hence the Standing Joint Committee of the A.P.S.W., the Society of Chief Administrative Mental Health Officers and the Society of Mental Welfare Officers). Other problems are perhaps less clearly formulated. Community care, as we have seen, has a dual origin in the pre-war supervision of mental defectives living in the community and experiments during the War in the social care of the mentally ill, following hospital treatment. With these origins the work of community care could assume a number of different guises. The mental deficiency origins, for example, could be repressed and the emphasis placed entirely on care of the mentally ill. We have seen that work with the subnormal has never attracted much attention or status and in the current enthusiasm for helping the mentally ill the special needs of the mentally subnormal and their parents (e.g. an effective counselling service for the parents of these children at least in their early years) may be neglected. On the other hand, a service could be interpreted as a means of helping patients of the mental hospital[10] (either to obtain treatment or after a period of hospitalization). The pivot on which a service of this kind would turn is the status of the person as a possible future or actual past patient of a mental hospital rather than as a mentally disturbed person living in the community.

This last possibility (i.e. providing a service for the mentally disturbed in the community) raises some important issues in both psychiatry and psychiatric social work. Does the community care service offer a service of general casework to the society at large (assuming a very wide notion of mental disturbance) and a consulatative service for the general casework problems of other social workers? Or does it offer a service of social work in conjunction with psychiatry for the problems of the psychiatric casualty and a consultative service for the psychiatric problems found in the work of other social workers? If the first interpretation is chosen, the caseworker appears as the key worker, with his specialized knowledge and skill in dealing with social problems. In this context it is the psychiatrist who might be considered the 'auxiliary'.[11] This suggestion raises two key problems implicit in most of the history of psychiatric social work, the authority for therapeutic intervention and the nature of the 'psychiatric' problems presented both to psychiatrists and psychiatric social workers.

Psychiatric social work began both as a specialized clinical function within psychiatry and as an attempt to bring the 'psychiatric viewpoint' into social work. The notion of a psychiatric viewpoint was, of course, ambiguous: it referred to a concern for psychiatric illness and its treatment and also to a recognition of something much wider, namely the significance of human relationship in the problems presented by the clients of different social agencies. We have seen that each interpretation has had its following amongst psychiatric social workers at different times in the history of the profession. In the discussions over generic training, for example, some assumed that psychiatric social work could no longer claim a unique place in social work because 'the psychiatric viewpoint' in the second sense outlined above had in fact permeated other branches of social work. What has now to be faced are the implications entailed in these different views.

The two views share a common emphasis on social work as an entity distinct from that of psychiatry, though the exact nature of its identity is far from clear. Those who see psychiatric social work as essentially connected through training and practice with psychiatry have to acknowledge that this does not produce as firm a sense of identity as at first appears. This is because the term

Conclusions

'psychiatrist' is used very widely. It refers always to a medical practitioner, but within that group it can encompass a doctor who is interested in mental illness, one who has been awarded a Diploma in Psychological Medicine (with the emphasis primarily on adult mental disorders), and to medically qualified analysts of all schools of thought. To claim to practice social work with such a heterogeneous collection of professionals is not to claim a very unified source of authority for one's work. In such a situation the psychiatrist's authority for therapeutic intervention must be re-examined, particularly in view of the fact that psychiatrists generally are coming to appreciate the limitations of an approach to mental disturbances based on ideas of discrete disease entities (e.g. schizophrenia) each with its own symptomatology. The significance of relationships in both the aetiology and treatment of mental disturbance is now more widely appreciated and, it must be admitted, psychiatric social workers are more trained to give this aspect much greater attention than are doctors in their professional education. This, however, entails a re-examination of the basis of psychiatric 'authorization'. There are, as psychiatric social workers have observed, many improvements to be made in psychiatric practice, but this does not necessarily imply a denial of the interpretation of their work as social work in conjunction with psychiatry. Treatment refers to a range of activities wider than help through a professional relationship and mental illness has very often implications for the body as well as the mind.

If these are some of the questions facing those who see psychiatry as the source of authority for one particular group of social workers, those who take a different view must answer other questions. Those who see casework as a kind of help *sui generis* for a particular (if wide) range of problems, those defined as 'social problems', must specify more clearly both their methods and the problems to which they are addressed. The way of help must be clearly distinguished from psychotherapy and psychoanalysis.

These views of psychiatric social work, particularly in the community care service, have obvious implications for training, but the training problems I wish to discuss here are those connected with the two movements towards 'generic' training, the earlier inside the university, the more recent in the Colleges of Advanced Technology. (These latter, 'Younghusband Courses', are at present training social workers only for local authority health and welfare services, but their syllabi and organization clearly reveal them as embryonic non-university generic courses). The psychiatric social worker was able to preserve her specialist training in the face of considerable pressure towards a general university training for all the branches of social work. Some of the pressure came from members of the Association and the result of the clash of opinion was the rather unsatisfactory compromise recorded in Chapter Nine. The compromise was made, but the basis of the psychiatric social worker's specialized function has still to be clearly formulated and the essential preconditions for its successful operation established. This would appear to be an important task for the future. It is hoped that the material in this book will not seem irrelevant to it.

In considering the Younghusband Courses, the Association of Psychiatric Social Workers has already shown itself aware of the importance of helping members to prepare for undertaking the supervision and consultation made necessary both by the C.A.T. training courses themselves and by the tripartite division of social work outlined in the Younghusband Report. The Report divided the needs of those using the health and welfare services into three categories (straightforward needs, more complex problems, problems of special difficulty) and allocated a differently trained worker to each general category. The hierarchy thus proposed places heavy responsibilities on the worker professionally trained at the university who would both carry cases of special difficulty and supervise all workers. Yet the capabilities of the professionally trained worker were simply assumed and no consideration given in the Report to the needs of the university courses to assess the products of their training and improve their quality. The A.P.S.W. in common with other professional bodies and University departments should consider the extent to which the needs of very disturbed clients for the most skilled service and of other workers for a service of supervision or consultation can be fully met without improvements in existing training and the establishment of an advanced university course in professional training (which would include specialization in research, advanced casework or groupwork, supervision and administration).

The other issue raised by the Younghusband Courses is, of course, the relationships between university training and non-

university training in social work and between the differently
trained personnel once they are employed. What are the differences
between the training courses? It was envisaged in the Younghusband Report that some who qualify on the Younghusband
Courses would go on to further professional training at the
University, but there are those inside and outside the universities
who question the necessity for this. Eventually, the Younghusband Courses will be training more social workers than any kind
of course and this will be an original and important contribution
to the problem of understaffed social services. The existence of
training courses under non-university auspices will also provide a
welcome stimulus to universities to appraise their own training.
What indeed is the special function of their training? To train
university graduates (as University departments of Education
train graduates for teaching) or to specialize in the teaching of
advanced studies in casework, groupwork, research, administration and social work education? These are primarily, but by no
means exclusively university matters, but a professional organization that has envisaged some of the possible lines of development
and likely problems will be able to exert some influence. One of
the most baleful facts of the present situation is the tendency of
social workers of all kinds to accept with little protest or enquiry
what is done in their name by those who have adopted their cause.

We have been concerned in this book with a group of people
who, for a number of different reasons, became qualified as psychiatric social workers through following a particular kind of training and who thereafter followed a variety of occupations. Through
membership of their professional organization and through their
writings—they have attempted to continue their own professional
education, to define and promote their work and training, to
protect their interests and to exercize an influence on social work
and social policy. Their numbers have been comparatively small,
and the unity of their professional association has sometimes been
threatened. In this book I have tried to record their significant
achievements and their interesting mistakes, not in order to strike
a balance or to arrive at a happy but featureless mean, but in order
to understand their situation in present-day society, its potentiality, uncertainty and limitations. Their main achievement has
been to add a new dimension to social work and to psychiatry,
and thus to extend the helpfulness of both institutions. The future

Conclusions

for the profession offers great opportunities. Psychiatric social work, because of its history and its situation, provides the paradigm case for judging whether social work in general has an independent existence apart from the knowledge it takes from other disciplines, and from the institutions it serves. What has emerged from this study is the image of a profession which has no body of knowledge of its own, but which is exploring the implications of various kinds of knowledge. The function of the agency (child guidance, mental hospital, local health authority) is served by combining and exploiting knowledge derived from sociology, psychiatry and related disciplines, but in the process of subjugation and selection a new entity is created and this is the basis of the identity of psychiatric social work. In reviewing the history of psychiatric social work, the profession can be seen to stand at a number of important crossing points in our society, where professional organization meets the university and also the trade union; where psychiatric medicine meets the complex of social relationships and norms; where the social services attempt to meet the specific needs of individuals and where sociological and psychological knowledge are also tested in use. In this situation identity can easily be lost, but if psychiatric social work can sustain and encompass its situation then social work, the psychiatric social worker and the society they exist to serve will derive continuing benefit.

NOTES

[1] And in the case of Southampton, Durham and Cardiff a psychiatric social worker should have completed the 'generic' year (with a placement in a mental hospital or child guidance clinic) and a further four months fieldwork in a second psychiatric placement.

[2] Emmett D., *Function, Purpose and Powers*, (1958), p. 242.

[3] *Ibid*, p. 285.

[4] As far as I can discover the following are the only published papers on supervision (to 1962) in Britain:—

Ashdown M., 'Some Notes on the Supervision of Students in Social Casework', *Social Work*, Vol. 3, No. 9, January 1946; *The Student—supervisor Relationship*, British Federation of Social Workers, 1947.

Howarth H. E., 'Some Aspects of Supervision as Education', *British Journal of Psychiatric Social Work*, Spring 1955. 'An Introduction to Casework Supervision', *Case Conference*, Vol. 8, No. 6, November 1961.

Conclusions

Hunnybun N., 'Supervision, Education and Social Casework I' in *The Boundaries of Casework*, A.P.S.W., 1956.

Lewis, K. M., 'Supervision, Education and Social Casework II', *ibid.*

[5] Williams R., *Culture and Society*, 1958, p. 213.

[6] By Irvine, for example, in 'Transference and Reality', *op. cit.*

[7] Polansky N., 'The Professional Identity in Social Work', in ed. Kahn A. J., *Issues in American Social Work*, 1959.

[8] Urwick J., 'Reciprocity', *Charity Organisation Quarterly*, April 1930.

[9] Of some importance in the developing *rationale* of work with a very disturbed personality who has already had various kinds of psychiatric treatment are the ideas developed in a short paper by Waldron F. E., 'The Choice of Goals in Casework Treatment', *British Journal of Psychiatric Social Work*, Vol. VI, No. 2, 1961.

[10] See, for example, Ratcliffe T. A.; and Jones E. V., 'Regional Community Care'. *Mental Health*, Vol. VIII, Nos. 3 and 4, 1948. In this article community care is seen essentially as after-care, though the authors emphasize that the work is not merely social welfare as usually understood but an active therapeutic process demanding special skills and techniques from team members. This emphasis on the clinical team in community care differs from most other accounts which stress the relative isolation (and independence) of the psychiatric social worker.

[11] This seems to be the position in Harbert W. B., 'The Role of the Community Services in Mental Health', *Case Conference*, Vol. 9, No. 5, October 1962.

INDEX OF SUBJECTS

Index of Subjects

Index of Subjects

INDEX OF NAMES

Index of Names

Hay-Shaw, C., 127n, 159n
Hayward, S., 113
Healy, W., 16, 17
Hill, O., 5
Horder, E., 19
Howarth, H. E., 264n
Huneeus, E., 128n
Hunnybun, N., 11, 19, 38, 109n, 165, 265n
Hutchinson, D., 100
Hutten, J., 116

Irvine, E. E., 66, 89n, 109n, 144, 148, 154, 155, 156, 158n, 181, 265n
Irvine, M., 65n

Jarrett, M., 16
Jones, E. V., 265n
Jones, K., 110, 128n
Joseph, B., 100
Jung, C. G., 142

Kenworthy, M., 17, 20
Kimber, W., 127n, 169
Kimmins, 16
Klee, P., 253
Klein, M., 142
Krapf, E., 65n

Lane, M., 158n
Laquer, A., 159n
Lederman, R., 150
Le Mesurier, A., 187n
Lewis, A., 136, 173
Lewis, J. B., 112
Lewis, K., 109n, 151, 265n

Macadam, E., 20
Mapother, Dr., 21
Mason, E., 142
McDougall, K., 12n, 23, 30, 65n, 88n, 114, 115, 158n
McGregor, O., 9
McKenzie, R., 242n
Moodie, Dr., 31
Morris, J., 12n
Morris, P., 134, 135, 219
Moser, J., 65n
Myers, E., 12n

Polansky, N., 256
Posthuma, Dr., 30
Price-Williams, D., 30

Rankin, T., 159n
Ratcliffe, Dr., 265n
Robinson, B., 158n
Robinson, D., 19
Robinson, K., 187n

Scoville, M., 17
Shaw, L., 158n
Sheppard, M., 88n
Shuttleworth, K., 15
Simmons, O., 127n
Simpson, J., 47n, 65
Slater, E., 158n
Strachey, St. Loe., 17, 18
Strauss, A., 47n
Swann, M., 127n

Taylor, K., 30
Thomas, Dr., 30
Thomas, R., 98, 111
Tickle, M., 159n
Tilley, M., 149, 150
Timms, N., 12n
Titmuss, R., 120, 187n
Tizard, J., 216n
Tredgold, Dr., 30

Urwick, J., 265n

Waldron, F., 147, 154, 158n, 265n
Williams, M., 147, 151
Williams, R., 265n
Winnicott, D., 108n, 173
Wisdom, J. O., 134
Woodroofe, K., 46n, 187n
Woodside, M., 158n
Woodward, L., 127n
Wootton, B., 9, 218, 253
Wright, R., 31

Yapp, B., 109n
Younghusband, E., 37, 38, 161, 186n

Zander, A., 108n

For Product Safety Concerns and Information please contact our EU
representative GPSR@taylorandfrancis.com
Taylor & Francis Verlag GmbH, Kaufingerstraße 24, 80331 München, Germany

www.ingramcontent.com/pod-product-compliance
Lightning Source LLC
Chambersburg PA
CBHW070610270326
41926CB00013B/2496